CASS LIBRARY OF WEST INDIAN STUDIES

No. 11

A True & Exact

HISTORY

Of the Island of

BARBADOES

A True & Exact

HISTORY

Of the Island of

BARBADOES

ILLUSTRATED WITH A MAP OF THE ISLAND,

as also the Principal Trees and Plants there,

Set forth in their due Proportions and Shapes, drawn out by their
several and respective Scales.

Together with

THE INGENIO THAT MAKES THE SUGAR,

with the Plots of the several Houses, Rooms, and other
places, that are used in the whole process of Sugar-making;

viz.

the Grinding-room, the Boyling-room,
the Filling-room, the Curing-house, Still-house,
and Furnaces.

By

RICHARD LIGON

FRANK CASS : LONDON

First Printed 1657, Second Edition 1673

First Published in 1970 in Great Britain by
FRANK CASS PUBLISHERS
Newbury House, 900 Eastern Avenue
London, IG2 7HH

and in the United States of America by
FRANK CASS PUBLISHERS
c/o ISBS, 5804 N.E. Hassalo Street
Portland, Oregon, 97213-3644

Website http://www.frankcass.com

Reprinted 1976 and 1998

British Library Cataloguing in Publication Data:

A catalogue record for this book is available
from the British Library

ISBN 0-7146-4886-8

Library of Congress Cataloging-in-Publication Data:

A catalog record for this book is available
from the Library of Congress

Printed in Great Britain by
Bookcraft (Bath) Ltd, Midsomer Norton, Avon

A TRUE & EXACT

HISTORY

Of the Island of

BARBADOES.

Illuſtrated with a Map of the Iſland, as alſo the
Principal Trees and Plants there, ſet forth in
their due Proportions and Shapes, drawn out by
their ſeveral and reſpective Scales.

Together with the Ingenio that makes the Sugar, with
the Plots of the ſeveral Houſes, Rooms, and other places, that
are uſed in the whole proceſs of Sugar-making; *viz.* the Grinding-
room, the Boyling-room, the Filling-room, the Curing-
houſe, Still-houſe, and Furnaces;
All cut in Copper.

By *RICHARD LIGON*, Gent.

LONDON,

Printed, and are to be ſold by *Peter Parker*, at his Shop at the *Leg* and *Star*
over againſt the *Royal Exchange*, and *Thomas Guy* at the corner
Shop of *Little Lumbard-ſtreet* and *Cornhill*, 1673.

THE CONTENTS

Of the several things mentioned in this

HISTORY.

Trees

The Contents.

ROCK

Steevens
Lee
Cole
Holand
Ware
Holland
Emerson
Ab: Turner
Parson
Foster
Wall
Donnman
Laurence
Cater
Patrick
Macock
Dutton
Wolfe
Gybson
Gybson
Par: men
Terill
Stevens
Terill
Curtis
Watters
Flatter
Biron
Ogle
Chapmyer
Conyers
Weeks
Jordam
Scriven
Bushell
Stevens
Hargrove
Cooly
Parvis
Streton
Browne
Bronne
Dobn
Paris Cop:
Hawley
Dukes
Part:
Cyates
Broff:
Senex
Care
Do
Elbrick
Henningworth
Sandforde
Humf
Webb
Ware
Nelson
Wright
Rowland
Boyd
Boythn
Adema
Wolcot
Tring
Math JoRead
Malmy
Smyth
Sympson
Hales
Wells
Buck
Senex
Buck
Walker
Buck
Buck
Saltonst.

Pryces men
Arnold
Pryce
Lewes
Sayers
Chapman
Marshall
Leonard Bowyer
Bowyer
Edwards
Matheves
Lee
Oyster Wood
Ellis
Go.

ROCK

Balues B.

Spykeses bay

The Hole

ROCK

Black Rock

A Scale of five Miles

Day
Powell
Powell
Russell
Treacle
Flei:h
Terill
Po:
Fr Ha:
Futter
Locustrees
Part
Marshall
Poarce
Smiths
Fo:
Holland
Futter
Go:
Woodhoyse
Legonch
Balls
Browne
Hutton
Tomyson
Weekes
Whitlak
Andrews
Andr:
Jurymen
Eyde
Statlong
Morgan
Stone
Partners
Reade
Elbrick
Howard
Swiney
Martinh
C. Balls
Cox Balls
Redf

Balls
Alums Frat:
Watts
Belo
Corne

A topographicall Description and Admeasurement of the YLAND of BARBADOS in the West INDYAES

with the Mrs. Names of the Seuerall plantacons ss

Clarkes Bay

Mylls
Io.
Th:
R.
Lyd:

Hady
Tom
Clarke
St. Ioyler
Conset Po:
Conset

Longe Bay
Go:

Poule Bay

Sabymngoe his Canome 35. foot longe

Georges hill
Spike
Royles fancy
Smyth

Hetherfolls
Fishers ponde
Alven
Newman
Masy
Iedham
Southell Syzmor
Townes

The tenn Thousande Acres of Lande which Belongeth to the Merchants of London.

Trott
Hayes
May
Sames
Lacy
Knott

Teridg
Battyn
Corne plantation
Redwood
Enghend
Square ponde

Advena
Buckly
Holdip
Erkins
Fisher
HILL
Grene
Holsu
Peter
Drax
Malnis
Stringer
Chamb
Rich
Mono
Mukly
Haw
Dighe
Bowyer
Howard
Lee
Pa:
Dorell
Coverly
Marten
Minor
N.
Marshall
Go:
Moss
Sander
Wood
Iedham
Needham
Webb
Birches
Downma
Iones
Butler
Wafer
Hamond
Kittridg
Warmll
3 Taylors
Fawcet
Bollen
Fryer
Royle
Baldwins
Byrch
Glegg
Hetherfoll
Ross
Scriven
Wetherfoll
Webb
Bar
Tempson
D:
Battyn
Knott
Trott
Ifham
Playr
Webb
Wach houses
Oyften

Allen
Brome
Hilliard

Austins bay
Maxvells bay
Cloves
Go:
16 mens
Yland
A ROCK
Bridg
River
Bix
Perk
Holdip

A TRUE AND EXACT
HISTORY
OF THE ISLAND OF
BARBADOES.

Aving been cenſur'd by ſome (whoſe Judgements I cannot controll, and therefore am glad to allow) for my weakneſs and Indiſcretion, that having never made proof of the Sea's operation, and the ſeveral faces that watry Element puts on, and the changes and chances that happen there, from Smooth to Rough, from Rough to Raging Seas, and High going Billows, (which are killing to ſome Conſtitutions,) I ſhould in the laſt Scene of my life, undertake to run ſo long a Riſco as from *England* to the *Barbadoes*; And truly I ſhould without their help conclude my ſelf guilty of that Cenſure, had I not the refuge of an old Proverb to fly to, which is, [*Need makes the old Wife trot*] for having loſt (by a Barbarous Riot) all that I had gotten by the painful travels and cares of my youth, by which means I was ſtript and rifled of all I had, left deſtitute of a ſubſiſtance, and brought to ſuch an Exigent, as I muſt famiſh or fly; and looking about for friends, who are the beſt ſupporters in ſo ſtaggering a condition, found none, or very few, whom griefs and afflictions had not depreſs'd, or worn out, Baniſhment abſented, or Death devour'd; ſo that in ſtead of theſe near and Native comforters, I found my ſelf a ſtranger in my own Countrey, and therefore reſolv'd to lay hold on the firſt opportunity that might convoy me to any other part of the World, how far diſtant ſoever, rather than abide here. I continued not many weeks in this expectation, when a friend, as willing to ſhift his ground as I, gave me an Overture which I accepted, and ſo upon the ſixteenth day of *June*, 1647. we embark'd in the *Downs*, on the good Ship called the *Achilles*; a veſſel of 350 tunns, the Maſter *Thomas Crowder* of *London*; & no ſooner were we all aboard, but we preſently weighed Anchor, and put to Sea; in ſo cold weather as at that time of the year, I have not felt the like; and continued ſo till we came to *Falmouth-Harbour :* where we put in, and reſted for a night; but in our paſſage thither, were very uncertain upon what Coaſt we were, by reaſon of the unſteadineſs of the winds, and cloudineſs of the weather; ſo that I perceived more troubles and

doubts

doubts in the Seamen in that fhort paffage, than in all the voyage after. But, the weather clearing up, the Mafter and Mates drew out
feveral plots and Landfcapes : which they had formerly taken upon
the Coaft of *France* and *England*, (which are of great ufe in the narrow Seas,) by which they were well affured where they were; for
there they feldome ufe *Loggline*, or *Backftaff*, but attend onely the
Tydes, Compafs, and Card; nor is there any ufe of other directors in
fo narrow a room. We were (as I remember) about 10 dayes
failing to *Falmouth*, and had with us a fmall fhip of about 180 tunns,
called the *Nonefuch*; of which Captain *Middleton* was owner, a very
good Seaman, and a Planter in *Barbadoes* : but himfelf then remaining in *London*.

The next day we put to Sea, and continued our courfe to the South-
weft, (with fomewhat a Scant wind,) partly to avoid the high going *Billowes* of the *Bay of Bifkey* : but chiefly to ftand aloof from
Pirats and *Pickaroones* : which are very frequent upon the *Coafts of
Spain*, and *Barbary*; and as we paft along, I perceiv'd a difference in
the way of our Ships : for in flack winds , our confort the *Nonefuch*
would run us out of fight in four or five hours fail; but in
ftrong and ftiff winds, we did the like with her. So that I
guefs'd the larger the fails, the fwifter the way; provided, they
were alike built in the model of their keeles : but I leave that to be
refolved by the Seamen , or that Admirable Architect of Moving-
Horfes, Mr. *Pett*.

About the Latitude of 45 degrees, we met with a Ship coming
from *Guinny*, but bound for *London*; the Captains name was *Blague*,
a very civil Gentleman, who hal'd us, came aboard us, and invited
divers Gentlemen that were there aboard his fhip : which was a Friggot of about 400 tuns, her Lading *Gold* and *Elephants teeth*; the Man
was exceeding civil to us, and gave to every Gentleman of our Company, a prefent of fuch rarities as he brought from *Guinny*, and *Binny*.
We ftayed together almoft a whole day, the weather being very calm,
and almoft no wind at all; in the evening , a frefh breefe began to
blow, which ferv'd us both in our feveral wayes, and fo faluting each
other with our Ordnance we took leave.

About this time, our Confort the *Nonefuch* parted with us, fhe
directly for the *Carabby* Iflands, we for St. *Jago*, one of the Iflands of
Cape Verd; where we were to trade for *Negroes* , Horfes , and Cattle;
which we were to fell at the *Barbadoes*. So, keeping our courfe about
80 Leagues from the Coaft of *Spain* and *Barbary*, the firft land we
difcovered, was the Ifle of *Porto Santo*; vvhich lyeth in 33 degrees to
the *Norward* ; vvhich vve left of our *Larboard* fide : When prefently
after, vve had fight of the *Maderas*, vvhich vve faild clofe by, and had
a full vievv of the place; fo Rocky, and Mountainous, and the ground
fo miferably burnt vvith the Sun , as vve could perceive no part of it
either Hill or Valley, that had the leaft appearance of green, nor any
tree bigger than a fmall Hathorn, and very fevv of thofe. Between
this and three inconfiderable Iflands called the *Deferts*, which appeared to us like the tops of large buildings; no unevennefs or rifings
and fallings, but level as the top of a large Church or Barn; but
burnt worfe than the other : fo that inftead of the frefh and lively
greens, other Countreys put on at this time of the year , thefe were
                                                      apparrel'd

apparrel'd with Ruffets, or at beft *Phyliamorts*. But it fell out that this year the Summer was there hotter than ufually, and the Sea-men that were with us, gave us to underftand, that they never had feen it fo burnt as now, and that the *Leeward* part of it was, at other times, exceeding fruitful and pleafant, abounding with all forts of excellent fruits, Corn, Wine, Oyl, and the beft Sugars; with Horfes, Cattle, Sheep, Goats, Hogs, Poultrey, of all forts, and the beft forts of Sea-fifh. Thefe Iflands lye near 33 degrees to the *Noreward*.

Having paft between thefe (leaving the *Maderas* on our *Starboard* fide) vve found a conftant trade-wind to carry us to the *Southward*, When the next Ifland that came in our view, was *Bona Vifta*; but at fuch a diftance, as vve could hardly difcern colours, but the general Landfcape of the Hills feemed to us very beautiful, gently rifing and falling, without Rocks or high precipices.

This Ifland is famous, for excellent Salt, and for Horfes, which in one property, excell all that ever I have feen; their hooves being to that degree of hardnefs, and toughnefs, that we ride them at the *Barbadoes*, dovvn fharp and fteep Rocks, vvithout fhooes; and no Goats go furer upon the fides of Rocks and Hills than they; and many of them very ftrong and clean limb'd.

This Ifland, vve left ten Leagues, or thereabouts, on our Larboard fide, and next to it, the Ifle of *May*; famous for ftore of excellent Salt.

The laft of thofe Iflands vvas *Palma*; a land fo high, as after vve firft difcovered it (vvhich vvas in the morning) vve thought to have reacht it that night, but found our felves far fhort of it next morning, though vve had a full gail all that night: fo much is the eye deceived in Land vvhich lyes high. This Ifland is about 28 degrees to the Norevvard, and from it to the Ifles of *Cape Verd* about 13 degrees a long vvay to be filent, for there is no land between; and therefore I purpofe to entertain you vvith fome Sea delights; for there is no place fo void and empty, vvhere fome lavvful pleafure is not to be had, for a man that hath a free heart, and a good Confcience. But thefe Sea-pleafures are fo mixt vvith Cruelties, as the trouble of the one, abates much the delight of the other; for here vve fee the great ones eat up the little ones, as they do at Land, and vvith as little remorfe; yet laying that confideration afide, the Chafe affords fome pleafure to the eyes: for fome kinds of fifhes fhew themfelves above vvater, for a long while together. I have feen 20 Porpifces very large of that kind, Crofs the Prow of our Ship, one behind another in fo fteady and conftant a courfe, in chafe of fome other fifhes; as I have feen a kennel of large Hounds, in *Windfor* Forreft, in the chafe of a Stag; one following another directly in a track; and the onely difference I find is, thefe do not fpend their mouths; but vvhat they vvant in that is fupplyed by the goodnefs of their nofes; for they never are at a fault, but go conftantly on. The Dolphins likevvife purfue the flying Fifh, forcing them to leave their knovvn watry Elements, and flye to an unknown one, where they meet with as mercilefs enemies; for there are birds that attend the rifing of thofe fifhes; and if they be within diftance, feldom fail to make them their own. Thefe birds, and no other but of their kind, love to ftraggle fo far from land; fo that it may be doubted, whether

the

the fea may not be counted their natural home; for we fee them 500 leagues from any land, at Sun fetting; and fo it is not poffible they fhould recover Land that night; and on the waves they cannot reft, without great hazzard. I have feen them fometimes light, and fit upon the waves, but with fuch Caution, for fear of being taken in by a fifh, as her reft is very unfafe; unlefs when fhe is covered by the nights dark wings. This Bird, is a kind of fea Hawk, fomewhat bigger than a Lanner, and of that colour; but of a far freer wing, and of a longer continuance, and when fhe is weary, fhe finds refting places, if the Seas be Calm; for then the Turtles lye and fleep upon the waves, for a long time together; and upon their backs they fit, and fleep fecurely; and there, mute, prune, and oyl their feathers; roufe, and do all their Offices of nature, and have room enough for all, for fome of thofe Turtles are a yard broad in the back: we took one with our Long Boat, as he lay fleeping on the water, whofe body afforded all the Gentleman, and Officers of the Ship, a very plentiful meal; and was the beft meat we tafted, all the time we were at Sea. There are of thefe kinds of Fifhes but two forts, that continue in the Main; the Loggerhead Turtle, and the Hawks bill Turtle, of which forts, the latter is the beft, and of that kind ours was that we took. There is a third kind, called the Green Turtle, which are of a leffer Magnitude, but far excelling the other two, in wholefomnefs, and Rarenefs of tafte; but of them hereafter, for I have no mind to part fo lightly, with the forenamed Birds of prey: For having been bred a Faulconer in my youth, I cannot but admire the admirable fwiftnefs of wing thefe birds make. They mount fometimes upon the trayne, to fo lofty a pitch: as, if a Faulcon were there, She might be allowed a double Cancellere in her ftooping to her game: they do it at one entire down-come. Her ordinary flying for her own pleafure, and not for prey, is commonly more free than the beft Haggard Faulcon, that I have ever feen; but the continuance of it makes it the more admirable. At the times they grow hungry, they attend the Dolphins, who are their Spaniels; and where they perceive the water to move, they know they are in Chafe of the flying fifh; and being near them, they rife like Coveys of Partridges by 12 and 16 in a Covey, and flye as far as young Partridges, that are forkers, and in their flight thefe birds make them their quarry.

Thefe frighted fifhes, fometimes in the night have crofs'd our fhip, and being ftopt by the fhrowds, have faln down; and with their bodies we have baited hooks, and taken their purfuers the Dolphins; which we have found very excellent meat, being drefs'd by a good hand, with Wine, Spice, and fweet herbs, which we never wanted. So here we have excellent hawking, no fear of lofing our hawk, by going out at Cheik, or to a Village to Poult, and yet eat of the quarry, and fometimes of the Spaniels, which is an advantage the beft Faulconers mifs at Land. As for the hunting here, we only fee the Chafe, but fuffer the hounds to flefh themfelves upon the quarry, or it may be, a royal fifh, fuch a one as may fill a difh to furnifh *Neptunes* table, and by that means we are cozen'd of our quarry. So that as I ever thought on Land, I find the fame at Sea, Hawking to be the better fport. I had almoft forgot, to tell what kind of fifh this flying fifh is, which is

the

the caufe of fuch excellent fport, both in himfelf and others, he is juft like a Pilchard, but his fins larger, both in breadth and length; and as long as they are wet, fo long he flyes; and for their mortal enemies the birds, they continue with us from 33 degrees till we come to 15, and then leave us.

At which time and place, another kind undertakes us, not much bigger than a Caftrill, and as near that colour as may be, but of another manner of flying: for thefe flye clofe to the water, and turn about every wave; fo that we often lofe fight of them, by interpofing of the waves, and think fomtimes that a wave has overwhelmed her. The pleafure fhe gives the eye, is by the giddinefs of her flying; and often feems to be loft, and yet (contrary to our expectation) appears again. But I will trouble you no longer with the inhabitants of the Plyant Air, but dive into the Deep, to try what pleafure that Element affords to give you delight.

There is a Fifh called a Shark, which as he is a common enemy to Saylers and all others that venture, in Calmes, to commit their naked bodies to the fea (for he often bites off Legs, fometimes Armes, and now and then fwallows the whole body, if the Fifh be great): So when the Saylers take them, they ufe them accordingly: Sometimes by putting out their eyes, and throwing them over board; fometimes by mangling and cutting their bodies, finns, and tailes, making them a prey to others, who were mercilefs Tyrants themfelves; And in this kind of juftice they are very Accurate.

Many of thefe fifhes we took; fome by ftriking with harping Irons, fome with Fifhgigs, fome with hookes; and amongft the reft, one very large, which followed the Ship four hours, before we went about to take him, and perceived before him, a little Fifh which they call the *Pilot Fifh*; This little guide of his, fwims fometimes a yard before him, fometimes more or lefs, at his pleafure; and in his greateft adverfity often cleaves to him, and like a dear friend, fticks clofeft when he needs him moft: for when he is taken, this little fifh never fails to faften himfelf to his head, or fome part near that, and refolves to dye with him. The experience of this we found not only in this great fifh, but in all the reft we had formerly taken, for we never took the one without the other. And the Engine we took this great Shark with, was a large Hook, baited with a piece of Beef; which he received into his mouth, his belly being turned upwards, for his mouth being fhort of his fnout a good deal, he could not take it conveniently, his back being upward, by reafon his fnout drove the line afore it, but as foon as we perceived the bait to be fwallowed, we gave a fudden pull, which faftened the hook fo, as we were fure the weight of his body would not tear it out: We drew him up, and laid him in the Waft of the Ship, where none durft abide, but the Seamen who dare do any thing.

We had aboard divers maftive Dogs, and amongft them, one fo large and fierce, as I have feldom feen any like him; this Dog flew to him with the greateft Courage that might be, but could take no hold of him, by reafon of his large roundnefs and fliminefs; but if by chance he got hold of one of his Fins, the Shark would throw him from fide to fide of the Ship, as if he had been nothing; and doubtlefs if he had encountred him in his own Element, the Sea, he would have made quick work with him.   Divers

Divers of this kind we took, but none so large; he was about 16 foot long, and 10 foot about the middle. Other fishes we took, as the *Bonito*, the *Spanish Maqnerell*, the *Albucore, Dolphin*, &c. which we found excellent meat, but especially the *Albucore*, which is a fish of such a shape, as it pleased me much to look on. Those we took were not much above a yard long, with forked tayles, the gristles very firm and strong, and the body near that, no bigger than a mans wrist; but suddenly growing upward to such a greatness, as I have seldom seen any like him, and so strong withall, as a sayler, a very strong man, holding one of them fast by the gill, when this fish mov'd but his tail to get loose, gave such a spring, as he had like to have put his arm out of joynt. These kind of fishes, in a clear Sun-shine evening, delight themselves and us, by trying which of them can leap highest above water; so that 'tis a pretty pastime, to see fishes so large, and gloriously colour'd, shew themselves so far above their natural Element, whose shapes and colours gave such variety. But this sport we saw not often.

I will trouble you no more, with mentioning the variety of shapes and colours of fishes, till I come to St. *Jago*; onely one, and that a very small one; for his body is not much bigger than a large Pomegranate, and yet his faculties are such, as may draw more eyes to look on him, and more minds to consider him, than the Vast *Whale*: for though it be true, that his large body, appearing above the surface of the water being in calmes a smooth level superficies, and suddenly appearing, is one of the strangest and most monstrous sights that can be in nature; (and the more admirable, when he is incountred by his two mortal enemies, the *Sword* and *Theshal* fishes : For to shake them off, he leaps more than his own length, above water, and in his fall, beats the sea with such violence, as the froth and foam is seen a quarter of an hour after, White; as when 'tis beaten by a strong West wind against a Rock; and at other times, spouts out the water in great quantities, the height of an ordinary Steeple.) Yet this great Master-piece of Nature, is not in my opinion so full of wonder, nor doth raise the consideration to such a height : as this little fish the *Carvil*, who can when he pleases, enjoy himself with his neighbour fishes, under water; And when he puts on a resolution to try his fortune in another Element, the *Air*, he riseth to the top of the sea, let the billow go never so high, and there without the help of a sayler, Raises up his Main Mast, spreads his sails, which he makes of his own sinews, fits his Rudder and Ballast, and begins his voyage; But to what Coast he is bound, or what Traffick he intends, himself and He that made him only can tell. Fishes there are none to prey on, nor flies, and therefore 'tis not for food he travels. I have seen them 500 leagues from any land : if his Voyage be to any Port, he must have a long time and much patience to get thither; if to sea, he's there already : in one thing he hath the advantage of any ship that ever sailed ; for he can go nearer the wind by a point, than the most yare Friggot that ever was built. Which shews how far Nature can exceed Art. Another advantage he has, that in the greatest Tempest, he never fears drowning. Compass, nor Card he needs not, for he is never out of his way; whether than his voyage be for pleasure or profit we are yet to seek.

But

But before we arrive at our next Harbour, St. *Jago,* one of the *Isles* of Cape *Verd,* and now revolted from the King of *Spain,* to the *Portugal* ; Let me tell you, one little observation I made of the Ships way ; which in slack winds, and dark nights, we saw nothing under water, but darkness ; but in stiff winds, and strong gayles, we saw perfectly the keel of the Ship; and fishes playing underneath, as lighted by a torch, and yet the nights of equal darkness. Which put me in mind of a point of Philosophy I had heard discours'd of, among the Learned ; That in the Air, Rough hard bodies, meeting with one another, by violent stroaks, Rarifie the Air, so as to make fire. So here, the Ship being of a hard substance, and in a violent motion, meeting with the strong resistance of the waves : (who though they be not hard, yet they are rough, by reason of their saltness,) do cause a light, though no fire, and I may guess, that that light would be fire, were it not quencht by the sea, in the instant it is made ; which in his own Element, hath the greater power and predominancy.

But before we came to St. *Jago,* we were to have visited a small Island called *Soll*; by the intreaty of a *Portugal* we carried with us, whose name was *Bernardo Mendes de Sousa*; who pretended, to have a great part of the Island (if not the whole) to be his own; but for that, it lay somewhat out of our way, and we could not recover it, by reason the wind was Cross; and partly for that we were informed by some of the Saylers, who told us it was uninhabited by any, but Goats, Dogs, and the like; and we guess'd, he would (out of a vain glory) shew us something that he call'd his. But the Master, who well knew the Condition of the place, would not lose so much time to no purpose. Which gave some discontentment to the *Portugal,* which he exprest in his Countenance, by a sullen dogged look, till we came to St. *Jago.* But that was but a whetstone, to sharpen a worse humour he was big with; for though our Merchants redeem'd him out of prison in *London,* intending him a Main director in the whole voyage, whose Credulous ears he highly abused, by telling them, That the *Padre Vagado* (Chief Governor of St. *Jago*) was his brother, and that by the power he had with him, to lay all trade open, for Negroes, Horses, and Cattle, which were the Contrabanded goods; By which perswasion, they gave him the power and Command of the ship and goods. But he intended nothing less than the performance of that trust, but instead of it, meant to make prey of both, and of our Liberties, and probably lives to boot, if we had not been very wary of him.

The first thing we perceiv'd in him, was a strange look he put on, when we came near the Island ; which caused us to suspect some great and bad design he was bent on, (for being Jolly and very good Company all the Voyage, to change his Countenance when we were near the place where we hop'd to enjoy our selves with happiness and Contentment, was a presage of some evil intent to be put in practice, which hourly we expected ; and were all at gaze what part of it was first to be acted; which he (more speedily than he needed) discovered; and it was thus.

Our water, being a good part spent in our passage thither, and we being to make new and large provisions for the remainder of our
Voyage,

Voyage, (carrying Horfes and Cattle with us) which we were to take in there; he Commanded the Mafter, by the power he had over him, to fend a fhore all the empty Cask he had aboard; with intent to detain them; and fo make us comply, by little and little, to his ends. But the Mafter abfolutely denied the Landing our great Cask, but told him he would fend our quarter Casks, in our Long boat, and fo by making often returns, to fill our Pipes and Buts. But finding himfelf at a lofs in this defign, thought good to keep us from any water at all; and fo appointed our men to dig in the valley under the Padres houfe, where he was well affured no Springs of water were to be found. But fome of our men, who fpoke good *Spanifh*, by their enquiries heard, That there was a very good well on the other fide of the hill, under the Caftle, and were brought to the fight of it by fome of the Country people; Which when he perceiv'd we had knowledge of, he was much out of Countenance, and ufed his beft eloquence to make us believe he had never heard of that Well.

So finding that this practice would not ferve his turn, he tryed another: and that was to command our Mafter, to carry a fhore that part of the Cargo foon that was confign'd for that place, which was Cloath, Bayes, Stuffs of feveral kinds, Linnen Cloath, Hats with broad brims, fuch as *Spaniards* ufe to wear, and were made in *London* purpofely to put off there; and thefe goods being valued, when they were receiv'd at Land, there fhould be a return made, in Horfes, and Cattle. But as we had Caufe to fufpect him for the Cask, fo we had for the Cargo, and fo return'd him this anfwer, that we would not land any of our goods, without receiving the like value in Cattle; and fo by parcels to receive the one, and deliver the other.

On which meffage, we fent the Purfer of our fhip, that fpoke good *Spanifh*; But *Bernardo*, being vext to the height that his Plot was difcovered, kept him prifoner. We fent another to demand him, which was likewife detained; then we fent three or four more, and fome of the Soldiers of the Caftle gave fire upon them. So that we refolv'd to weigh Anchor and put to Sea for a week or ten dayes, and return in the night (the weather being dark and fit for our purpofe) and furprife the Padres houfe with 50 Musquettiers, which we could mufter very well of the Gentlemen and other paffengers in the fhip, and fome of the Saylers, and take the *Padre Vagago*, and *Bernardo Mendes de Soufa*, and carry them to the *Barbadoes*. But the Padre not knowing of this defign in *Bernardo*, fent to us a very kind meffage, inviting himfelf aboard our fhip, receiving hoftages from us, and fo upon treaty with him aboard, fettled a trade, and got our prifoners releas'd; whereupon we were invited to his houfe, or rather his Rock, for it was moft part of it form'd in a Rock, with a fteep and very high precipice.

But I am mifled into this digreffion by this wicked *Portugal*, whofe unlucky Countenance before we came to the *Ifland*, gave me the occafion to fay fomewhat of him, and his mifcarriage in the *Ifland*, before I came at it.

But when we came within fight of it, it appeared to us full of high and fteep Rocks, (the higheft of which were meer ftone, without any foyl at all) and they of fo great a height, as we feldom faw the tops, whilft we lay before it; being interpofed by mifts, and Clouds, which rife and darken the sky in the time of the *Turnado*. But the day

we

we had the first sight of it, being very clear ; and we being at a competent distance, had a perfect view of it.)   But those of the second altitude, appear'd not so white, but had a grayish colour, as if covered with light and sandy earth.   But the lowest of those , seem'd rather Hills, than Rocks ; but yet no russet, as we were in doubt whether grass did ever grow on them.   But when we came within distance of discerning colour perfectly ; we expected the valleys, as they opened to us, would have afforded our eyes a richer prospect, with more variety of colours, but we found very little or no amendment , only the trees of *Coconuts*, with some other that were large and beautiful, whose tops (giving amply proportionable shadows to their roots) held their greenness, and were extream beautiful.   But the time of our stay there , being the *Turnado*, when the Sun (being in his return from the Tropique of Cancer, to that of Capricorn , to visit and refresh the Southern world,) became *Zenith* to the Inhabitants of that part of the world ; which is about the beginning of *August* : At which time the rains fall in abundance, and is accompted winter, to those parts where the *Zenith* is, and we staying there 19 or 20 dayes, (the rain falling a good part of that time,) we perceived the valleys to put on new liveries : so fresh, so full of various greens, intermixt with flowers of several kinds , some growing on stalks , some on trees, so full of variety, of the most beautiful colours, as if Nature had made choice of that place to shew her Master piece.   So that, having feasted our eyes with this delighted object, we desired to try whether their smell was as pleasant and odoriferous, as their beauty was admirable ; and to satisfie our selves of this curiosity, would willingly have gone ashoar, but we were advised to stay a little, till we were better assured of our *Portugal Bernardo*.   Which stay, gave us time to take a view of the Harbour or *Bay*, which they call the *Pry*, and is about a league over from Land to Land.   And, as I guess'd, somewhat more ; from the points of Land, to the bottom ; and, as we enter, we leave a small Island on our Larboard side.

This *Bay* or *Pry*, lyes to the *Leeward* of the Island ; by reason whereof we found so great, so insufferable heat , as you will hardly imagine that bodies coming out of cold Climates, could indure such scorching without being suffocated.

I had in a Cabinet two pieces of hard wax, in the hold of the ship both melted and clave together ; and the Cement of that Cabinet, that was made to hold the Ink, melted and became flat.

So that finding the *Air* so torridly hot , I thought good to make tryal of the water ; and I leapt into the Sea, which appeared to my sense no more colder than the *Air* ; than the Queens bath (at *Bathe*) is hotter in *June* here in *England*.

At the bottom, or inward part of the *Pry*, there appeared to us, a fair round rising hill, near half the breadth of the *Pry*, not much unlike the *How* at *Plimouth*, with a valley on either side ; And on the brow of the Hill towards the right hand, a very high and steep precipice of a Rock ; in which stood the house of the *Padre Vagado*, fixt on the top of the Rock.   A house fit enough for such a Master ; for though he were the chief Commander of the Island : yet by his port and house he kept he was more like a *Hermite*, than a Governour.   His family consisting of a *Mollotto* of his own getting, three *Negroes*, a Fidler, and a Wench.

Himself

Himself a man grave enough to be wife, but certainly of no great learning; for upon the differences between *Bernardo* and us, Colonel *Modiford* writ him a Letter in *Latine*, which he did his beft endeavour to anfwer, but fell the two bows fhort, fubftance and language; and though his Quarrel were to us, yet he revenged himfelf on *Prifcian*, whofe head he broke three or four times in his Letter.

The firft time we faw him, was at his own houfe, by his own invitation: to which almoft inacceffible habitation, when we had climed with infinite difficulty; and indeed fo painful and violent was our motion (our legs finding the motion of elevation, much more violent then of diftention,) as we were almoft fcalded within; and the torrid heat of the Sun, being then our *Zenith*, did fo fcald us without, as we were in fitter condition to be fricafed for the *Padres* dinner, than to eat any dinner our felves.

Being painfully and pipeing hot, arriv'd at this exalted manfion; we found none to entertain us but *Bernardo*; whofe countenance was not fo well reconcil'd to himfelf, as to give us a hearty welcome. He told us that the *Padre* was gone forth about fome affairs of the Ifland, but would return time enough to dinner. And whilft we were ftaying there, expecting his coming, we thought good not to be idle, for the ftructure of that Fabrick, did not minifter to our eyes much of delight; Onely that it had a fair profpect to fea. So we walk'd along upon that round hill, enquiring what we could of the place; and were inform'd that there had been formerly a very ftately Town, beautified with fair buildings, and ftreets fo contrived, as to make the beft ufe of fuch a profpect; But burnt and demolifh'd by Sir *Francis Drake*, in the time of the wars, between Queen *Elizabeth*, and the King of *Spain*, which made us give more reverence to the place; for that fome of our Countreymen had there facrificed their lives for the Honour of our Nation.

About the hour that our ftomachs told us, it was full high time to pay Nature her due, we lookt about us, and perceived at a good diftance, a horfe coming towards us, with a man on his back, as hard as his heels could carry him; and within a very little time, made a fudden ftop at the *Padres* houfe, from whofe back (being taken by two *Negroes*) was fet on the ground a great fat man, with a gown on his back, his face not fo black as to be counted a *Mollotto*, yet I believe full out as black as the Knight of the Sun; his eyes blacker if poffible, and fo far funk into his head, as with a large pin you might have prick'd them out in the nape of his neck. Upon his alighting we perceiv'd him very much difcompofed, for the pace he rid, was not his ufual manner of riding, as by our enquiry afterwards we underftood; and that he very feldom rid at all, but his bufinefs having held him over long, caus'd him to take horfe, who intended to come a foot; and being mounted, (and he none of the beft Horfemen,) was made fubject to the will of his horfe; which being a Barb, and very fwift of foot, coming towards the place where he was kept, ran with fuch violence, as it was a wonder his burthen had not been caft by the way; for the Horfe having a bit in his mouth, and the ftirrops being extream fhort, as the manner of their riding there is, if he had ever checkt him with the bridle, that he had been put to bound, he had undoubtedly lay'd him on the ground. But the rider that thought

of

of nothing more, then holding faſt by the pummel with both hands, was miraculouſly preſerv'd.

In this great diſcompoſure, he was taken off by two *Negroes*, and ſet on his own legs : but in ſuch a trance, as for ſome minutes, he was not in a Condition to ſpeak to us : So ſenſible an impreſſion had the fear of falling made in him. But being at laſt come to himſelf, he made his addreſs to us, and in his language bid us welcom, beginning to excuſe his too long ſtay : to redeem which fault, he had put himſelf in ſuch a hazard, as in his whole life he had not known the like. We anſwered, that it argued a great reſpect and civility to us, that he would expoſe his gravity, which was accuſtomed to a moderate pace, to ſuch a ſwiftneſs of motion, as might in any kind indanger his health, or hazard his perſon. But he being a man much reſerv'd, and ſlow of language, ſaid no more; but brought us into his houſe; which was upon a level at the entrance, but the other ſide of the Rooms a ſteep precipice, and ſome of the rooms like galleries, ſuch as are in the meaneſt *Inns* upon *London*-way. There were not in the houſe above four rooms, beſides two galleries and a Kitchin; and thoſe all on a floor; and the floors of earth, not ſo much as made Level, nor ſo even as to deſerve ſweeping; and the moſt of them were juſtly dealt withall : for they had no more than they deſerv'd, both above and below; for the Cobwebs ſerv'd for hangings, and frying pans and grid-irons for pictures.

By this equipage, you may gueſs what the trading is of this Iſland, when the Governour is thus accoutred; but by and by, a Cloath was laid of Calico, with four or five Napkins of the ſame, to ſerve a dozen men. The firſt Courſe was ſet on the table, uſher'd in by the *Padre* himſelf, (*Bernardo*, the *Mollotto*, and *Negroes* following after,) with every one a diſh of fruit, ſix in all; the firſt was Millions, Plantines the ſecond, the third Bonanos, the fourth of Guavers, the fifth of Prickled Pears, the ſixth the Cuſtard Apple : but to fill up the table, and make the feaſt yet more ſumptuous, the *Padre* ſent his *Mollotto*, into his own Chamber, for a diſh which he reſerv'd for the Cloſe of all the reſt; Three *Pines* in a diſh, which were the firſt that ever I had ſeen, and as far beyond the beſt fruit that grows in *England*, as the beſt Abricot is beyond the worſt Slow or Crab.

Having well refreſh'd our ſelves with theſe excellent fruits, we drank a glaſs or two of Red Sack; a kind of wine growing in the *Maderas*; very ſtrong, but not very pleaſant; for in this Iſland, there is made no wine at all; nor as I think any of grapes, ſo near the Line upon Iſlands in all the world. Having made an end of our fruit, the diſhes were taken away, and another Courſe fetcht in; which was of fleſh, fiſh, and ſallets; the ſallets being firſt plac'd upon the table : which I took great heed of, being all Novelties to me, but the beſt and moſt ſavoury herbs that ever I taſted, very well ſeaſoned with ſalt, Oyle, and the beſt Vinegar. Several ſorts we had, but not mixt, but in ſeveral diſhes, all ſtrange, and all excellent. The firſt diſh of fleſh, was a leg of a young ſturk, or a wild Calf, of a year old; which was of the Colour of ſtags fleſh, and taſted very like it, full of Nerves and ſinews, ſtrong meat, and very well Condited : boyl'd tender, and the ſauce of ſavoury herbs, with *Spaniſh* Vinager. Turkies and Hens we had roaſted; a gigget of young goat; fiſh in abundance of ſeveral kinds

kinds, whoſe name I have forgotten, Snappers, grey and red ; Cavallos, Carpions, &c. with others of rare colours and ſhapes, too many
to be named in this leaf ; ſome fryed in oyl, and eaten hot, ſome ſouc't,
ſome marinated : of all theſe we taſted, and were much delighted.

Dinner being near half done, (the Padre, *Bernardo*, and the other
black attendants, waiting on us) in comes an old fellow, whoſe com-
plexion was raiſed out of the red Sack ; for near that Colour it was :
his head and beard milk white, his Gountenance bold and cheerful ,
a Lute in his hand, and play'd us for a Novelty , The *Paſſame ſares
galiard* ; a tune in great eſteem, in *Harry* the fourths dayes ; for when
Sir *John Falſtaff* makes his Amours to Miſtreſs *Doll Tear-ſheet*, *Sneake*
and his Company, the admired fidlers of that age, playes this Tune,
which put a thought into my head, that if Time and Tune be the Com-
poſits of Muſick, what a long time this Tune had in ſayling from *England* to this place.   But we being ſufficiently ſatisfied with this kind of
Harmony, deſired a ſong ; which he performed in as Antique a manner ;
both ſavouring much of Antiquity ; no Graces, Double Reliſhes,
Trillos, Gropos, or Piano forte's, but plain as a packſtaff ; his Lute
too, was but of ten ſtrings, and that was in faſhion in King *David's*
dayes ; ſo that the rarity of this Antique piece, pleas'd me beyond
meaſure.

Dinner being ended, and the *Padre* well near weary of his waiting, we roſe, and made room for better Company ; for now the
Padre , and his black Miſtreſs were to take their turns ; A *Negro*
of the greateſt beauty and majeſty together : that ever I ſaw in one
woman.   Her ſtature large, and excellently ſhap'd, well favour'd, full
ey'd, and admirably grac'd ; ſhe wore on her head a roll of green Taffaty,
ſtrip'd with white and Philiamort, made up in manner of a Turbant ,
and over that a ſleight vayle, which ſhe took off at pleaſure.   On her
body next her Linnen, a Peticoat of Orange Tawny and Sky colour ;
not done with Strait ſtripes, but wav'd ; and upon that a mantle of purple ſilk, ingrayld with ſtraw colour.   This Mantle was large, and tyed
with a knot of very broad black Ribbon , with a rich Jewel on her
right ſhoulder, which came under her left arm, and ſo hung looſe and
careleſly , almoſt to the ground.   On her Legs, ſhe wore buskins of
wetched Silk, deck'd with Silver lace, and Fringe ; Her ſhooes, of white
Leather, lac'd with sky colour, and pink'd between thoſe laces. In her
ears, ſhe wore large Pendants ; about her neck, and on her arms, fair
Pearls.   But her eyes were her richeſt Jewels, for they were the largeſt, and moſt oriental that I have ever ſeen.

Seeing all theſe perfections in her only at paſſage , but not yet
heard her Speak ; I was reſolv'd after dinner, to make an Eſſay what
a preſent of rich ſilver, ſilk, and gold Ribbon would do, to perſwade
her to open her lips : Partly out of a Curioſity, to ſee whether her
teeth were exactly white, and clean, as I hop'd they were ; for 'tis a
general opinion, that all *Negroes* have white teeth ; but that is a Common error, for the black and white, being ſo near together, they ſet off
one another with the greater advantage.   But look nearer to them ,
and you ſhall find thoſe teeth, which at a diſtance appear'd rarely
white, are yellow and foul.   This knowledge wrought this Curioſity
in me, but it was not the main end of my enquiry ; for there was now,
but one thing more, to ſet her off in my opinion , the rareſt black

Swan

swan that I had ever seen, and that was her language, and graceful delivery of that, which was to unite and confirm a perfection in all the rest. And to that end I took a Gentleman that spoke good *Spanish* with me, and awaited her coming out, which was with far greater Majesty, and gracefulness, than I have seen Queen *Anne*, descend from the Chair of State, to dance the Measures with a Baron of *England*, at a Masque in the Banquetting house. And truly, had her followers and friends, with other perquisits (that ought to be the attendants on such a state and beauty) waited on her, I had made a stop, and gone no farther. But finding her but slightly attended, and considering she was but the *Padres* Mistress, & therefore the more accessible, I made my addresses to her, by my interpreter; and told her, I had some Trifles made by the people of *England*, which for their value were not worthy her acceptance, yet for their Novelty, they might be of some esteem, such having been worn by the great Queens of *Europe*, and intreated her to vouchsafe to receive them. She with much gravity, and reservedness, opened the paper; but when she lookt on them, the colours pleased her so, as she put her gravity into the loveliest smile that I have ever seen. And then shew'd her rows of pearls, so clean, white, orient, and wel shaped, as *Neptunes* Court was never pav'd with such as these; and to shew whether was whiter, or more Orient, those or the whites of her eyes, she turn'd them up, & gave me such a look, as was a sufficient return for a far greater present, and withall wisht, I would think of somewhat wherein she might pleasure me, and I should find her both ready & willing. And so with a graceful bow of her neck, she took her way towards her own house; which was not above a stones cast from the *Padres*. Other addresses were not to be made, without the dislike of the *Padre*, for they are there as jealous of their Mistresses, as the *Italians* of their wives.

In the afternoon we took leave, and went aboard; where we remained three or four dayes; about which time, some passengers of the ship, who had no great store of linnen for shift, desired leave to go ashoar, and took divers women along with them, to wash their linnen. But (it seem'd) the *Portugals*, and *Negroes* too, found them handsome and fit for their turns, and were a little Rude, I cannot say Ravish'd them; for the Major part of them, being taken from *Bridewel, Turnball* street, and such like places of education, were better natur'd than to suffer such violence; yet complaints were made, when they came aboard, both of such abuses, and stealing their linnen.

But such a praise they gave of the place, as we all were desirous to see it : for, after the Rain, every day gave an increase to the beauty of the place, by the budding out of new fruits and flowers.

This was the valley on the left side of the Hill, more spacious and beautiful by much than that on the right hand, where the *Padre* dwelt. The next day, a dozen Gentlemen of our company, resolv'd to go and see this so much admired valley; and when our Saylers with their long boat went to fetch water, (as daily they did,) we went along with them, and landed there, in as high going Billows, as I have ever seen, so near the land. Much adoe we had, to be carried to land, though on mens backs; and yet the grapple came as near the shoar as they durst bring it, for bulging against the bottom.

No sooner were we landed, but the Captain of the Castle, with one Soldier with him; came towards us, with a slow formal pace;

who

who defired to fpeak with one of us alone. Colonel *Modiford*, being the chief man in the Company, went with an Interpreter to meet him; and being at the diftance of fpeech, defired to know his pleafure; which he told him was this. That he underftood divers of our women had been afhoar, the day before; and received fome injury, from the people of the Ifland, and that it was conceiv'd, we were come Arm'd to take revenge on thofe that did the affront. He therefore advifed us, either to make fpeedy return to the boat that brought us. or to fend back our fwords and piftols, and commit our felves to his protection; and if one of thofe were not prefently put in act, we fhould in a very fhort time have all our throats Cut.

We told him vve had no intention of revenge for any wrong done, and that the only caufe of our landing, was to fee the beauty of the place vve had heard fo much Commended, by our people that were afhoar, of vvhich they had given a very large teftimony, both of the pleafantnefs and fruitfulnefs of it, and that our vifit was out of love, both to the place and people. But for fending our weapons back to the boat, we defired his pardon; for this reafon, that the Billovvs going fo very high at that time, we could not fend them to the boat vvithout being dipt in the Sea water, which would fpoil them; and the moft of them, being rich fwords and piftols, vve vvere loath to have their beauty covered vvith ruft, which the falt vvater would be the occafion of. We defired rather, that he would Command a Soldier of his, to ftay with a man of ours, and keep them fafe, till our return; which he being content to do, we committed our felves to his protection, who put a guard upon us of 10 Soldiers, part *Portugals*, part *Negroes*; the moft part of either kind, as proper men as I have feen, and as handfomely cloathed.

Their garments made with much Art, and all feem'd to be done by the Tayler; the Coverings for their heads, were not unlike Helmets; of blew and white ftrip'd filk, fome tawny, and yellow, others of other forts of Colours; but all of one fafhion, their doublets clofe to their bodies, with Caflocks, made of the fafhion of the Kings guard: loofe fleeves, which came to their elbows; but large and gathered fo as to fit loofe from their arms; with four large skirts, reaching down to the middle of their thighs; but thefe of a different colour from their fuits, their breeches indifferently large, coming down below the knee; and the upper part, fo wrought with Whalebones within, as to keep them hollow, from touching their backs; to avoid heat, which they were much troubled with; upon their legs, buskins of the colour of their fuits, yet fome made a difference: their fhooes colour'd for the moft part; fome white, but very few black. Their weapons, as Swords, Piftols, Mufquets, Pikes, and Partifans, kept very bright, and worn comelily and gracefully; which argued a decency in the Commander, as their awful refpect did of his aufterity.

Being now under a Guard, we marcht into this valley, one of the delightfulleft places that I have ever feen, for befides the high and lofty trees, as the *Palmeto, Royal, Coco, Cedar, Locuft, Maftick, Mangrave, Bully, Redwood, Pickled yellow wood, Caffia, Fiftula, Calibafh, Cherry, Figtree*, whofe body is large enough for Timber, *Cittrons, Cuftard apple, Gnavers, Macow, Cipres, Oranges, Lemons, Lymes, Pomegranat, Anotto, Prickled apple, Prickled pear, Papa*, thefe & more may be accounted wood: & yet a
good

good part of them bearing excellent fruit; But then there are of a lesser sort, that bear the rarest fruit; whose bodies cannot be accompted wood, as the *Plantine, Pine, Bonano, Melon, water Millon,* &c. and some few grapes, but those inconsiderable, by reason they can never make wine : because they have no winter, and so by that means, they can never ripe together, but one is green, another ripe, another rotten, which reason will ever hold, that no wine can be made on Islands, where there is no winter: or within twenty degrees of the line on either side. I have heard that wine is made in the *East Indies,* within less than fifteen Degrees; but 'tis of the Palm-tree; out of whose body, they draw both wine and oyle; which wine will not keep above a day, but no wine of grapes, for the reasons aforesaid. Other kinds of trees, we found good to smell to, as *Mirtle, Jesaman, Tamarisk,* with a tree somewhat of that bigness, bearing a very beautiful flower. The first half next the stalk, of a deep yellow or gold colour; the other half, being the larger, of a rich Scarlet : shap'd like a Carnation, and when the flowers fall off, there grows a Cod, with seven or eight seeds in it, divers of which, we carried to the *Barbadoes,* and planted there : and they grew and multiplyed abundantly, and they call them there, the St. *Jago* flower, which is a beautiful, but no sweet flower.

From these woods of pleasant trees, we saw flying divers birds, some one way, some another, of the fairest, and most beautiful colours, that can be imagined in Nature: others whose colours and shapes come short of these, did so excel in sweetness, and loudness of voyce, as our Nightingals in *England,* are short of them, in either of those two properties; but in variety of tunes, our birds are beyond them, for in that they are defective.

In this valley of pleasure, adorn'd as you have heard, we march'd with our Guard, fair and softly, near a quarter of a mile; before we came to the much praised fountain; from whence we fetcht our water. The circle whereof, was about 60 foot, the Diameter about 20 from the ground to the top of the Well, (which was of free-stone,) threee foot and a half; from thence within, down to the surface of the water, about fifteen foot. The spring it self, not so much to be praised for the excellency of the taste, though clear enough, as for the Nymphs that repair thither. For whil'st we stayed there seeing the Saylers fill their Casks; and withall contemplating the glory of the place : there appear'd to our view, many pretty young *Negro* Virgins, playing about the Well. But amongst those; two, that came down with either of them a natural Pitcher, a Calibash upon their arm, to fetch water from this fountain. Creatures, of such shapes, as would have puzzel'd *Albert Durer,* the great Master of Proportion, but to have imitated; and *Tition,* or *Andrea de Sarta,* for softness of muscles, and curiosity of Colouring, though with a studied diligence; and a love both to the party and the work. To express all the perfections of Nature, and Parts, these Virgins were owners of, would ask a more skilful pen, or pencil than mine; Sure I am, though all were excellent, their motions were the highest, and that is a beauty no Painter can express, and therefore my pen may well be silent; yet a word or two, vvould not be amiss, to express the difference betvven these, and those of high *Africa*; as of *Morocco, Guinny, Binny, Cutchow, Angola, Æthiopia,* and *Mauritania,* or those that dvvel near the River of of *Gambia*, vvho are thick lipt, ſhort nos'd, and commonly lovv fore-heads. But theſe, are compos'd of ſuch features, as would mar the judgment of the beſt Painters, to undertake to mend. Wanton, as the ſoyl that bred them, ſweet as the fruits they fed on; for being come ſo near, as their motions, and graces might perfectly be diſcern'd, I gueſs'd that Nature could not, without help of Art, frame ſuch ac-compliſh'd beauties, not only of colours, and favour, but of motion too, which is the higheſt part of beauty. If dancing had been in faſhion in this *Iſland*, I might have been perſwaded, that they had been taught thoſe motions, by ſome who had ſtudied that Art. But conſidering the *Padre's* Muſick to be the beſt the Iſland afforded, I could not but caſt avvay that thought, and attribute all to pure nature; Innocent, as youthful, their ages about fifteen. Seeing their beauties ſo freſh and youthful, withall the perfections I have named, I thought good to try, whether the uttering of their language, would be as ſweet and harmo-nious, as their other parts were comely. And by the help of a Gen-tleman that ſpoke *Portugal*, I accoſted them; and began to praiſe their beauties, ſhapes, and manner of dreſſings; which was extreamly pret-ty. Their hair not ſhorn as the *Negroes* in the places I have named, cloſe to their heads; nor in quarters, and mazes, as they uſe to wear it, which is ridiculous to all that ſee them, but themſelves: But in a due proportion of length, ſo as having their ſhortenings by the na-tural Curls, they appeared as Wyers, and Artificial Dreſſings to their faces. On the ſides of their Cheeks, they plat little of it, of purpoſe to tye ſmall Ribbon; or ſome ſmall beads, of white Amber, or blew bugle, ſometimes of the rare flowers that grow there; Their ears hung with Pendants, their necks and arms adorn'd with bracelets of Counterfeit pearls, and blew bugle; ſuch as the *Portugals* beſtow on them, for theſe are free *Negroes*, and wear upon the ſmall of one of their legs, the badge of their freedom; which is a ſmall piece of ſil-ver, or tin, as big as the ſtale of a Spoon; which comes round about the leg: and by reaſon of the ſmoothneſs, and lightneſs, is no impedi-ment to their going. Their cloaths, were Petticoats of Strip'd ſilk, next to their linnen, which reach to their middle leg: and upon that a mantle of blew Taffity, tyed with a Ribbon on the right ſhoulder: which coming under the left arm, hung down careleſly ſomewhat lower than the Petticoat, ſo as a great part of the natural beauty of their backs and necks before, lay open to the view, their breaſt round, firm, and beautifully ſhaped.

Upon my addreſſes to them, they appear'd a little diſturb'd; and whiſpered to one another, but had not the Confidence to ſpeak aloud; I had in my hat a piece of ſilver and ſilk Ribbon, which I perceiv'd their well ſhap'd eyes, often to dart at; but their modeſties would not give them Confidence to ask. I took it out, and divided it between them, which they accepted with much alacrity; and in return, drank to one another my health in the liquor of the pure fountain, which I perceiv'd by their vvanton ſmiles, and jeſticulations, and caſt-ing their eyes tovvards me: vvhen they thought they had expreſt enough, they vvould take in their Countenances, and put themſelves in the modeſteſt poſtures that could be, but vve having brought a Caſe of bottles, of *Engliſh* ſpirits, vvith us; I call'd for ſome, and drank a health to them, in a ſmall dram cup; and gave it to one

of

of them which they smelt to; and finding it too strong for their temper, pour'd some of it into one of their Calibashes : And put to it as much water, as would temper it to their palats; They drank again, but all this would not give them the confidence to speak, but in mute language, and extream pretty motions, shewed they wanted neither wit nor discretion to make an Answer.   But it seem'd it was not the fashion there for young Maids to speak to strangers in so publick a place.

I thought I had been sufficiently arm'd with the perfections I found in the Padre's Mistress, as to be free from the darts of any other beauty of that place in so short a time; but I found the difference between young fresh beauties, and those that are made up with the addition of State and Majesty : for though they counsel and perswade our loves; yet young beauties force, and so commit rapes upon our affections.   In summe, had not my heart been fixed fast in my breast, and dwelt there above sixty years, and therefore loth to leave its long kept habitation, I had undoubtedly left it between them for a Legacy : For so equal were their beauties, and my love as it was not, nor could be particular to either.

I have heard it a question disputed, whether if a horse, being plac'd at an equal distance between two bottles of Hey equally good, and his appetite being equally fix'd upon either, whether that horse must not equally starve.   For if he feed on either, it must argue that his appetite was more fixt on that, or else that bottle was better than the other; Otherwise, what should move him to choose one before the other.

In this posture was I with my two Mistresses, or rather my two halves of one Mistress; for had they been conjoyn'd, and so made one, the point of my love had met there; but being divided, and my affection not forked, it was impossible to fix but in one centre.

In this doubtful condition I took my leave, with an assurance that I should never find two such parallel Paragons in my whole search through the world : And the reason of their so great likeness and lustre, was, they were Sisters and Twins, as I was after inform'd by a Hermite that came often to visit us when we came on Land, as we often did, and not far off from his Cell.

But you will think it strange, that a man of my age and gravity should have so much to do with beauty and love : But I have three arguments to protect me; the first is, I have in my younger dayes been much enclin'd unto painting, in which, art, colour, favour and shape, is exercised; and these beauties being a proper subject of all these perfections (being in themselves perfect) I could not but consider them with a studied diligence.

Next, I had been long at Sea without setting foot on any Land, and that hath a property to make all Land-objects beautiful; and these being in the highest degree Paramount, could not but surprize my fancy. Besides, the place being extream beautiful and lovely, could not but secretly harbour in it the spirit of love, a passion not to be govern'd. And therefore I hope you will pardon my wild extravagancy.

But the main reason of this flying out, is, I had little else to say, for the Island being a place of very little or no Traffique, could not afford much of discourse. Cattle they have very good and large, which they sell at very easie rates.   And likewise horses of excellent shapes and mettle, but they are Contrabanded goods, and whosoever deals in them (without special licence) forfeits both Ship and Goods, if they have power to compel them.

But I believe they have not, being partly inform'd by the Hermite, who came often to us to hear news, and beg somewhat of us, which being obtain'd, he would not stick to impart somewhat of the weakness of the Island, that would have cost him dear, if it had been known to the Padre. And some of that which he inform'd us, was, the Forts and Block-houses on either side the *Pry*, on which we saw the appearance of Ordnances good store and large; but we understood by him, that those Forts were neither regular, nor the Guns Brass or Iron, but such as *Henry* the 8th. took *Bulloyne* with, and this we found by experience to be true, for upon our first difference with *Bernardo* and the Padre, we weighed Anchor, and removed our selves out of the distance of the Castle which stood in the bottom of the *Pry*, and expected to be shot at from those Forts and Block-houses, but saw no fire given; and if they had been furnish'd with such Artillery as would have reached us, we should certainly have heard from them.

We also enquired of our Intelligencer, the Hermite, what Trades or Manufactures were practised there; but were answered, that they were few and inconsiderable: Sugar, Sweet-meats, and Coco-nuts, being the greatest Trade they had. Yet by the Padre's leave, we carried away with us 50 head of Cattle, and eight Horses, which *Bernardo* made us pay double, for the usual price being 25 *s*. a piece, for which he made us pay 50 *s*. and for horses 10 *l*. a piece, which others have had for 4 or 5 pound, but he was content we should rate our Commodities accordingly, and so we were no great losers by the exchange.

Having dispatch'd our business, we got leave to go ashoar upon the little Island, at the entrance of the *Pry*, there to cut and pull grass for our Horses and Cattle, which we made up into Hay, a work quickly done where so much Sun-shine was our helper; it being perfectly dryed, we stowed it in our Ship, which was our last work, and so weighed Anchor and hoysed Sail, steering our Course for the *Barbadoes*, leaving *Bernardo* (according to his own desire) behind us, having but two degrees to the Southward, to vary in the running of 620 leagues Westward, St. *Jago* lying in 15, and the *Barbadoes* in 13 degrees and 30 Minutes to the Northward of the Line.

There are seven more Islands, which are call'd the Islands of *Cape Verd*, viz. St. *Michaels*, St. *Vincents*, St. *Anthonies*, St. *Lucia*, *Bravo*, *Fogo*, and *Soll*; some of which are much larger, but none so considerable as this of St. *Jago*.

As we lay at Anchor in the entrance of the *Pry*, we perceiv'd at Sunset, between the Sun and us, the Island called *Fogo*, which was at such a distance, that none of us could discern it all the day till that hour, and then the Island interposing between the Sun and us, we saw it perfectly shap'd like the neither half of a Sugar-loaf, the upper half being cut off even, and in the midst of the top of that, a smoak and fire rising out, from which we guess'd it took its name.

About the 10th. of *August* we put out to Sea, and as we sailed, we left the Island of our Starboard-side, and did not part with the sight of it till we discern'd a little Town near to the Shoar, which we were told

was

was the best in the Island, and a place meant for the chief Port for all Traffick in the Island; but by means of a great mischief that Ships were subject to in that Harbour, it was almost totally deserted, for the Sea there was so Rocky in the bottom, and those Rocks so thick together, and sharp withall, as they cut the Cables off near to the Anchor, and so the Anchor is often left in the bottom. There was a *Dutch* man that lay there but three dayes, and in that little stay lost two Anchors.

From this Island to the *Barbadoes*, we account 620 leagues, which by reason of the constancy of the winds, which blow seldom in any other point than Nore East and by East, they have usually sail'd it in sixteen or seventeen dayes; but we, for that it was the time of *Tornado*, when the winds chop about into the South, were somewhat retarded in our passage, and made it twenty two dayes e're we came thither; and many have made it a far longer time, for in the time of *Tornado*, the clouds interpose so thick, and darken the sky, so much as we are not able to make any observation for a fortnight together; and so being doubtful of our Latitude, dare not make the best use of our Sails and way, for fear of slipping by the Island, and being past it, can hardly beat it up again, without putting out into the Main, and so by painful traverses recover our selves to the Eastward of the Island, and then fall back again to the due Latitude upon it at 13 degrees, and 30 minutes.

Besides this pains and loss of time, when we miss the Island, we many times run hazards by falling upon the Leeward Islands in the night, of which the Bay of *Mexico* is well stor'd.

In this long reach (which may be call'd a Voyage it self) I had only two things to make the way seem short, the one was pleasure, the other business; that of pleasure, was to view the heavens and the beauty of them, which were objects of so great glory, that the Inhabitants of the world from 40 degrees to either pole, can never be witness of. And this happens at the time when the *Tornado* is with those of that Latitude where we were, for the clouds being exhal'd in great quantities, some thick and gross, some thin and aerial, and being hurl'd and roll'd about with great and lesser curles, the Sun then and there being far brighter than with us here in *England*, caused such glorious colours to rest upon those clouds, as 'tis not possible to be believed by him that hath not seen it, nor can imagination frame so great a beauty; the reason is, the nearness and propinquity of the place we are in, which makes us see the glory of the Sun, and of those Stars which move in that Horizon much more perfectly, than at a further distance, the proof of this I found by looking on the Stars that appear large and bright to us in *England*, which being seen there, do not only lose much of their light, but of their magnitude, for instance, there is a little Star call'd *Auriga* near the *Charles Waine*, which in *England* I have seen very perfectly in bright nights, but at that distance I could never see it in the clearest night, though I have often attempted it. And upon my return to *England*, I found it as I left it; which argues it was no decay or impediment in my sight that made me lose it, but only the distance of place. I deny not but a better sight than mine may see this Star *Auriga* at the *Barbadoes*; but then so good a sight may see it more perfectly in *England* than I can, and so the comparison holds. But another reason to prove the Cælestial bodies brighter at a nearer

distance

diſtance, is, that the Moon being near the full (at which time it gives a plentiful light) I have obſerv'd in the night, the having been for two hours or thereabouts, and at ſuch a time as the clouds being in a fit poſition to reflect the beams which the Moon then gives to the place where you are, you ſhall ſee a perfect Rainbow in the night ; but this does not happen at all times, though there be clouds for the beams to reſt on, but only ſuch as are in an angle where theſe beams reflect and meet in a juſt point. Divers new conſtellations we found to the South-ward, which in our Horizon are never ſeen, and amongſt them one which we call the *Cruſeros*, which is made up of four Stars, which ſtand almoſt ſquare, or rather like the claws of a birds foot, and the Seamen told us, that two of them point at the South pole, as the Painters of the *Charles Wain* do to the North Star ; but the South pole cannot be ſeen by us that come from the Northern parts, till we be under the Line, and then we ſee both North and South, as we do the Sun in morning and evening, at ſix and ſix. And thus much for pleaſure.

Now for buſineſs it was only this, to inform my ſelf, the beſt I could, of the accompt the Maſter and his Mates kept of the Ships way, both for Compaſs, Card, and Log-line, together with the obſervations at Noon, by that excellent and uſeful inſtrument the back-ſtaff, by which we know to a mile the Latitude we are in ; and if we had an inſtrument to find out the Longitude, as perfectly, every man might guide a Ship, that could but keep an account.

To the knowledge of this great ſecret of the Ships courſe, divers Gentlemen of our Company applyed themſelves very diligently, for the Maſter was not forward to communicate his skill to all that were of his Meſs. And to ſuch a proficiency we were grown, as to lay a wager with the Boatſwain, a very good Seaman, upon the firſt ſight of the Iſland of *Barbadoes* : he would lay we ſhould not ſee it till the af-ternoon, or late in the evening ; we, that we ſhould make it before noon ; whether it were chance, or our skilfulneſs, I know not, but we won the wager, which was a couple of very fat Hens, which we cauſed to be dreſs'd, and eat them in ſight of the Iſland, with a double joy ; firſt, that we had won the wager, next, that we were grown ſo near our wiſhed Harbour.

Being now come in ſight of this happy Iſland, the nearer we came, the more beautiful it appeared to our eyes, for that being in it ſelf extreamly beautiful, was beſt diſcern'd and beſt judged of, when our eyes became full Maſters of the object ; there we ſaw the high large and lofty trees, with their ſpreading branches and flouriſhing tops, ſeem'd to be beholding to the earth and roots that gave them ſuch plenty of ſap for their nouriſhment, as to grow to that perfection of beauty and largeneſs, whilſt they in gratitude return their cool ſhade to ſecure and ſhelter them from the Suns heat, vvhich vvithout it vvould ſcorch and dry avvay ; ſo that bounty and goodneſs in the one, and gratefulneſs in the other, ſerve to make up this beauty, vvhich othervviſe vvould lye empty and vvaſt ; and truly theſe Vegetatives may teach both the ſen-ſible and reaſonable creatures, vvhat it is that makes up vvealth, beauty, and all harmony in that Leviathan, a vvell govern'd Common-vvealth, vvhere the Mighty men and Rulers of the earth by their prudent and careful protection, ſecure them from harms, vvhilſt they retribute

their

their pains, and faithful obedience, to serve them in all just Commands. And both these, interchangeably and mutually in love, which is the Cord that binds up all in perfect Harmony. And where these are wanting, the roots dry, and leaves fall away, and a general decay, and devastation ensues. Witness the woeful experience of these sad times we live in.

Being now come to the distance of two or three leagues, my first observation was, the form of the Island in general, which is highest in the middle; by which commodity of situation, the Inhabitants within, have these advantages; a free prospect to Sea, and a reception of pure refreshing air, and breezes that come from thence : the plantations overlooking one another so, as the most inland parts, are not bar'd nor restrained the liberties of their view to sea, by those that dwell between them and it. For as we past along near the shoar, the Plantations appear'd to us one above another : like several stories in stately buildings, which afforded us a large proportion of delight. So that we begg'd of the Master, to take down those of his sails, that gave the ship the greatest motion, that we might not be depriv'd on a sudden, of a sight we all were so much pleased with. But our Cattle and Horses (who were under hatches ; and therefore no partners of this object,) having devoured all their fodder, and were now ready to come to that necessity, as the next thing to be thought on, was to plain deal boards, and feed them with the shavings ; Which deadly hunger, caused such lowing and bellowing of the poor Cattle, as their cry stopped the Masters ears, so as the smoothest, and most persuasive language, we could use : could not force a passage, but with all the haste he could, put into *Carlisle Bay* ; which is the best in the Island, where we found riding at Anchor, 22 good ships, with boats plying to and fro, with Sails and Oars, which carried commodities from place to place : so quick stirring, and numerous, as I have seen it below the bridge at *London*.

Yet notwithstanding all this appearance of trade, the Inhabitants of the Islands, and shipping too, were so grievously visited with the plague, (or as killing a disease,) that before a month was expired, after our arrival, the living were hardly able to bury the dead. Whether it were brought thither in shipping : (for in long voyages, diseases grow at Sea, and take away many passengers, and those diseases prove contagious,) or by the distempers of the people of the Island : who by the ill dyet they keep, and drinking strong waters, bring diseases upon themselves, was not certainly known. But I have this reason to believe the latter : because for one woman that dyed, there were ten men ; and the men were the greater deboystes.

In this sad time, we arriv'd in this Island; and it was a doubt whether this disease, or famine threatned most ; There being a general scarcity of Victuals throughout the whole Island.

Our intention at first, was not to stay long there, but onely to sell our Goods, Cattle, and Horses ; and so away to *Antigoa* ; where we intended to plant : but the ships being (for the most part) infected with this disease, and our selves being unprovided of hands for a new Plantation (by reason of the miscarrying of a ship, which set out before us from *Plimouth*, a month before, with men victuals, and all utensils fitted for a Plantation, we were compelled to stay longer in the

Island

Ifland than we intended. Befides, the fhip we came in, was configned
to another part in *Africa*, called *Cutchew*, to trade for *Negroes*.

But during the time of our ftay there, we made enquires of fome
fmall Plantation to reft us on, till the times became better, and fitter
for our remove; with intent to make ufe of thofe few hands we
had, to fettle that, till we had fupplies, and new directions from
England.

And fo upon difcourfe with fome of the moft knowing men of
the Ifland, we found that it was far better, for a man that had money,
goods, or Credit, to purchafe a Plantation there ready furnifh'd, and
ftockt with Servants, Slaves, Horfes, Cattle, Affinigoes, Camels, *&c.* with
a Sugar work, and an Ingenio: than to begin upon a place, where land
is to be had for nothing, but a trivial Rent, and to indure all hard-
fhips, and a tedious expectation, of what profit or pleafure may arife,
in many years patience: and that, not to be expected, without large
and frequent fupplies from *England*; and yet fare, and labour hard. This
knowledge, was a fpur to fet on Colonel *Modiford*, who had both
goods and credit, to make enquiry for fuch a purchafe, which in very few dayes he lighted on; making a vifit to the Governour
Mr. *Phillip Bell*, met there with Major *William Hilliard*, an eminent
Planter of the Ifland, and a Councellor, who had been long there, and
was now defirous to fuck in fome of the fweet air of *England*: And
glad to find a man likely to perform with him, took him home to his
houfe, and began to treat with him, for half the Plantation upon which
he lived; which had in it 500 Acres of Land, with a fair dwelling houfe,
an Ingenio plac'd in a room of 400 foot fquare; a boyling houfe,
filling room, Cifterns, and Still-houfe; with a Carding houfe, of 100
foot long, and 40 foot broad; with ftables, Smiths forge, and rooms
to lay provifions, of Corn, and Bonavift; Houfes for *Negroes* and *Indian*
flaves, with 96 *Negroes*, and three *Indian* women, with their Children;
28 Chriftians, 45 Cattle for work, 8 Milch Cows, a dozen Horfes and
Mares, 16 Affinigoes.

After a Months treaty, the bargain was concluded, and Colonel
Modiford was to pay for the Moity of this Plantation, 7000 *l.* to be pay-
ed, 1000 *l.* in hand, the reft 2000 *l.* a time, at fix and fix months,
and Colonel *Modiford* to receive the profit of half the Plantation
as it rofe, keeping the account together, both of the expence and
profit.

In this Plantation of 500 acres of land, there was imployed for fugar
fomewhat more than 200 acres; above 80 acres for pafture, 120 for
wood, 30 for Tobacco, 5 for Ginger, as many for Cotton wool, and 70
acres for provifions; *viz.* Corn, Potatoes, Plantines, Caffavie, and Bonavift; fome few acres of which for fruit; *viz.* Pines, Plantines, Milions,
Bonanoes, Gnavers, Water Milions, Oranges, Limon Limes, *&c.* moft
of thefe onely for the table.

Upon this Plantation I lived with thefe two partners a while, But
with Colonel *Modiford* three years; for the other went for *England*,
and left Colonel *Modiford* to manage the imployment alone; and I to
give what affiftance I could for the benefit of both: which I did, partly
at their requefts, and partly at the inftance of Mr. *Thomas Kendal*, who
repofed much confidence in me, in cafe Colonel *Modiford* fhould mif-
carry in the Voyage.

I only speak thus much, that you may perceive, I had time enough to improve my self, in the knowledge of the management of a Plantation of this bulk ; and therefore, you may give the more credit in what I am to say, concerning the profit and value of this Plantation ; which I intend as a Scale, for those that go upon the like ; or to vary it to greater or less proportions, at their pleasure. And indeed, I wanted no tutridge, in the learning this mysterie, for, to do him right, I hold Collonel *Modiford* as able, to undertake and perform such a charge, as any I know. And therefore I might (according to my ability) be able to say something, which I will, as briefly as I can, deliver to you, in such plain language as I have.

But before I come to say any thing of the Island, as it was when I arrived there, I will beg leave, to deliver you a word or two , what hath been told me by the most ancient Planters, that we found there , and what they had by tradition from their Predecessors. For, few or none of them that first set foot there, were now living.

About the year   a Ship of Sir *William Curteens*, returning from *Fernambock* in *Brasil*, being driven by foul weather upon this coast, chanc'd to fall upon this Island, which is not far out of the way , being the most windwardly Island of all the *Caribbies*, (*Tobago* only excepted;) and Anchoring before it , stayed some time, to inform themselves of the nature of the place ; which they found by tryals in several parts, to be so overgrown with Wood, as there could be found no Champions, or *Savannas* for men to dwell in ; nor found they any beasts to inhabit there, only Hogs, and those in abundance : the *Portugals* having long before, put some ashoar for breed , in case they should at any time be driven by foul weather, to be cast upon the Island, they might there find fresh meat, to serve them upon such an extremity : And the fruits and roots that grew there, afforded them so great plenty of food, as they multiplyed abundantly. So that the Natives of the leeward Islands, that were at the distance of sight, coming thither in their *Cannoas* , and *Periagos* , and finding such Game to hunt, as these hogs, and the flesh so sweet and excellent in taste , they came often thither a hunting , and stayed sometimes a month together, and so returned again at pleasure, leaving behind them certain tokens of their being there, which were, Pots, of several sizes, in which they boyled their meat, made of clay, so finely tempered, and turned with such art, as I have not seen any like them, for fineness of mettle, and curiosity of turning, in *England*. This information I received from the Planters in *Barbadoes*. But being here a Prisoner, in the *Upper Bench* Prison, my chance was to meet with an ancient Captain, and one of those that first landed on the Island ; and had the managing of a good part of the Island, under *William* late Earl of *Pembrook*, before my Lord of *Carlisle* begg'd it of King *James*. This Captain *Canon* (for so was his name)) inform'd me for certain, that this was a gross mistake in the Planters, and that no *Indians* ever came there : But those Pots were brought by the *Negroes* , which they fetcht from *Angola*, and some other parts of *Africa* ; and that he had seen them make of them at *Angola*, with the greatest art that may be. Though I am willing to believe this Captain , who delivered upon his knowledge, that the *Negroes* brought some Pots thither, and very finely and artificially made ; yet, it does not hinder any man from believing ,
that

that the *Indians* brought fome too , and who knows, which were the moft exactly made. For, 'tis certain, that from fome part of the Ifland, you may fee (in a clear day) St. *Vincents* perfectly : And if we can fee them, why may not they fee us; and they will certainly venture to any place they fee, fo far as they know they can reach before night, fetting out very early in the morning. But I leave you to credit which of thefe you pleafe, either, or both.

But I have a great inclination to believe , the *Indians* have been there, for this reafon, that the Ifland of St. *Vincents*, lying in the fame Climate with this of *Barbadoes*, the Clay may be of the fame nature and quality ; and they, having the skill to bring their Clay to fo fine a temper, as to burn and not break, may fhew us the way, to temper ours of the *Barbadoes* fo, as we may make Bricks to burn, without chopping or cracking ; which thofe of *Angola*, being far off, and it may be, their Clay of different temper, cannot help us in. And it is no hard matter, to procure an *Indian* or two, to come from that Ifland, and give us direction, which would be of infinite ufe and advantage, to our buildings in *Barbadoes*. But this digreffion muft not lead me out of the way of my bufinefs.

This difcovery being made, and advice given to their friends in *England*, other Ships were fent, with men, provifions, and working tools, to cut down the Woods, and clear the ground, fo as they might plant provifions to keep them alive, which, till then, they found but ftraglingly amongft the Woods. But having clear'd fome part of it, they planted *Potatoes*, *Plantines*, and *Mayes*, with fome other fruits; which, with the Hogs-flefh they found, ferv'd only to keep life and foul together. And their fupplies from *England* coming fo flow, and fo uncertainly, they were often driven to great extremities : And the Tobacco that grew there, fo earthy and worthlefs, as it could give them little or no return from *England*, or elfewhere; fo that for a while they lingred on in a lamentable condition. For, the Woods were fo thick, and moft of the Trees fo large and maffie, as they were not to be faln with fo few hands ; and when they were lay'd along, the branches were fo thick and boyfterous, as required more help, and thofe ftrong and active men, to lop and remove them off the ground. At the time we came firft there, we found both *Potatoes*, *Maies*, and *Bonavifts*, planted between the boughs, the Trees lying along upon the ground; fo far fhort was the ground then of being clear'd. Yet, we found *Indico* planted, and fo well ordered, as it fold in *London* at very good rates , and their Cotton wool, and Fuftick wood, prov'd very good and ftaple commodities. So that having thefe four forts of goods to traffick with, fome fhips were invited (in hope of gain by that trade) to come and vifit them, bringing for exchange, fuch commodities as they wanted, working Tools, Iron, Steel, Cloaths, Shirts, and Drawers, Hofe and Shooes, Hats, and more Hands. So that beginning to tafte the fweet of this Trade, they fet themfelves hard to work, and lived in much better condition.

But when the Canes had been planted three or four years, they found that to be the main Plant , to improve the value of the whole Ifland : And fo, bent all their endeavours to advance their knowledge in the planting, and making Sugar : Which knowledge, though they ftudied hard, was long a learning. But I will forbear to fay any thing

of

of that, till I bring in the Plants ; where you shall find not only the colour, shape, and quality of this Plant, but the worth and value of it, together the whole process of the great work of Sugar making, which is the thing I mainly aim at : But, in my way to that, I will give you a sleight description or view, of the Island in general : and first, of the Scituation.

It were a crime, not to believe, but that you are well vers'd in the knowledge of all parts of the known habitable world ; and I shall seem impertinent, if I go about to inform you of the scituation of this Island. But, because there have been some disputes between Seamen, whether it lye in bare 13 Degrees, or in 13 Degrees and 30 Minutes, I shall easily be led by the most voices, of the most able Seamen, to give for granted, that *Carlisle Bay*, which is the Harbour where most of them put in, is 13 Degrees and 30 Minutes from the Line, to the Northern Latitude.

The Scituation.

This Bay is, without exception, the best in the Island, and is somewhat more than a league over ; and from the points of Land to the bottom of the Bay, is twice as much.

Upon the most inward part of the Bay, stands the Town, which is about the bigness of *Hounslo*, and is called the *Bridge* ; for that a long Bridge was made at first over a little nook of the Sea, which was rather a Bog than Sea.

A Town ill scituate ; for if they had considered health, as they did conveniency, they would never have set it there ; or, if they had any intention at first, to have built a Town there, they could not have been so improvident, as not to foresee the main inconveniences that must ensue, by making choice of so unhealthy a place to live in. But, one house being set up, another was erected, and so a third, and a fourth, till at last it came to take the name of a Town ; Divers Store-houses being there built, to stow their goods in, for their convenience, being near the Harbour. But the main oversight was, to build their Town upon so unwholsome a place. For, the ground being somewhat lower within the Land, than the Sea-banks are, the spring Tides flow over, and there remains, making a great part of that flat, a kind of Bog or Morass, which vents out so loathsome a savour, as cannot but breed ill blood, and is (no doubt) the occasion of much sickness to those that live there.

At the time of our arrival, and a month or two after, the sickness raign'd so extreamly, as the living could hardly bury the dead ; and for that this place was near to them, they threw the dead carcases into the bog, which infected so the water, as divers that drunk of it were absolutely poysoned, and dyed in few hours after ; but others, taking warning by their harms, forbear to taste any more of it.

The ground on either side the Bay, (but chiefly that to the Eastward) is much firmer, and lies higher ; and, I believe, they will in time, remove the Town upon that ground, for their habitations, though they suffer the Store-houses to remain where they are, for their convenience. But the other scituation, may be made with some charge as convenient as that, and abundantly more healthful.

Three Bayes there are more of note in this Island ; one, to the Eastward of this, which they call *Austin's Bay*, not in commemoration of any Saint, but of a wild mad drunken fellow, whose lewd and extra-

vagant

travagant carriage, made him infamous in the Ifland ; and his Plantation ftanding near this Bay, it was called by his name.   The other two
are to the Weft of *Carlifle Bay* ; and the firft is called *Mackfields Bay*, the
other *Spikes Bay* ; but neither of thefe three are environ'd with Land,
as *Carlifle Bay* is : but being to the Leeward of the Ifland, and good
Anchorage, they feldom are in danger ; unlefs in the time of *Turnado*,
when the wind turns about to the South ; and then, if they be not
well moor'd, they are fubject to fall foul on one another, and fometimes driven aground. For, the Leeward part of the Ifland being rather
fhelvy than rocky, they feldom or never are caft away.

The Extent.   The length and breadth of this Ifland, I muft deliver you only upon
truft ; for, I could not go my felf about it, being full of other bufinefs ;
but I had fome fpeech with the antienteft, and moft knowing Sur-
veyer there , one Captain *Swan*, who told me, that he once took an
exact plot of the whole Ifland, but it was commanded out of his hands
by the then Governour, Sir *Henry Hunks*, who carried it into *England* ;
fince which time, neither himfelf, nor any other, to his knowledge ,
had taken any ; nor did he believe, there was any extant. I defired him
yet that he would rub up his memory, and take a little pains in the
furvey of his Papers, to try what could be found out there, that might
give me fome light in the extent of the Ifland , which he promifed to
do ; and within a while after, told me , that he had found by fome
Papers, that lay fcattered in his Study, the length of it ; but for the
breadth, it was very uncertain, by reafon of the nooks and corners
that reach'd out into the Sea, fo that it muft of neceffity be broad in
fome places, and narrow in others. I defired then to know , how
many miles the broadeft, and how few the narroweft parts might be. He
told me, that he guefs'd the broadeft place could not be above feventeen miles, nor the narroweft under twelve ; and that the length, he
was affured, was twenty eight miles.   Out of thefe uncertain grounds,
it was a hard matter to conclude upon any certainties ; and therefore
the eveneft way I can go, is, upon a *Medium*, between twelve and
feventeen ; and, I will be as modeft as I can in my computation ; and
take but 14. which is lefs than the *Medium*, and multiply 14. which
is fuppofed to be the breadth, 28. which is affured to be the length,
and they make 292 fquare miles in the Ifland.   Beyond this, my enquiries could not reach, and therefore was compell'd to make my efti-
mate upon this bare Suppofition.   But, for the form of the *Superficies*
of the Ifland, I am utterly ignorant ; and for the Upright, I have
given it you in my firft view of the Ifland, that it rifes higheft in the
middle.

The Length   When the Sun is in the *Æquinoctial*, or within 10 Degrees of either
of dayes.   fide, we find little change in the dayes length; for at fix and fix the Sun
rifes and fets : but when he is near the Tropick of *Capricorn*, and is 37
Degrees from us, we find a difference ; for then, the day is fomewhat
fhorter, and we perceive that fhortning, to begin about the end of *Octo-
ber* ; the *Crepufculum* being then not much longer than at other times,
which is not half the length, as 'tis with us in *England*.

At the time of new *Moon*, we find both her Corners equally high,
when the Sun is near us ; but when it is at the diftance of 37 Degrees
to the Southward, we find fome difference; for then it hangs not fo
equal, but one end is higher than the other, by reafon of the pofition
we are in.   Eight

Eight months of the year, the weather is very hot, yet not so scalding, but that servants, both Christians, and slaves, labour and travel ten hours in a day.

As the Sun rises, there arises with him cool breezes of wind , and the higher and hotter the Sun shines, the stronger and cooler the breezes are, and blow alwayes from the Nore East, and by East, except in the time of the *Turnado :* And then it sometimes chops about into the South, for an hour or two, and then returns again to the same point where it was. The other four months it is not so hot, but is near the temper of the air in *England,* in the middle of *May,* and though in the hot seasons we sweat much, yet we do not find that faintness, that we find here, in the end of *July,* or beginning of *August.* With this great heat, there is such a moisture, as must of necessity cause the air to be very unwholsome.

We are seldom dry or thirsty, unless we overheat our bodies with extraordinary labour , or drinking strong drinks ; as of our *English* spirits , which we carry over, of *French* Brandy , or the drink of the Island, which is made of the skimmings of the Coppers, that boyl the Sugar, which they call kill-Devil. And though some of these be needful if they be used with temper ; yet the immoderate use of them, over-heats the body, which causes Costiveness , and Tortions in the bowels ; which is a disease very frequent there ; and hardly cur'd, and of which many have dyed, but certainly strong drinks are very re-quisite, where so much heat is ; for the spirits being exhausted with much sweating, the inner parts are left cold and faint , and shall need comforting, and reviving. Besides, our bodies having been used to colder Climates , find a debility, and a great failing in the vigour , and sprightlmess we have in colder Climates ; our blood too, is thin-ner and paler than in our own Countreys. Nor is the meat so well relish'd as in *England* ; but flat and insipid, the hogs flesh onely ex-cepted, which is indeed the best of that kind that I think is in the world.

Our Horses and Cattle seldom drink, and when they do, it is in very small quantities ; except such as have their bodies over heated with working.

This moisture of the air, causes all our Knives, Etweese, Keys, Needles, Swords, and Ammunition, to rust ; and that in an instant for take your knife to the grindstone, and grind away all the rust ; which done, wipe it dry, and put it up into your sheath, and so into your pocket, and in a very little time, draw it out ; and you shall find it beginning to rust all over ; which in more time, will eat deep into the steel, and spoil the blade. Our locks too , that are not often made use of, will rust in the wards, and so become useless, and Clocks, and Watches will seldome or never go true ; and all this occasion'd by the moistness of the Air. And this we found at sea : for before we came near this Island, we perceiv'd a kind of weather , which is neither rain nor mist, and continued with us sometimes four or five dayes together, which the Seamen call a Heysey weather, and rises to such a height, as though the Sun shine out bright , yet we cannot see his body, till nine a clock in the morning, nor after three in the after-noon. And we see the sky over our heads clear : a close and very unhealthful weather, and no pleasure at all in it.

This

This great heat and moisture together, is certainly the occasion that the trees and plants grow to such vast height, and largeness as they are.

How wate-red.

There is nothing in this Island so much wanting, as Springs and Rivers of water; there being but very few, and those very small and inconsiderable. I know but only one River, and that may rather be term'd a Lake, than a River; The Springs that run into it, are never able to fill it, they are so small; out fall to Sea it has none; but at spring tides, the Sea comes in and fills it; and at Nepe tides, it cannot run out again, the Sea banks being higher than it. But some of it issues out through the Sands, and leaves behind it a mixt water, of fresh and salt: at the time the tide comes in, it brings with it some fishes, which are content to remain there; being better pleased to live in this mixt water, than the Salt. Colonel *Humphrey Walrond*, who is owner of the land of both sides, and therefore of it; has told me, that he has taken fishes there, as big as Salmons, which have been overgrown with fat, as you have seen Porpisces; but extreamly sweet and firm.

But it has not been often, that such fish, or any other, have been taken in that place, by reason the whole Lake is filled with trees and roots.

So that no Net can be drawn, nor any Hook laid; for they will wind the lines about the roots, and so get away; or the lines break in pulling up, being fastned to the roots.

This River, or Lake, reaches not within the Land above twelve score yards, or a flight shot at most; and there is no part of it so broad, but you may cast a Coyte over it.

The spring tides there, seldom rise above four or five foot upright: there come from the sea into these small bibling rivolets, little Lobsters, but wanting the great claws afore, which are the sweetest and fullest of fish, that I have seen; *Chichester* Lobsters are not to be compared to them.

But the water which the people of this Island most relye upon, is rain water; which they keep in ponds, that have descents of ground to them, so that what falls on other ground, may run thither. And the place in which the Pond is set, must be low, and clay in the bottom: or if it be not naturally of Clay, it must be made so. For if it find any Leak to the rocky part, it gets between those clifts, and sinks in an instant. About the end of *December*, these ponds are fill'd; and with the help it hath by the weekly showrs that fall, they continue so, yet sometimes they feel a want. This pond water, they use upon all occasions, and to all purposes; to boyl their meat, to make their drink, to wash their linnen, for it will bear soap. But one thing seem'd to me a little loathsome, and that was the *Negroes* washing themselves in the Ponds, in hot weather; whose bodies have none of the sweetest savours. But the Planters are pleased to say, that the Sun with his virtual heat, draws up all noisome vapours, and so the waters become rarified, and pure again. But it was a great satisfaction to me, that a little Rivulet was near us, from whence we fetcht daily, as much as served us, both for meat, and drink.

In these ponds, I have never seen any small fish, fry, or any thing that lives or moves in it, except some flies that fall into it; but the water

ter is clear and well tasted. And because their Cattle shall not be in danger of miring or drowning, the best Husbands rail in a part of the Pond, where it is of a competent depth, for the water to stand, and pave that in the bottom with stone; and so the Cattle neither raise the mud, nor sink in with their feet; and so the water comes clear to them.

Water they save likewise from their houses, by gutters at the eves, which carry it down to cisterns. And the water which is kept there, being within the limits of their houses, many of which are built in manner of Fortifications, and have Lines, Bulwarks, and Bastions to defend themselves, in case there should be any uproar or commotion in the Island, either by the Christian servants, or *Negro* slaves; serves them for drink whilst they are besieged; as also, to throw down upon the naked bodies of the *Negroes*, scalding hot; which is as good a defence against their underminings, as any other weapons.

If any tumult or disorder be in the Island, the next neighbour to it, discharges a Musquet, which gives the Alarum to the whole Island; for, upon the report of that, the next shoots, and so the next, and next, till it go through the Island : Upon which warning, they make ready.

Bread, which is accounted the staff, or main supporter of mans life, has not here that full taste it has in *England*; but yet they account it nourishing and strengthening. It is made of the root of a small tree or shrub, which they call *Cassavie*; the manner of his growth I will let alone, till I come to speak of Trees and Plants in general.

His root only, which we are now to consider, (because our bread is made of it) is large and round, like the body of a small Still or retort; and as we gather it, we cut sticks that grow nearest to it, of the same tree, which we put into the ground, and they grow. And as we gather, we plant. This root, before it come to be eaten, suffers a strange conversion; for, being an absolute poyson when 'tis gathered, by good ordering, comes to be wholsom and nourishing; and the manner of doing it, is this : They wash the outside of the root clean, and lean it against a Wheel, whose sole is about a foot broad, and covered with Lattin, made rough like a large Grater. The Wheel to be turned about with a foot, as a Cutler turns his Wheel. And as it grates the root, it falls down in a large Trough, which is the receiver appointed for that purpose. This root thus grated, is as rank poyson, as can be made by the art of an Apothecary, of the most venomous simples he can put together : but being put into a strong piece of double Canvas, or Sackcloth, and press'd hard, that all the juice be squeezed out, and then opened upon a cloath, and dryed in the Sun, 'tis ready to make bread. And thus 'tis done.

They have a piece of Iron, which I guess is cast round, the diameter of which, is about twenty inches, a little hollowed in the middle, not unlike the mould that the Spectacle-makers grinde their glasses on, but not so much concave as that ; about half an inch thick at the brim or verge, but thicker towards the middle, with three feet like a pot, about six inches high , that fire may be underneath. To such a temper they heat this Pone, (as they call it) as to bake, but not burn. When 'tis made thus hot, the *Indians*, whom we trust to make it, because they are best acquainted with it, cast the meal upon the Pone, the whole breadth of it, and put it down with their hands, and

Meat and Drink for supportation of life:

and it will prefently ftick together : And when they think that fide almoft enough, with a thing like a Battle-dore, they turn the other; and fo turn and re-turn it fo often, till it be enough, which is prefently done. So they lay this Cake upon a flat board, and make another, and fo another, till they have made enough for the whole Family. This bread they made, when we came firft there, as thick as a pancake; but after that, they grew to a higher degree of curiofity , and made it as thin as a wafer, and yet purely white and crifp, as a new made wafer. Salt they never ufe in it, which I wonder at ; for the bread being taftelefs of it felf, they fhould give it fome little feafoning. There is no way it eats fo well, as in milk, and there it taftes like Almonds. They offer to make Pye-cruft, but very few attain to the skil of that ; for, as you work it up with your hand, or roll it out with a roller, it will alwayes crackle and chop, fo that it will not be raifed to hold any liquor, neither with, nor without, butter or eggs.

But after many tryals, and as often failings, at laft, I learnt the fecret of an *Indian* woman, who fhew'd me the right way of it, and that was, by fearfing it very fine, (and it will fall out as fine , as the fineft wheat-flower in *England*) if not finer. Yet, this is not all the fecret , for all this will not cure the cracking. But this is the main skill of the bufinefs : Set water on the fire in a skillet, and put to it as much of this fine flower, as will temper it to the thicknefs of ftarch or pap; and let it boyl a little, keeping it ftirring with a flice ; and mix this with the maffe of flower you mean to make into pye-cruft , which being very well mingled, and wrought together, you may add what coft you will of butter and eggs, and it will rife and ftand near as well as our paft in *England.*

But thofe that have not Cows, and cannot make butter upon the place, but muft make ufe of fuch as is brought from *England* or *Holland,* were better leave it out, and be content to eat their pye-cruft dry. Yet I make a main difference, between butter that is brought from either of thofe places, in refpect of the times it is brought. For, if a fhip fet out from *England* in *November,* and that fhip arrive at the *Barbadoes* at the middle, or near the end of *December,* when the Sun is at the fartheft diftance, the butter may come thither in very good condition; and being fet in cool places, may retain the tafte for a while: But, if the fhip fet out in Spring or Summer, that brings this butter, it is not then to be endured, it is fo reftie and loathfome. Nor can Cheefe be brought from thence without fpoyl, at that time of the year, except you put it in oyl. Neither are Candles to be brought, for the whole barrel will ftick together in one lump, and ftink fo profoundly, as neither Rats nor Mice will come near them, much lefs eat of them. For which reafon, the Planters, who are much troubled with this annoyance, as alfo, for that thefe candles cannot be taken out of the barrel whole, nor will ftand in the candleftick without drooping, and hanging down; they burn for the moft part wax lights, which they make themfelves, of wax they fetch from *Africa,* and have it at a reafonable rate, there being no Bees in the *Barbadoes.*

But I am too apt to fly out in extravagant digreffions ; for, the thing I went to fpeak of, was bread only, and the feveral kinds of it; and having faid as much of the bread of *Caffavie* as I know, I will give you one word of another kind of bread they make , which is a

mixt

mixt fort of bread, and is made of the flower of *Mayes* and *Caffavie* mixt together; for the *Mayes* it felf will make no bread, it is fo extream heavy and lumpifh: But thefe two being mixt, they make it into large Cakes, two inches thick; and that, in my opinion, taftes the likeft to *Englifh* bread of any.

But the *Negroes* ufe the *Mayes* another way, which is, toafting the ears of it at the fire, and fo eating it warm off the ear. And we have a way, to feed our Chriftian fervants with this *Mayes*, which is, by pounding it in a large Morter, and boyling it in water, to the thick-hefs of Frumenty; and fo put in a Tray fuch a quantity, as will ferve a mefs of feven or eight people; give it them cold, and fcarce afford them falt with it. This we call *Lob-lollie*. But the *Negroes*, when they come to be fed with this, are much difcontented, and cry out, *O!O! no more Lob-lob.*

The third fort of bread we ufe, is only Potatoes, which are cho-fen out of the dryeft and largeft they can choofe: And at rhe time we firft came, there was little elfe ufed, at many good Planters Tables in the Ifland. And thefe are all the forts of bread that I know growing upon the place.

The next thing that comes in order, is Drink, which being made of feveral materials, afford more variety in the defcription. The firft, and that which is moft ufed in the Ifland, is *Mobbie*, a drink made of Potatoes, and thus done. Put the Potatoes into a tub of water, and, with a broom, ftir them up and down, till they are wafht clean; then take them out, and put them into a large iron or brafs pot, fuch as you boyl beef in, in *England*; and put to them as much water, as will only cover a quarter part of them; and cover the top of the pot with a piece of thick canvas doubled, or fuch cloth as facks are made with, covering it clofe, that the fteam go not out. Then make a little fire underneath, fo much only as will caufe thefe roots to ftew; and when they are foft, take them out, and with your hands, fqueeze, break, and mafh them very fmall, in fair water; letting them ftay there, till the water has drawn and fuckt out all the fpirit of the roots; which will be done in an hour or two. Then put the liquor and roots into a large woollen bag, like a jelly-bag, pointed at the bottom; and let it run through that, into a Jar, and within two hours it will begin to work. Cover it, and let it ftand till the next day, and then 'tis fit to be drunk. And as you will have it ftronger or fmaller, put in greater or leffer quantities of roots; fome make it fo ftrong, as to be drunk with fmall quantities. But the drink it felf, being temperately made, does not at all fly up into the head, but is a fprightly thirft-quenching drink. If it be put up in fmall casks, as Rundlets, or Firkins, it will laft four or five dayes good, and drink much more fprightly than out of the Jar. I cannot liken it to any thing fo near, as *Rhenifh-wine* in the Muft; but it is fhort of it in the ftrength of the fpirit, and finenefs of the tafte.

There are two feveral layers, in which thefe roots grow; one makes the skins of the Potatoes white, the other red: And where the red roots grow, the *Mobbie*, will be red like *Claret-wine*; the other white.

Though this be the drink moft generally ufed in the Ifland, yet I cannot commend the wholfomnefs of it, for, the moft part of the

roots

Drink of Mobbie.

roots have a moiſt quality in them, and are the cauſe of Hydropick humours. Mr. *Phillip Bell*, then the Governour of the Iſland, told me that when he was Governour of the Iſle of *Providence*, that there chanc'd ſome *Spaniards* to land there, and taſting of this drink, wondred that any of thoſe that continually drink it were alive; ſo unwholſome and Hydropick he conceived this drink to be.

Perino.   Another drink they have which is accounted much wholſomer, though not altogether ſo pleaſant, and that is *Perino*; a drink which the *Indians* make for their own drinking, and is made of the *Caſſavy* root, which I told you is a ſtrong poyſon; and this they cauſe their old wives, who have a ſmall remainder of teeth, to chaw and ſpit out into water, (for the better breaking and macerating of the root). This juyce in three or four hours will work, and purge it ſelf of the poyſonous quality.

Having ſhewed you, in the making of Bread, that the moyſture being preſs'd out, which is accounted the poyſonous quality that root has; by drying and baking it is made uſeful and wholſome, and now having the juyce and root both uſed, and both theſe put into water, which is moiſt, I know not which way to reconcile theſe direct contraries, but this; that the poyſon of the old womens breath and teeth having been tainted with many ſeveral poxes, (a diſeaſe common amongſt them, though they have many and the beſt cures for it,) are ſuch oppoſites to the poyſon of the *Caſſavy*, as they bend their forces ſo vehemently one againſt another, as they both ſpend their poyſonous qualities in that conflict; and ſo the relict of them both, becomes leſs unwholſome; and the water, which is in it ſelf pure, caſts out the remainder of the ill qualities they leave behind : which is manifeſted by the extraordinary working, which is far beyond that of Beer, Wine, or Sider with us in *Europe*. This drink will keep a month or two, being put into barrels, and taſtes the likeſt to *Engliſh* beer of any drink we have there.

Grippo.   *Grippo* is a third ſort of drink, but few make it well; it was never my chance to taſte it, which made me the leſs curious to enquire after it.

Punch.   *Punch* is a fourth ſort, and of that I have drunk; it is made of water and ſugar put together, which in ten dayes ſtanding will be very ſtrong, and fit for labourers.

Plum-drink.   A fifth, is made of wild Plumbs, which grow here in great abundance, upon very large trees, which being preſs'd, and ſtrayned, give a very ſharp, and poynant flaver; but there is not much of it made, becauſe of the trouble of making it, and they are not there very indulgent to their palats.

Plantine-drink   But the drink of the Plantine, is far beyond all theſe; gathering them full ripe, and in the height of their ſweetneſs, we pill off the skin, and maſh them in water well boyl'd; and after we have let them ſtay there a night, we ſtrain it, and bottle it up, and in a week drink it; and it is very ſtrong and pleaſant drink, but it is to be drunk but ſparingly, for it is much ſtronger than Sack, and is apt to mount up into the head.

The ſeventh ſort of drink is that we make of the skimming of ſugar, which is infinitely ſtrong, but not very pleaſant in taſte; it is common, and therefore the leſs eſteem'd; the value of it is half a Crown

a

a gallon, the people drink much of it, indeed too much; for it often layes them afleep on the ground, and that is accounted a very unwholfome lodging.

The eighth fort of drink is Beveridge, made of fpring water, white fugar, and juyce of Oranges, and this is not onely pleafant but wholfome.

Beveridge.

The laft and beft fort of drink that this Ifland or the world affords, is the incomparable wine of Pines; And is certainly the Nectar which the Gods drunk; for on earth there is none like it; and that is made of the pure juyce of the fruit it felf, without commixture of water, or any other creature, having in it felf, a natural compound of all taftes excellent, that the world can yield. This drink is too pure to keep long; in three or four dayes it will be fine; 'tis made by preffing the fruit and ftraining the liquor, and it is kept in bottles.

Wine of Pines.

Having given you a tafte of the Bread and Drink this Ifland affords, which will ferve any mans palate, that is not over curious; I could tell you what we have of both forts that is brought to us from other parts of the world; as Biskets, both fine and courfe, Barrels of meal clofe put up; which comes to us very fweet from *England*, and *Holland*; of which we make Bread, Pye-cruft, and Puddings. And for drink, good *Englifh* Beer, *French* and *Spanifh* Wines, with others, fome from the *Maderas*, fome from *Fiall*, one of the Iflands of *Afores*; So we cannot juftly complain of want, either of bread or drink, and, from *England*, Spirits, fome of Annifeeds, fome of Mint, fome of Wormwood, *&c.* And from *France, Brandy,* which is extream ftrong, but accounted very wholfome.

Having given you a juft account, as near as my memory will ferve of the bread and drink of this Ifland: The next thing is the feveral forts of meat we have there; and becaufe Hogs flefh is the moft general meat, and indeed the beft the Ifland affords, I will begin with that, which is (without queftion) as good, as any can be of that kind: for their feeding being as good, as can grow any where, the flefh muft needs be anfwerable; fruit, the nuts of Locuft, Pompians of a rare kind, almoft as fweet as Milions, the bodies of the Plantines, and Bonanoes, Sugar-canes, and Mayes, being their daily food.

Meat of all kinds.

When we came firft upon the Ifland, I perceiv'd the fties they made to hold them, were trees, with the ends lying crofs upon one another, and the inclofure they made, was not large enough to hold the numbers of Hogs were in them, with convenient diftance to play and ftir themfelves for their health, and pleafure; fo that they were in a manner pefter'd, and choakt up, with their own ftink, which is fure the moft noyfome of any other beaft, and by reafon of the Suns heat much worfe; I have fmelt the ftink of one of thofe fties down the wind, near a mile, through all the wood: and the crowding and thrufting them fo clofe together, was certainly the caufe of their want of health, which much hindred their growth; So that they were neither fo large, nor their flefh fo fweet, as when they were wild, and at their own liberty, and choice of feeding.

For I have heard Major *Hilliard* fay: that at their firft coming there, they found Hogs, that one of them weighed (the intrals being taken out, and the head off) 400 weight. And now at the time of

my

my being there, the moſt ſort of thoſe, that were in ours and our neighbours ſtyes, were hardly ſo big as the ordinary ſwine in *England*. So finding this decay in their growth, by ſtowing them too cloſe together, I adviſed Collonel *Modiford* to make a larger ſtye, and to wall it about with ſtone ; which he did, and made it a mile about, ſo that it was rather a Park than a Stye ; and ſet it on the ſide of a dry Hill, the greateſt part Rock, with a competent Pond of water in the bottom ; and plac'd it between his two Plantations, that from either, food might be brought, and caſt over to them, with great convenience: And made ſeveral diviſions in the Park, for the Sowes with Pig, with little houſes ſtanding ſhelving, that their foulneſs by gutters might fall away, and they lye dry ; Other diviſions for the Barrow-Hogs, and ſome for Boars.

This good ordering cauſed them to grow ſo large and fat, as they wanted very little of their largeneſs when they were wild. They are the ſweeteſt fleſh of that kind, that ever I taſted, and the lovlieſt to look on in a diſh, either boyl'd, roaſted, or bak'd : With a little help of art. I will deceive a very good palate, with a ſhoulder of it for Mutton, or a leg for Veal, taking off the skin, with which they were wont to make minc't Pies, ſeaſoning it with ſalt, cloves, and mace, and ſome ſweet herbs minc'd. And being bak'd, and taken out of the Oven, opening the lid, put in a dram-cup of *Kill-Devil* ; and being ſtirr'd together, ſet it on the Table ; and that they call'd a *Calvesfoot Pye* ; and, till I knew what it vvas made of, I thought it very good meat : When I came firſt upon the Iſland, I found the Pork dreſs'd the plain wayes of boyling, roaſting, and ſometimes baking : But I gave them ſome taſtes of my Cookery, in haſhing, and fricaſing this fleſh ; and they all were much taken with it ; and in a week, every one was practiſing the Art of Cookery. And indeed, no fleſh taſtes ſo well in Collops, Haſhes, or Fricaſes, as this. And when I bak'd it, I alwayes laid a Side of a young Goat underneath, and a ſide of a Shot (which is a young Hog of a quarter old) a top. And this, well ſeaſoned, and well bak'd, is as good meat, as the beſt Paſty of Fallow-Deer, that ever I taſted.

In the cooleſt time of the year, I have made an eſſay to powder it, and hang it up for Bacon : But there is ſuch loſs in't, as 'tis very ill Husbandry to practiſe it ; for, it muſt be cut through in ſo many places, to let the ſalt in, as when 'tis to be dreſs'd, much goes to waſte. And therefore I made no more attempts that way. But a little corning with ſalt, makes this fleſh very ſavoury, either boyled or roaſted.

About *Chriſtmas*, we kill a Boar, and of the ſides of it, make three or four Collers of Brawn ; for then the weather is ſo cool, as, with ſome art, it may be kept ſweet a week : and to make the ſouc't drink give it the ſpeedier and quicker ſeaſoning, we make it of *Mobbie*, with ſtore of Salt, Lemons, and Lymes, ſliced in it, with ſome Nutmeg, which gives it an excellent flaver.

Beef, we have very ſeldome any, that feeds upon the ſoil of this place, except it be of Gods killing, (as they tearm it) ; for very few are kill'd there by mens hands ; it were too ill Husbandry, for they coſt too dear, and they cannot be ſpared from their work, which they muſt advance by all the means they can. Such a Planter as Collonel *James Drax* (who lives like a Prince) may kill now and then one ;
but

but very few in the Iſland did ſo when I was there.

The next to Swines-fleſh in goodneſs, are. Turkies, large, fat, and full of gravy. Next to them, Pullen or Dunghill-foul : and laſt of all, Muſcovia-Ducks, which being larded with the fat of this Pork, (being ſeaſoned with pepper and ſalt) are an excellent bak'd-meat. All theſe, with their Eggs and Chickens, we eat.

Turtle-Doves they have of two ſorts, and both very good meat ; but there is a ſort of Pidgeons, which come from the leeward Iſlands at one time of the year, and it is in *September* ; and ſtay till *Chriſtmas* be paſt, and then return again : But very many of them ne'r make returns, to tell news of the good fruit they found there : For, they are ſo fat, and of ſuch excellent taſtes, as many fowlers kill them with guns, upon the trees ; and ſome of them are ſo fat, as their weight with the fall, cauſes them to burſt in pieces. They are good roaſted, boyl'd, or bak'd, but beſt cut in halves, and ſtewed ; to which Cookery, there needs no liquor, for their own gravy will abundantly ſerve to ſtew them.

Rabbets we have, but tame ones, and they have but faint taſtes, more like a Chicken than a Rabbet.

And though they have divers other Birds, which I will not forget to recount in their due times, and place ; yet, none for food for the Table, which is the buſineſs I intend at this preſent. Other fleſh-meat, I do not remember.

Now for fiſh, though the Iſland ſtands as all Iſlands do, invironed with the Sea, (and therefore is not like to be unfurniſh'd of that proviſion) yet, the Planters are ſo good husbands, and tend their profits ſo much, as they will not ſpare a *Negroes* abſence ſo long, as to go to the *Bridge* and fetch it. And the Fiſhermen ſeeing their fiſh lye upon their hands, and ſtink (which it will do in leſs than ſix hours) forbear to go to Sea to take it ; only ſo much as they can have preſent vent for, at the Taverns at the *Bridge* ; and thither the Planters come, when they have a mind to feaſt themſelves with fiſh, to Mr. *Jobſons*, or *Joan Fullers*, where they have it well dreſs'd ; for they were both my Pupils. Butter they ſeldom have, that will beat thick, but in ſtead of that, we are fain to uſe vinegar and ſpice, and much of it fryed in oyle, and eaten hot ; and ſome marinated, and ſouc't in pickle, and eaten cold. Collonel *Humphrey Walrond* has the advantage of all the Planters in the Iſland ; for, having a Plantation near the Sea, he hath of his own a Sain to catch fiſh withall, which his own ſervants and ſlaves put out to Sea, and, twice or thrice a week, bring home all ſorts of ſuch ſmall and great fiſhes, as are near the ſhoar ; amongſt which, ſome are very large, and excellently well taſted. For, he being a Gentleman, that had been bred with much freedom, liberty, and plenty, in *England*, could not ſet his mind ſo earneſtly upon his profit, as to forget his accuſtomed lawful pleaſures, but would have his Table well furniſh'd, with all ſorts of good meat the Land and Sea afforded ; and as freely bid his friends welcom to it. And I, as the pooreſt of his friends, in a lingring ſickneſs, and near death, found ſuch a charity with him, as I ſhall never forget to pay my thanks for, to the laſt hour of my life ; and I ſhall account it as a great happineſs, (if ever it fall in the compaſs of my power) to be ſerviceable to him or his, as any thing that can befall me in the world.

Amongſt

Amongſt other fiſhes that were taken by his Sain , (as the Snappers, red and grey, Cavallos, Macquerels, Mullets, Cony-fiſh , with divers others, firm and excellent ſweet fiſh) he took four , that were about a yard long at the leaſt, all at one draught, and, to that length , bigger grown than Salmonds, of the rareſt colour that ever I beheld ; from the back-finn, which is the middle of the fiſh, to the end of the tail, the pureſt graſſe-green that ever I ſaw, and as ſhining as Satin : but the fins and tail dapled or ſpotted with as pure a hair-colour, and from the back finn to the head, pure hair colour dapled with green ; the ſcales as big for the moſt part, as a half-crown piece of ſilver. This fiſh is no fiſh of prey, but lives by what he finds in the bottom of the Sea, as I perceived by what was in his maw.   An excellent ſweet fiſh ; I dreſſed them ſeveral wayes, and all proved excellent. There is one fiſh wanting to this Iſland , whoſe kindes are very frequent upon moſt of the *Charibby* and *Lucaick* Iſlands ; and that is the green *Turtle*, which is the beſt food the Sea affords , and the greateſt ſtore of them ; but I have ſeen very few of that kind in the *Barbadoes*, and thoſe neither fat nor kindly ; and the reaſon is , there are no ſhelves nor ſands to lay their eggs , or to ayre themſelves on : For, theſe fiſhes delight to be on the ſands, and can remain there twelve hours, all the time the Tyde is out ; and then ſuffer themſelves to be carried away by the return of the next Tyde.   They take infinite numbers of them, by turning them on their backs with ſtaves, where they lye till they are fetcht away.   A large *Turtle* will have in her body half a buſhel of eggs, which ſhe layes in the ſand, and that being warm, they are hatcht in the heat.

When you are to kill one of theſe fiſhes, the manner is, to lay him on his back on a table, and when he ſees you come with a knife in your hand to kill him, he vapours out the grievouſeſt ſighs, that ever you heard any creature make, and ſheds as large tears as a Stag, that has a far greater body, and larger eyes. He has a joynt or crevis, about an inch within the utmoſt edge of his ſhell, which goes round about his body, from his head to his tail, on his belly-ſide ; into which joynt or crevis, you put your knife, beginning at the head, and ſo rip up that ſide, and then do as much to the other ; then lifting up his belly, which we call his *Calipee*, we lay open all his bowels, and taking them out, come next to his heart, which has three diſtinct points, but all meet above where the fat is ; and if you take it out, and lay it in a diſh, it will ſtir and pant ten hours after the fiſh is dead.   Sure , there is no creature on the Earth, nor in the Seas, that enjoyes life with ſo much ſweetneſs and delight, as this poor fiſh the *Turtle* , nor none more delicate in taſte, and more nouriſhing, than he.

Next to the fleſh and fiſh this Iſland affords, 'tis fit to conſider what *Quelquechoſes* there are to be found , that may ſerve to furniſh out a Table of ſuch Viands, as are there to be had ; which are eggs ſeveral wayes, *viz.* poch'd, and laid upon ſippets of bread, ſoak'd in butter and juice of limes, and ſugar, with plumpt currans ſtrewed upon them , and Cloves, Mace, and Cinamon beaten, ſtrewed on that, with a little ſalt. Eggs boyl'd and roaſted, fryed with Collops of the fat of Pork well powdered.   Buttered eggs, an Amulet of eggs, with the juice of Limes and Sugar, a Froize, and a Tanſey ; Cuſtards, as good as any at my Lord Mayors Table ; Cheeſ-cakes, Puffs, ſecond Porrage, which

is

is cream boyl'd to a height, with yolk of eggs and season'd with sugar, and spice, Jelly which we make of the flesh of young pigs, calves feet, and a cock, and is excellent good, but must presently be eaten, for it will not last.   Cream alone, and some done several wayes, of which there is great variety, having Lemons, Lymes, and Oranges ready at hand; and some wherein we put Plantines, Gnavers and Bonanoes, stew'd, or preserv'd with sugar, and the same fruits also preserv'd and put in dishes by themselves, without Cream; and for a whetstone, to pull on a cup of wine, we have dryed Neats tongues, brought from new and old *England*; and from *Holland*, *Westphalia* Bacon, and Caviare; as also pickl'd Herring, and Macquerel, which we have from new *England*, and from *Virginia Botargo*, of which sort I have eaten the best at Collonel *Draxes* that ever I tasted.

The fruits that this Island affords, I have already named, and therefore it will be needless to name them twice; you may take your choice, whether you will have them set on the Table before or after meat; they use as they do in *Italy*, to eat them before meat.

The victuals brought from forraign parts are these, Beef which we have from *Holland*, from Old and New *England*, *Virginia*, and some from *Russia*; and yet comes to us sweet. Pork from all these places, with the most sorts of salt fish; as Ling, Haberdine, Cod, poor-John, pickled Macquerels, pickled Herrings, all very good. Sturgeon from New *England*, but so ill Cook'd, as 'tis hardly to be eaten; for they want the skil both of boyling and seasoning it; they first over-boyl it, and next over-salt it, and so the fish being over tender by boyling, the salt frets and eats upon it all the way; for when we come to open it, being carried far from the Bridge, and shaken in the carriage: there is scarce a whole piece, but the Sturgeon and pickle all in a mash, & so vehemently salt, as I could never eat any of it, but at Collonel *Wallronds* Plantation it is less broken.

Pickled Turtle, we have from the Leeward Islands, but so uncleanly ordered, as we could hardly find in our hearts to eat it; for they gather the Salt and Sand together, for hast, upon the Island where it is taken up as; though we wash it never so well, yet the grit cracks in our teeth; it has a taste being salted, almost as ill as puffins, which we have from the Iles of *Silly*, but this kind of food, is only for servants; sometimes the *Negroes* get a little, but seldome the one or the other did eat any bone meat, at our first coming thither.

But now at my coming away from thence, it was much better'd, for by the care and good Husbandry of the Planters, there was greater plenty, both of the victuals they were wont to eat, as Potatoes, Bonavist, Loblolly, as also of the bone meat, *viz.* Pork, salt Fish, and powder'd beef, which came thither by sea, from forraign parts, in so much as the *Negroes* were allowed each man two Macquerels a week, and every woman one; which were given out to them on *Saturday* in the evening, after they had their allowance of Plantines, which was every one a large bunch, or two little ones, to serve them for a weeks provision; and if any cattle dyed by mischance, or by any disease: the servants eat the bodies, and the *Negroes* the skins, head, and intrails which was divided amongst them by the Overseers; or if any horse, than the whole bodies of them were distributed amongst the *Negroes*, and that they thought a high feast, with which   never poor souls were more contented; and the drink to the servants with this dyet,
                                                                nothing

nothing but *Mobbie*, and fometimes a little Beveridge; but the *Negroes* nothing but fair water.   And now I think, I have given you a juft account of the victuals that feeds the Mafters, the Servants, and the Slaves of this Ifland : and now you fee the provifion the Ifland affords, give me leave to fhew you vvhat feafts they can (vvhen they vvill) make for their friends, upon their Plantations, vvhich that I may the better do, I vvill make tvvo bills of fare; the one for an Inland Plantation , the other for a Plantation near the fea, of fuch meat and fuch plenty of that, as I have feen and eaten of, at either of thofe Plantations; And for the Inland Plantation, I will make choice of Collonel *James Draxes*, at vvhofe Table I have found vvell drefs'd, thefe follovving meats; for the firft Courfe vvhereof there hath been tvvo meffes of meat and both equally good, and this feaft is alvvayes vvhen he kills a beef, vvhich he feeds extreamly fat, giving him a dozen acres of Bonavift to go loofe in, and due times of vvatering.

Firft then (becaufe beef being the greateft rarity in the Ifland, efpecially fuch as this is) I vvill begin vvith it , and of that fort there are thefe difhes at either mefs, a Rump boyl'd, a Chine roafted, a large piece of the breaft roafted, the Cheeks bak'd, of which is a difh to either mefs, the tongue and part of the tripes minc'd for Pyes, feafon'd with fweet Herbs finely minc'd, Suet, Spice and Currans; the Legs, Pallets and other ingredients for an *Olio Podrido* to either mefs, a difh of Marrow-bones, fo here are 14 difhes at the Table and all of Beef; and this he intends as the great *Regalio* , to which he invites his fellow Planters; who having well eaten of it, the difhes are taken away, and another Courfe brought in, which is a Potato pudding, a difh of Scots Collops of a leg of Pork, as good as any in the world , a fricacy of the fame, a difh of boyl'd Chickens, a fhoulder of a young Goat drefs'd with his Blood and Time, a Kid with a pudding in his belly, a fucking Pig, which is there the fatteft, whiteft, and fweeteft in the world, with the poynant-fauce of the Brains, Salt, Sage, and Nutmeg done with Claret-wine, a Shoulder of Mutton which is there a rare difh, a Pafty of the fide of a young Goat, and a fide of a fat young Shot upon it, well feafon'd with Pepper and Salt, and with fome Nutmeg , a Loyn of Veal, to which there wants no fauce being fo well furnifh'd with Oranges, Lemons, and Lymes, three young Turkies in a difh, two Capons, of which fort I have feen fome extream large and very fat, two Hens with eggs in a difh, four Ducklings, eight Turtle doves , and three Rabbets; and for cold bak'd meats, two *Mufcovia* Ducks larded, and feafon'd well with Pepper and Salt : and thefe being taken off the Table, another courfe is fet on, and that is of *Weftphalia* or *Spanifh* bacon, dryed Neats Tongues, Botargo, pickled Oyfters, Caviare, Anchovies, Olives, and (intermixt with thefe) Cuftards, Creams, fome alone, fome with preferves of Plantines, Bonano, Gnavers, put in, and thofe preferv'd alone by themfelves, Cheefe-cakes, Puffes , which are to be made with *Englifh* flower, and bread; for the Caffavie will not ferve for this kind of Cookery; fometimes Tanfies, fometimes Froizes, or Amulets, and for fruit, Plantines, Bonanoes, Gnavers, Milions , prickled Pear, Anchove Pear, prickled Apple, Cuftard Apple, water Milions, and Pines worth all that went before.   To this meat you feldom fail of this drink, Mobbie, Beveridge , Brandy, Kill-Devil , Drink of the Plantine, Claret-wine, White-wine, and Rhenifh-wine,

Sherry,

Sherry, Canary, Red sack, wine of Fiall, with all Spirits that come from *England*, and with all this, you shall find as chearful a look, and as hearty a welcome, as any man can give to his best friends. And so much for a Feast of an inland Plantation.

Now for a Plantation near the Sea, which shall be Collonel *Walrond's*, he being the best seated for a Feast, of any I know : I must say this, that though he be wanting in the first Course, which is Beef; yet, it will be plentifully supplyed in the last, which is Fish; and that the other wants. And though Collonel *Walrond*, have not that infinite store of the provisions Collonel *Drax* abounds in; yet, he is not wanting in all the kinds he has, unless it be Sheep, Goats, and Beef, and so for all the sorts of meats, that are in my Bill of Fare, in Collonel *Drax* his Feast, you shall find the same in Collonel *Walronds*, except these three, and these are supplyed with all these sorts of fish I shall name, to wit, *Mullets, Macquerels, Parrat fish, Snappers,* red and grey, *Cavallos, Terbums, Crabs, Lobsters,* and *Cony fish,* with divers sorts more, for which we have no names. And having these rare kinds of fishes, 'twere a vain superfluity, to make use of all those dishes I have named before, but only such as shall serve to fill up the Table; and when he has the ordering it, you must expect to have it excellent; his fancy and contrivance of a Feast, being as far beyond any mans there, as the place where he dwells is better scituate, for such a purpose. And his Land touching the Sea, his House being not half a quarter of a mile from it, and not interposed by any unlevel ground, all rarities that are brought to the Island, from any part of the world, are taken up, brought to him, and stowed in his Cellars, in two hours time, and that in the night; as, Wine, of all kinds, Oyl, Olives, Capers, Sturgeon, Neats tongues, Anchovies, Caviare, Botargo, with all sorts of salted meats, both flesh and fish for his Family; as, Beef, Pork, *English* Pease, Ling, Haberdine, Cod, Poor John, and Jerkin Beef, which is husled, and flasht through, hung up and dryed in the Sun; no salt at all put to it. And thus ordered in *Hispaniola,* as hot a place as *Barbadoes,* and yet it will keep longer than powdred Beef, and is as dry as Stock-fish, and just such meat for flesh, as that is for fish, and as little nourishment in it; but it fills the belly, and serves the turn, where no other meat is. Though some of these may be brought to the inland Plantations well conditioned; yet, the Wines cannot possibly come good; for the wayes are such, as no Carts can pass; and to bring up a Butt of Sack, or a Hogshead of any other Wine, upon *Negroes* backs, will very hardly be done in a night, so long a time it requires, to hand it up and down the Gullies; and if it be carried in the day-time, the Sun will heat and taint it, so as it will lose much of his spirit and pure taste; and if it be drawn out in bottles at the *Bridge,* the spirits fly away in the drawing, and you shall find a very great difference in the taste and quickness of it. Oyle will endure the carriage better than Wine, but over-much heat will abate something of the purity, and excellent taste it has naturally. And for Olives, 'tis well known, that jogging in the carriage causes them to bruise one another; and some of them being bruised, will grow rotten, and infect the rest. So that Wine, Oyle, and Olives, cannot possibly be brought to such Plantations, as are eight or ten miles from the *Bridge*; and from thence, the most part of these commodities are to be fetch'd. So that you may

imagine

imagine, what advantage Collonel *Walrond* has, of any inland Plantation, having these materials, which are the main *Regalia's* in a Feaft,
and his own contrivance to boot, besides all I have formerly nam'd,
concerning raw and preserv'd fruits, with all the other *Quelquechofes*.
And thus much I thought good to say for the honour of the Island,
which is no more than truth; because I have heard it fleighted by some,
that seem'd to know much of it.

Commodi-
ties Expor-
ted.

About a hundred fail of Ships yearly vifit this Island, and receive,
during the time of their ftay in the Harbours, for their fuftenance, the
native Victuals growing in the Island, such as I have already named;
besides what they carry away, and what is carried away by Planters
of the Isle, that vifit other parts of the world. The commodities this
Island trades in, are *Indico, Cotton-wool, Tobacco, Sugar, Ginger,* and
Fuftick-wood.

Commodi-
ties Impor-
ted.

The Commodities these Ships bring to this Island, are, *Servants* and
Slaves, both men and women; *Horfes, Cattle, Affinigoes, Camels, Uten-*
fils for boyling Sugar as, *Coppers, Taches, Goudges,* and *Sockets*; all manner
of working tooles for Tradefmen, as, *Carpenters, Joyners, Smiths, Ma-*
fons, Mill-wrights, Wheel-wrights, Tinkers, Coopers, &c. *Iron, Steel, Lead,*
Brafs, Pewter, Cloth of all kinds, both *Linnen* and *Woollen*; *Stuffs, Hats,*
Hofe, Shooes, Gloves, Swords, Knives, Locks, Keys, &c. *Victuals* of all
kinds, that will endure the Sea, in fo long a voyage. *Olives, Capers,*
Anchovies, falted Flefh and *Fifh, pickled Macquerels* and *Herrings, Wine*
of all forts, and the boon Beer, *d' Angleterre.*

What Buil-
ding, we
found at our
firft coming
upon the
Ifland.

I had it in my thought before I came there, what kind of Buildings
would be fit for a Country, that was fo much troubled with heat, as
I have heard this was; and did expect to find thick walls, high roofs, and
deep cellers; but found neither the one nor the other, but clean contrary; timber houfes, with low roofs, fo low, as for the moft part of
them, I could hardly ftand upright with my hat on, and no cellars at
all: befides, another courfe they took, which was more wonder to me
than all that; which was, ftopping, or barring out the wind, which
fhould give them the greateft comfort, when they were neer ftifled
with heat. For, the wind blowing alwayes one way, which was Eaft-
wardly, they fhould have made all the openings they could to the
Eaft, thereby to let in the cool breezes, to refrefh them when the heat
of the day came. But they, clean contrary, clofed up all their houfes to
the Eaft, and opened all to the Weft; fo that in the afternoons, when
the Sun came to the Weft, thofe little low roofed rooms were like
Stoves, or heated Ovens. And truly, in a very hot day, it might raife
a doubt, whether fo much heat without, and fo much Tobacco and
kill-devil within, might not fet the houfe a fire; for thefe three ingredients are ftrong motives to provoke it, and they were ever
there.

But at laft I found by them, the reafons of this ftrange prepofterous
manner of building, which was grounded upon the weakeft and filli-
eft foundation that could be: For they alledged, that at the times of
rain, which was very often, the wind drave the rain in at their
windows fo faft, as the houfes within were much annoyed with it;
for having no glafs to keep it out, they could feldom fit or lye dry;
and fo being conftrained to keep out the air on that fide, for fear of
letting in the water, would open the Weft ends of their houfes fo
                                                                        wide

wide, (as was beyond the proportion of windows to repair that want) and fo let in the fire ; not confidering at all, that there was fuch a thing as fhutters for windows, to keep out the rain that hurt them, and let in the wind to refrefh them, and do them good at their plea-fure. But this was a confideration laid afide by all, or the moft part of the meaner fort of Planters. But at laft I found the true reafon, was their poverty and indigence, which wanted the means to make fuch conveniences; and fo, being compelled by that, had rather fuffer painfully, and patiently abide this inconvenience, than fell or part with any of their goods, to prevent fo great a mifchief : So loath poor people are to part with that, which is their next immediate help, to fupport them in their great want of fuftenance. For, at that lock they often were, and fome good Planters too, that far'd very hard, when we came firft into the Ifland. So that hard la-bour, and want of victuals, had fo much deprefs'd their fpirits, as they were come to a declining and yielding condition. Nor can this be called flothfulnefs or fluggifhnefs in them, as fome will have it, but a decay of their fpirits, by long and tedious hard labour, fleight feeding, and ill lodging, which is able to wear out and quell the beft fpirit of the world.

The *Locuft* is a tree of fuch a growth, both for length and bignefs, as may ferve for beams in a very large room : I have feen many of them, whofe ftraight bodies are above fifty foot high, the diameter of the ftem or body, three foot and half. The timber of this tree is a hard clofe fubftance, heavy, but firm, and not apt to bend, fome-what hard for tooles to cut ; brittle, but lafting. *Maftick*, not alto-gether fo large as he, but of a tougher fubftance, and not accounted fo brittle. The *Bully-tree* wants fomething of the largenefs of thefe, but in his other qualities goes beyond either ; for, he is full out as la-fting, and as ftrong, but not fo heavy, nor fo hard for tooles to work. The *Redwood* and *prickled yellow wood*, good for pofts or beams, and are lighter than the *Locuft*; both are accounted very lafting, and good for building. The *Cedar* is, without controul, the beft of all ; but by reafon it works fmooth, and looks beautiful, we ufe it moft in Wain-fcot, Tables, and Stools. Other timber we have, as the *Iron-wood*, and another fort, which are excellent good to endure wet and dry ; and of thofe we make Shingles, which being fuch a kind of wood, as will not warp nor rive, are the beft coverings for a houfe that can be, full out as good as Tiles, and lye lighter upon the Rafters.

What mate-rials grow in the Ifland fit to build with, which may be call'd the Elements of Archite-cture. And firft, for Timber.

We have two forts of Stone, and either will ferve indifferently well in building : The one we find on fides of fmall Hills, and it lyes as ours do in *England*, in Quarries ; but they are very fmall, rough, and ill fhaped, fome of them porous, like Honey combes ; but being burnt, they make excellent Lyme, the whiteft and firmeft when 'tis dry, that I have feen ; and by the help of this, we make the better fhift with our ill fhap'd ftone; for this lime binds it faft together, and keeps it firm to endure the weather. Other Stone we have, which we find in great Rocks, and maffie pieces in the ground, but fo foft, as with your finger you may bore a hole into it ; and this foftnefs gives us the means of cutting it with two-handed Sawes, which being hard, we could not fo eafily do, and the eafinefs caufes the expedition ; for by that, we the more fpeedily fit it for our walls, taking a juft breadth

Stone fit for Building.

of

of the walls, and cutting it accordingly ; so that we need very little hewing.   This stone, as we cut it in the quarry, is no harder than ordinary morter , but being set out in the weather, by pieces as we cut it, grows indifferently hard, and is able to bear all the weight that lyes on it , and the longer it lyes, the harder it grows.   Many essayes we made, whilst I was there, for the making and burning of bricks, but never could attain to the perfection of it ; and the reason was, the over fatness of the clay , which would alwayes crackle and break, when it felt the great heat of the fire in the Clampe ; and by no means could we find the true temper of it , though we made often tryals.   There was an ingenious *Jew* upon the I sland, whose name was *Solomon*, that undertook to teach the making of it ; yet for all that, when it came to the touch his wisdom failed , and we were deceived in our expectation, I doubt not but there is a way of tempering, to make it far better than ours in *England* ; for the pots which we find in the Island , wherein the *Indians* boyl'd their Pork, were of the same kind of Clay, and they were the best and finest temper'd ware of earth that ever I saw.   If we could find the true temper of it, a great advantage might be made to the Island ; for the air being moist , the stones often sweat, and by their moisture rot the timbers they touch, which to prevent we cover the ends of our beams and girders with boards, pitch'd on both sides, but the walls being made of bricks, or but lin'd with brick, would be much the wholesomer ; and besides keep our wainscot from rotting.   Hangings we dare not use, for being spoyl'd by Ants, and eaten by the Cockroaches, and Rats, yet some of the Planters that meant to handsom their houses, were minded to send for gilt leather , and hang their rooms with that , which they were more than perswaded those vermine would not eat , and in that resolution I left them.

Carpenters, and Masons, were newly come upon the Island, and some of these very great Masters in their Art : and such as could draw a plot, and pursue the design they framed with great diligence, and beautifie the tops of their Doors , Windows , and Chimney-peeces , very prettily ; but not many of those, nor is it needful that there should be many, for though the Planters talk of building houses, and wish them up, yet when they weigh the want of those hands in their sugar work, that must be employed in their building , they fall back, and put on their considering caps.   I drew out at least twenty plots when I came first into the Islands which they all lik'd well enough, and yet but two of them us'd, one by Captain *Midleton* , and one by Captain *Standfast*, and those were the two best houses , I left finish'd in the Island when I came away.   Cellars I would not make under ground, unless the house be set on the side of a Hill ; for though the air be moist above, yet I found it by experience much moister under ground ; so that no moist thing can be set there , but it will in a very short time grow mouldy, and rotten ; and if for coolness you think to keep any raw flesh, it will much sooner taint there, than being hung up in a garret , where the Sun continually shines upon.   Nay the pipe-staves hoops, and heads of barrels, and hogsheads, will grow mouldy and rotten : Pavements and foundations of bricks would much help this with glass windows, to keep out the air.

If I were to build a house for my self in that place, I would have

a

a third part of my building to be of an Eaft and Weft line, and the other two thirds to crofs that, at the Weft end : in a North and South line, and this latter to be a ftory higher than that of the Eaft and Weft line, fo that at four a clock in the afternoon, the higher buildings will begin to fhade the other , and fo afford more and more fhade to my Eaft and Weft building till night; and not only to the houfe, but to all the walks that I make on either fide that building, and then I would raife my foundation of that part of my houfe wherein my beft rooms were three foot above ground; leaving it hollow underneath for Ventiducts , which I would have come into every room in the houfe, and by that means you fhall feel the cool breeze all the day, and in the evening, when they flacken, a cool fhade from my North and South building, both which are great refrefhings, in hot Countreys : and according to this Model, I drew many plots, of feveral fizes and contrivances, but they did not or would not underftand them : at laft I grew weary of cafting ftones againft the wind, and fo gave over.

It were fomewhat difficult, to give you an exact account , of the number of perfons upon the Ifland ; there being fuch ftore of fhipping that brings paffengers daily to the place, but it has been conjectur'd, by thofe that are long acquainted, and beft feen in the knowledge of the Ifland , that there are not lefs than 50 thoufand fouls, befides Negroes; and fome of them who began upon fmall fortunes, are now rifen to very great and vaft eftates.

The number and nature of the Inhabitants.

The Ifland is divided into three forts of men, *viz.* Mafters, Servants, and Slaves. The flaves and their pofterity, being fubject to their Mafters for ever, are kept and preferv'd with greater care than the fervants, who are theirs but for five years, according to the law of the Ifland. So that for the time, the fervants have the worfer lives, for they are put to very hard labour, ill lodging, and their dyet very fleight. When we came firft on the Ifland , fome Planters themfelves did not eat bone meat, above twice a week : the reft of the feven dayes, Potatoes, Loblolly, and Bonavift. But the fervants no bone meat at all, unlefs an Oxe dyed : and then they were feafted, as long as that lafted. And till they had planted good ftore of Plantines, the *Negroes* were fed with this kind of food ; but moft of it Bonavift, and Loblolly, with fome ears of Mayes toafted , which food (efpecially Loblolly,) gave them much difcontent : But when they had Plantines enough to ferve them , they were heard no more to complain; for 'tis a food they take great delight in, and their manner of dreffing, and eating it, is this : 'tis gathered for them (fomewhat before it be ripe, for fo they defire to have it,) upon *Saturday*, by the keeper of the Plantine grove; who is an able *Negro*, and knowes well the number of thofe that are to be fed with this fruit; and as he gathers, layes them all together, till they fetch them away, which is about five a clock in the afternoon, for that day they break off work fooner by an hour : partly for this purpofe, and partly for that the fire in the furnaces is to be put out, and the Ingenio and the rooms made clean ; befides they are to wafh, fhave and trim themfelves againft *Sunday*. But 'tis a lovely fight to fee a hundred handfom *Negroes*, men and women, with every one a graffe-green bunch of thefe fruits

on

on their heads, every bunch twice as big as their heads, all coming in a train one after another, the black and green so well becoming one another. Having brought this fruit home to their own houses, and pilling off the skin of so much as they will use, they boyl it in water, making it into balls, and so they eat it. One bunch a week is a *Negroe's* allowance. To this, no bread nor drink, but water. Their lodging at night a board, with nothing under, nor any thing a top of them. They are happy people, whom so little contents. Very good servants, if they be not spoyled by the *English*. But more of them hereafter.

As for the usage of the Servants, it is much as the Master is, merciful or cruel; Those that are merciful, treat their Servants well, both in their meat, drink, and lodging, and give them such work, as is not unfit for Christians to do. But if the Masters be cruel, the Servants have very wearisome and miserable lives. Upon the arrival of any ship, that brings servants to the Island, the Planters go aboard; and having bought such of them as they like, send them with a guid to his Plantation; and being come, commands them instantly to make their Cabins, which they not knowing how to do, are to be advised by other of their servants, that are their Seniors; but, if they be churlish, and will not shevv them, or if materials be vvanting, to make them Cabins, then they are to lye on the ground that night. These Cabins are to be made of sticks, vviths, and Plantine leaves, under some little shade that may keep the rain off; Their suppers being a fevv Potatoes for meat, and vvater or Mobbie for drink. The next day they are rung out with a Bell to work, at six a clock in the morning, with a severe Overseer to command them, till the Bell ring again, which is at eleven a clock; and then they return, and are set to dinner, either with a mess of Lob-lolly, Bonavist, or Potatoes. At one a clock, they are rung out again to the field, there to work till six, and then home again, to a supper of the same. And if it chance to rain, and wet them through, they have no shift, but must lye so all night. If they put off their cloaths, the cold of the night will strike into them; and if they be not strong men, this ill lodging will put them into a sickness: if they complain, they are beaten by the Overseer; if they resist, their time is doubled. I have seen an Overseer beat a Servant with a cane about the head, till the blood has followed, for a fault that is not worth the speaking of; and yet he must have patience, or worse will follow. Truly, I have seen such cruelty there done to Servants, as I did not think one Christian could have done to another. But, as discreeter and better natur'd men have come to rule there, the servants lives have been much bettered; for now, most of the servants lie in Hamocks, and in warm rooms, and when they come in wet, have shift of shirts and drawers, which is all the cloths they wear, and are fed with *bone meat* twice or thrice a week. Collonel *Walrond* seeing his servants when they came home, toyled with their labour, and wet through with their sweating, thought that shifting of their linnen not sufficient refreshing, nor warmth for their bodies, their pores being much opened by their sweating; and therefore resolved to send into *England* for rug Gowns, such as poor people wear in Hospitals, that so when

they

they had shifted themselves, they might put on those Gowns, and lye down and rest them in their Hamocks : For the Hamocks being but thin, and they having nothing on but Shirts and Drawers, when they awak'd out of their sleeps, they found themselves very cold; and a cold taken there, is harder to be recovered, than in *England*, by how much the body is infeebled by the great toyl, and the Sun's heat, which cannot but very much exhaust the spirits of bodies unaccustomed to it. But this care and charity of Collonel *Walrond's*, lost him nothing in the conclusion; for, he got such love of his servants, as they thought all too little they could do for him; and the love of the servants there, is of much concernment to the Masters, not only in their diligent and painful labour, but in fore-seeing and preventing mischiefs that often happen, by the carelessness and slothfulness of retchless servants; sometimes by laying fire so negligently, as whole lands of Canes and Houses too, are burnt down and consumed, to the utter ruine and undoing of their Masters : For, the materials there being all combustible, and apt to take fire, a little oversight, as the fire of a Tobacco-pipe, being knockt out against a dry stump of a tree, has set it on fire, and the wind fanning that fire, if a land of Canes be but near, and they once take fire, all that are down the wind will be burnt up. Water there is none to quench it, or if it were, a hundred *Negroes* with buckets were not able to do it; so violent and spreading a fire this is, and such a noise it makes, as if two Armies, with a thousand shot of either side, were continually giving fire, every knot of every Cane, giving as great a report as a Pistol. So that there is no way to stop the going on of this flame, but by cutting down and removing all the Canes that grow before it, for the breadth of twenty or thirty foot down the wind, and there the *Negroes* to stand and beat out the fire, as it creeps upon the ground, where the Canes are cut down. And I have seen some *Negroes* so earnest to stop this fire, as with their naked feet to tread, and with their naked bodies to tumble, and roll upon it; so little they regard their own smart or safety, in respect of their Masters benefit. The are before I came away, there were two eminent Planters in the Island, that with such an accident as this, lost at least 10000 l. sterling, in the value of the Canes that were burnt; the one, Mr. *James Holduppe*, the other, Mr. *Constantine Silvester* : And the latter had not only his Canes, but his house burnt down to the ground. This, and much more mischief has been done, by the negligence and wilfulness of servants. And yet some cruel Masters will provoke their Servants so, by extream ill usage, and often and cruel beating them, as they grow desperate, and so joyn together to revenge themselves upon them.

A little before I came from thence, there was such a combination amongst them, as the like was never seen there before. Their sufferings being grown to a great height, and their daily complainings to one another (of the intolerable burdens they labour'd under) being spread throughout the Island; at the last, some amongst them, whose spirits were not able to endure such slavery, resolved to break through it, or dye in the act; and so conspired with some others of their acquaintance, whose sufferings were equal, if not above theirs; and

their

their spirits no way inferiour, resolved to draw as many of the discontented party into this plot, as possibly they could; and those of this perswasion, were the greatest numbers of Servants in the Island. So that a day was appointed to fall upon their Masters, and cut all their throats, and by that means, to make themselves only freemen, but Masters of the Island. And so closely was this plot carried, as no discovery was made, till the day before they were to put it in act: And then one of them, either by the failing of his courage, or some new obligation from the love of his Master, revealed this long plotted conspiracy; and so by this timely advertisement, the Masters were saved: Justice *Hethersall* (whose servant this was) sending Letters to all his friends, and they to theirs, and so one to another, till they were all secured; and, by examination, found out the greatest part of them; whereof eighteen of the principal men in the conspiracy, and they the first leaders and contrivers of the plot, were put to death, for example to the rest. And the reason why they made examples of so many, was, they found these so haughty in their resolutions, and so incorrigible, as they were like enough to become Actors in a second plot, and so they thought good to secure them; and for the rest, to have a special eye over them.

Negroes. It has been accounted a strange thing, that the *Negroes*, being more than double the numbers of the Christians that are there, and they accounted a bloody people, where they think they have power or advantages; and the more bloody, by how much they are more fearful than others: that these should not commit some horrid massacre upon the Christians, thereby to enfranchise themselves, and become Masters of the Island. But there are three reasons that take away this wonder; the one is, They are not suffered to touch or handle any weapons: The other, That they are held in such awe and slavery, as they are fearful to appear in any daring act; and seeing the mustering of our men, and hearing their Gun-shot, (than which nothing is more terrible to them) their spirits are subjugated to so low a condition, as they dare not look up to any bold attempt. Besides these, there is a third reason, which stops all designs of that kind, and that is, They are fetch'd from several parts of *Africa*, who speak several languages, and by that means, one of them understands not another: For, some of them are fetch'd from *Guinny* and *Binny*, some from *Cutchew*, some from *Angola*, and some from the River of *Gambia*. And in some of these places where petty Kingdomes are, they sell their Subjects, and such as they take in Battle, whom they make slaves; and some mean men sell their Servants, their Children, and sometimes their Wives; and think all good traffick, for such commodities as our Merchants send them.

When they are brought to us, the Planters buy them out of the Ship, where they find them stark naked, and therefore cannot be deceived in any outward infirmity. They choose them as they do Horses in a Market; the strongest, youthfullest, and most beautiful, yield the greatest prices. Thirty pound sterling is a price for the best man *Negroe*; and twenty five, twenty six, or twenty seven pound for a Woman; the Children are at easier rates. And we buy them so, as
the

the sexes may be equal ; for, if they have more Men than Women, the men who are unmarried will come to their Masters, and complain , that they cannot live without Wives, and desire him, they may have Wives.   And he tells them, that the next ship that comes, he will buy them Wives, which satisfies them for the present ; and so they expect the good time : which the Master performing with them, the bravest fellow is to choose first, and so in order, as they are in place , and every one of them knows his better , and gives him the precedence, as Cows do one another, in passing through a narrow gate ; for, the most of them are as near beasts as may be, setting their souls aside.   Religion they know none ; yet most of them acknowledge a God , as appears by their motions and gestures : For, if one of them do another wrong, and he cannot revenge himself , he looks up to Heaven for vengeance, and holds up both his hands, as if the power must come from thence, that must do him right.   Chast they are as any people under the Sun ; for, when the men and women are together naked , they never cast their eyes towards the parts that ought to be covered ; and those amongst us, that have Breeches and Petticoats, I never saw so much as a kiss, or embrace , or a wanton glance with their eyes between them.   Jealous they are of their Wives, and hold it for a great injury and scorn, if another man make the least courtship to his Wife.   And if any of their Wives have two Children at a birth, they conclude her false to his Bed, and so no more adoe but hang her. We had an excellent *Negro* in the Plantation , whose name was *Macow*, and was our chief Musician ; a very valiant man, and was keeper of our Plantine-Grove.   This *Negroe*'s Wife was brought to bed of two Children, and her Husband, as their manner is, had provided a cord to hang her.   But the Overseer finding what he was about to do , enformed the Master of it, who sent for *Macow*, to disswade him from this cruel act, of murdering his Wife, and used all perswasions that possibly he could, to let him see, that such double births are in Nature, and that divers presidents were to be found amongst us of the like ; so that we rather praised our Wives, for their fertility, than blamed them for their falseness. But this prevailed little with him, upon whom custom had taken so deep an impression ; but resolved , the next thing he did, should be to hang her.   Which when the Master perceived, and that the ignorance of the man, should take away the life of the woman , who was innocent of the crime her Husband condemned her for, told him plainly , that if he hang'd her , he himself should be hang'd by her, upon the same bough ; and therefore wish'd him to consider what he did. This threatning wrought more with him than all the reasons of Philosophy that could be given him ; and so let her alone ; but he never car'd much for her afterward , but chose another which he lik'd better.   For the Planters there deny not a slave, that is a brave fellow, and one that has extraordinary qualities, two or three Wives, and above that number they seldom go : But no woman is allowed above one Husband.

At the time the wife is to be brought a bed, her Husband removes his board, (which is his bed) to another room (for many several divisions they have, in their little houses,) and none above six foot square)

And

And leaves his wife to God, and her good fortune, in the room, and upon the board alone, and calls a neighbour to come to her, who gives little help to her delivery, but when the child is born, (which she calls her Pickaninny) she helps to make a little fire near her feet, and that serves instead of Possets, Broaths, and Caudles. In a fortnight, this woman is at work with her Pickaninny at her back, as merry a soul as any is there . If the Overseer be discreet , she is suffer'd to rest her self a little more than ordinary ; but if not, she is compelled to do as others do. Times they have of suckling their Children in the fields, and refreshing themselves ; and good reason, for they carry burthens on their backs ; and yet work too. Some women, whose Pickaninnies are three years old, will, as they work at weeding, which is a stooping work, suffer the hee Pickaninny, to sit a stride upon their backs , like St. *George* a Horse-back ; and there Spur his mother with his heels, and sings and crows on her back, clapping his hands, as if he meant to flye ; which the mother is so pleas'd with, as she continues her painful stooping posture, longer than she would do, rather than discompose her Jovial Pickaninny of his pleasure, so glad she is to see him merry. The work which the women do, is most of it weeding, a stooping and painful work ; at noon and night they are call'd home by the ring of a Bell, where they have two hours time for their repast at noon ; and at night, they rest from six, till six a Clock next morning.

On *Sunday* they rest, and have the whole day at their pleasure ; and the most of them use it as a day of rest and pleasure ; but some of them who will make benefit of that dayes liberty , go where the Mangrave trees grow, and gather the bark, of which they make ropes , which they truck away for other Commodities , as Shirts and Drawers.

In the afternoons on *Sundayes* , they have their Musick , which is of kettle drums, and those of several sizes ; upon the smallest the best Musitian playes, and the other come in as Chorasses : the drum all men know, has but one tone ; and therefore variety of tunes have little to do in this musick ; and yet so strangely they varie their time, as 'tis a pleasure to the most curious ears, and it was to me one of the strangest noises that ever I heard made of one tone ; and if they had the variety of tune, which gives the greater scope in Musick, as they have of time, they would do wonders in that Art. And if I had not faln sick before my coming away, at least seven months in one sickness , I had given them some hints of tunes, which being understood, would have serv'd as a great addition to their harmony ; for time without tune , is not an eighth part of the Science of Musick.

I found *Macow* very apt for it of himself , and one day coming into the house, (which none of the *Negroes* use to do, unless an Officer, as he was,) he found me playing on a Theorbo , and singing to it, which he hearkened very attentively to ; and when I had done, he took the Theorbo in his hand, and strook one string, stopping it by degrees upon every fret, and finding the notes to varie, till it came to the body of the instrument ; and that the nearer the body of the instrument
strument

ſtrument he ſtopt, the ſmaller or higher the ſound was, which he found was by the ſhortning of the ſtring, conſidered with himſelf, how he might make ſome tryal of this experiment upon ſuch an inſtrument as he could come by; having no hope ever to have any inſtrument of this kind to practice on.   In a day or two after, walking in the Plantine grove, to refreſh me in that cool ſhade, and to delight my ſelf with the ſight of thoſe plants, which are ſo beautiful, as though they left a freſh impreſſion in me when I parted with them, yet upon a review, ſomething is diſcern'd in their beauty more than I remembred at parting: which cauſed me to make often repair thither, I found this *Negro* (whoſe office it was to attend there) being the keeper of that grove, ſitting on the ground, and before him a piece of large timber, upon which he had laid croſs, ſix Billets, and having a handſaw and a hatchet by him, would cut the billets by little and little, till he had brought them to the tunes, he would fit them to; for the ſhorter they were, the higher the Notes, which he tryed by knocking upon the ends of them with a ſtick, which he had in his hand. When I found him at it, I took the ſtick out of his hand, and tryed the ſound, finding the ſix billets to have ſix diſtinct notes, one above another, which put me in a wonder, how he of himſelf, ſhould without teaching do ſo much.   I then ſhewed him the difference between flats and ſharps, which he preſently apprehended, as between *Fa*, and *Mi* : and he would have cut two more billets to thoſe tunes, but I had then no time to ſee it done, and ſo left him to his own enquiries. I ſay thus much to let you ſee that ſome of theſe people are capable of learning Arts.

Another, of another kind of ſpeculation I found; but more ingenious than he : and this man with three or four more, were to attend me into the woods, to cut Church wayes, for I was employed ſometimes upon publick works; and thoſe men were excellent Axe-men, and becauſe there were many gullies in the way, which were impaſſable, and by that means I was compell'd to make traverſes, up and down in the wood; and was by that in danger to miſs of the point, to which I was to make my paſſage to the Church, and therefore was fain to take a Compaſs with me, which was a Circumferenter, to make my traverſes the more exact, and indeed without which, it could not be done, ſetting up the Circumferenter, and obſerving the Needle : This *Negre Sambo* comes to me, and ſeeing the needle wag, deſired to know the reaſon of its ſtirring, and whether it were alive : I told him no, but it ſtood upon a point, and for a while it would ſtir, but by and by ſtand ſtill, which he obſerv'd and found it to be true.

The next queſtion was, why it ſtood one way, and would not remove to any other point, I told him that it would ſtand no way but North and South, and upon that ſhew'd him the four Cardinal points of the compaſs, Eaſt, Weſt, North, South, which he preſently learnt by heart, and promis'd me never to forget it. His laſt queſtion was, why it would ſtand North, I gave this reaſon, becauſe of the huge Rocks of Loadſtone that were in the North part of the world, which had a quality to draw Iron to it; and this Needle being of Iron, and touch'd with a Loadſtone, it would alwayes ſtand that way.

This

This point of Philoſophy was a little too hard for him, and ſo he ſtood in a ſtrange muſe; which to put him out of, I bad him reach his axe, and put it near to the Compaſs, and remove it about; and as he did ſo, the Needle turned with it, which put him in the greateſt admiration that ever I ſaw a man, and ſo quite gave over his queſtions, and deſired me, that he might be made a Chriſtian; for, he thought to be a Chriſtian, was to be endued with all thoſe knowledges he wanted.

I promiſed to do my beſt endeavour; and when I came home, ſpoke to the Maſter of the Plantation, and told him, that poor *Sambo* deſired much to be a Chriſtian. But his anſwer was, That the people of that Iſland were governed by the Lawes of *England*, and by thoſe Lawes, we could not make a Chriſtian a Slave. I told him, my requeſt was far different from that, for I deſired him to make a Slave a Chriſtian. His anſwer was, That it was true, there was a great difference in that: But, being once a Chriſtian, he could no more account him a Slave, and ſo loſe the hold they had of them as Slaves, by making them Chriſtians; and by that means ſhould open ſuch a gap, as all the Planters in the Iſland would curſe him. So I was ſtruck mute, and poor *Sambo* kept out of the Church; as ingenious, as honeſt, and as good a natur'd poor ſoul, as ever wore black, or eat green.

On *Sundayes* in the afternoon, their Muſick playes, and to dancing they go, the men by themſelves, and the women by themſelves, no mixt dancing. Their motions are rather what they aim at, than what they do; and by that means, tranſgreſs the leſs upon the *Sunday*; their hands having more of motion than their feet, and their heads more than their hands. They may dance a whole day, and ne'r heat themſelves; yet, now and then, one of the activeſt amongſt them will leap bolt upright, and fall in his place again, but without cutting a capre. When they have danc'd an hour or two, the men fall to wreſtle, (the Muſick playing all the while) and their manner of wreſtling is, to ſtand like two Cocks, with heads as low as their hips; and thruſting their heads one againſt another, hoping to catch one another by the leg, which ſometimes they do: But if both parties be weary, and that they cannot get that advantage, then they raiſe their heads, by preſſing hard one againſt another, and ſo having nothing to take hold of but their bare fleſh, they cloſe, and graſp one another about the middle, and have one another in the hug, and then a fair fall is given on the back. And thus two or three couples of them are engaged at once, for an hour together, the women looking on: for when the men begin to wreſtle, the women leave off their dancing, and come to be ſpectators of the ſport.

When any of them dye, they dig a grave, and at evening they bury him, clapping and wringing their hands, and making a doleful ſound with their voices. They are a people of a timerous and fearful diſpoſition, and conſequently bloody, when they find advantages. If any of them commit a fault, give him preſent puniſhment, but do not threaten him; for if you do, it is an even lay, he will go and hang himſelf, to avoid the puniſhment.

What

What their other opinions are in matter of Religion, I know not; but certainly, they are not altogether of the sect of the *Sadduces:* For, they believe a Resurrection, and that they shall go into their own Countrey again, and have their youth renewed. And lodging this opinion in their hearts, they make it an ordinary practice, upon any great fright, or threatning of their Masters, to hang themselves.

But Collonel *Walrond* having lost three or four of his best *Negroes* this way, and in a very little time, caused one of their heads to be cut off, and set upon a pole a dozen foot high; and having done that, caused all his *Negroes* to come forth, and march round about this head, and bid them look on it, whether this were not the head of such an one that hang'd himself. Which they acknowledging, he then told them, That they were in a main errour, in thinking they went into their own Countreys, after they were dead; for, this mans head was here, as they all were witnesses of; and how was it possible, the body could go without a head. Being convinc'd by this sad, yet lively spectacle, they changed their opinions; and after that, no more hanged themselves.

When they are sick, there are two remedies that cure them; the one, an outward, the other, an inward medicine. The outward medicine is a thing they call *Negro-oyle*, and 'tis made in *Barbary*, yellow it is as Bees wax, but soft as butter. When they feel themselves ill, they call for some of that, and annoint their bodies, as their breasts, bellies, and sides, and in two dayes they are perfectly well. But this does the greatest cures upon such, as have bruises or strains in their bodies. The inward medicine is taken, when they find any weaknes or decay in their spirits and stomachs, and then a dram or two of *kill-devil* revives and comforts them much.

I have been very strict, in observing the shapes of these people; and for the men, they are very well timber'd, that is, broad between the shoulders, full breasted, well filletted, and clean leg'd and may hold good with *Albert Durers* rules, who allowes *twice the length of the head*, to the breadth of the shoulders, and twice the *length of the face*, to the breadth of the hips, and according to this rule these men are shap'd. But the women not; for the same great Master of Proportions, allowes to each woman, twice the length of the face to the breadth of the shoulders, and twice the length of her own head to the breadth of the hips. And in that, these women are faulty; for I have seen very few of them, whose hips have been broader than their shoulders, unless they have been very fat. The young Maids have ordinarily very large breasts, which stand strutting out so hard and firm, as no leaping, jumping, or stirring, will cause them to shake any more, than the brawns of their arms. But when they come to be old, and have had five or six Children, their breasts hang down below their Navels, so that when they stoop at their common work of weeding, they hang almost down to the ground, that at a distance, you would think they had six legs: And the reason of this is, they tye the cloaths about their Children's backs, which comes upon their breasts, which by pressing very hard, causes them to heng down to that length. Their
Children

Children, when they are firſt born, have the palms of their hands and the ſoles of their feet, of a whitiſh colour, and the ſight of their eyes of a blewiſh colour, not unlike the eyes of a young Kitling ; but, as they grow older, they become black.

Their way of reckoning their ages, or any other notable accident they would remember, is by the Moon ; and ſo accounting from the time of their Childrens births, the time they were brought out of their own Countrey, or the time of their being taken Priſoners, by ſome Prince or Potentate of their own Country, or any other notorious accidents, that they are reſolved to remember, they account by the Moon ; as, ſo many Moons ſince one of theſe, and ſo many Moons ſince another ; and this account they keep as long as they can : But if any of them live long, their Arithmetick fails them, and then they are at a dead fault, and ſo give over the chaſe, wanting the skill to hunt counter. For what can poor people do, that are without Letters and Numbers, which is the ſoul of all buſineſs that is acted by Mortals, upon the Globe of this World.

Some of them, who have been bred up amongſt the *Portugals*, have ſome extraordinary qualities, which the others have not ; as ſinging and fencing. I have ſeen ſome of theſe *Portugal Negroes*, at Collonel *James Draxes*, play at Rapier and Dagger very skilfully, with their Stookados, their Imbrocados, and their Paſſes: And at ſingle Rapier too, after the manner of *Charanza*, with ſuch comelineſs ; as, if the skill had been wanting, the motions would have pleaſed you ; but they were skilful too, which I perceived by their binding with their points, and nimble and ſubtle avoidings with their bodies, and the advantages the ſtrongeſt man had in the cloſe, which the other avoided by the nimbleneſs and skilfulneſs of his motion. For, in this Science, I had been ſo well vers'd in my youth, as I was now able to be a competent Judge. Upon their firſt appearance upon the Stage, they march towards one another, with a ſlow majeſtick pace, and a bold commanding look, as if they meant both to conquer ; and coming near together, they ſhake hands, and embrace one another, with a chearful look. But their retreat is much quicker than their advance, and, being at firſt diſtance, change their countenance, and put themſelves into their poſture ; and ſo after a paſs or two, retire, and then to't again : And when they have done their play, they embrace, ſhake hands, and putting on their ſmoother countenances, give their reſpects to their Maſter, and ſo go off. For their Singing, I cannot much commend that, having heard ſo good in *Europe* ; but for their voices, I have heard many of them very loud and ſweet.

Excellent Swimmers and Divers they are, both men and women. Collonel *Drax* (*who was not ſo ſtrict an obſerver of* Sundayes, as to deny himſelf lawful recreations) would ſometimes, to ſhew me ſport, upon that day in the afternoon, ſend for one of the *Muſcovia* Ducks, and have her put into his largeſt Pond, and calling for ſome of his beſt ſwimming *Negroes*, commanded them to ſwim and take this Duck ; but forbad them to dive, for if they were not bar'd that play, they would riſe up under the Duck, and take her as ſhe ſwome, or meet her in her diving, and ſo the ſport would have too quick an end.

But

but that play being forbidden, the duck would make them good sport, for they are stronger Ducks, and better Divers by far than ours : and in this chase, there was much of pleasure, to see the various swimmings of the *Negroes* ; some the ordinary wayes, upon their bellies, some on their backs, some by striking out their right leg and left arm, and then turning on the other side, and changing both their leg and arm, which is a stronger and swifter way of swimming, than any of the others : and while vve vvere seeing this sport, and observing the diversities, of their svvimmings, a *Negro* maid, vvho vvas not there at the beginning of the sport, and therefore heard nothing of the forbidding them to dive, put off her peticoat behind a bush, that was at one end of the Pond, and closely sunk down into the water, and at one diving got to the Duck, pull'd her under water, and went back again the same way she came to the bush, all at one dive. We all thought the Duck had div'd : and expected her appearance above water, but nothing could be seen, till the subtilty was discovered, by a Christian that saw her go in, and so the duck was taken from her. But the trick being so finely and so closely done, I beg'd that the Duck might be given her again, which was granted, and the young girle much pleased.

Though there be a mark set upon these people, which will hardly ever be vvip'd off, as of their cruelties vvhen they have advantages, and of their fearfulness and falseness ; yet no rule so general but hath his acception : for I believe, and I have strong motives to cause me to be of that persvvasion, that there are as honest, faithful, and conscionable people amongst them, as amongst those of *Europe*, or any other part of the vvorld.

A hint of this, I vvill give you in a lively example ; and it vvas in a time vvhen Victuals vvere scarce, and Plantins vvere not then so frequently planted, as to afford them enough. So that some of the high spirited and turbulent amongst them, began to mutiny, and had a plot, secretly to be reveng'd on their Master ; and one or two of these were Firemen that made the fires in the furnaces, who were never without store of dry wood by them. These villains, were resolved to make fire to such part of the boyling-house, as they were sure would fire the rest, and so burn all, and yet seem ignorant of the fact, as a thing done by accident. But this plot was discovered, by some of the others who hated mischief, as much as they lov'd it ; and so traduc'd them to their Master, and brought in so many witnesses against them, as they were forc'd to confess, what they meant should have been put in act the next night : so giving them condign punishment, the Master gave order to the overseer that the rest should have a dayes liberty to themselves and their wives, to do what they would ; and withall to allow them a double proportion of victual for three dayes, both which they refus'd : which we all wonder'd at, knowing well how much they lov'd their liberties, and their meat, having been lately pinch'd of the one, and not having overmuch of the other ; and therefore being doubtful what their meaning was in this, suspecting some discontent amongst them, sent for three or four of the best of them, and desir'd to know why they refus'd this favour that was offer'd them, but

receiv'd

receiv'd such an answer : as we little expected ; for they told us, it was not sullenness, or slighting the gratuity their Master bestow'd on them, but they would not accept any thing as a recompence for doing that which became them in their duties to do, nor would they have him think, it was hope of reward, that made them to accuse their fellow servants, but an act of Justice, which they thought themselves bound in duty to do, and they thought themselves sufficiently rewarded in the Act. The substance of this, in such language as they had, they delivered, and poor *Sambo* was the Orator; by whose example the others were led both in the discovery of the Plot, and refusal of the gratuity. And withall they said, that if it pleas'd their Master, at any time, to bestow a voluntary boon upon them, be it never so sleight, they would willingly and thankfully accept it : and this act might have beseem'd the best Christians, though some of them were denyed Christianity, when they earnestly sought it. Let others have what opinion they please, yet I am of this belief; that there are to be found amongst them, some who are as morally honest, as Conscionable, as humble, as loving to their friends, and as loyal to their Masters, as any that live under the Sun; and one reason they have to be so, is, they set no great value upon their lives : And this is all I can remember concerning the *Negroes*, except of their games, which I could never learn, because they wanted language to teach me.

As for the *Indians*, we have but few, and those fetcht from other Countries ; some from the neighboaring Islands, some from the Main, which we make slaves : the women who are better vers'd in ordering the Cassavie and making bread, then the *Negroes*, we imploy for that purpose, as also for making Mobbie : the men we use for footmen, and killing of fish, vvhich they are good at ; vvith their ovvn bovves and arrovvs they vvill go out ; and in a dayes time, kill as much fish, as vvill serve a family of a dozen persons, tvvo or three dayes, if you can keep the fish so long. They are very active men, and apt to learn any thing, sooner than the *Negroes* ; and as different from them in shape, almost as in colour; the men very broad shoulder'd, deep breasted, with large heads, and their faces almost three square, broad about the eyes and temples, and sharp at the chin, their skins some of them brown, some a bright Bay, they are much craftier, and subtiler then the *Negroes* ; and in their nature falser ; but in their bodies more active : their women have very small breasts, and have more of the shape of the *Europeans* than the *Negroes*, their hair black and long, a great part whereof hangs down upon their backs, as low as their hanches, with a large lock hanging over either breast, which seldom or never curles : cloaths they scorn to wear, especially if they be well shap'd ; a girdle they use of tape, covered with little smooth shels of fishes, white, and from their flank of one side, to their flank on the other side, a fringe of blew *Bugle*; which hangs so low as to cover their privities. We had an *Indian* woman, a slave in the house, who was of excellent shape and colour, for it was a pure bright bay; small breasts, with the niples of a porphyrie colour, this woman would not be woo'd by any means to wear Cloaths. She chanc'd to be with Child, by a Christian servant, and lodging in the *Indian* house, amongst other

women,

women of her own Country, where the Christian servants, both men
and women came; and being very great, and that her time was come
to be delivered, loath to fall in labour before the men, walk'd down
to a Wood, in which was a Pond of water, and there by the side of the
Pond, brought her self a bed; and presently washing her Child in some
of the water of the Pond, lap'd it up in such rags, as she had begg'd
of the Christians; and in three hours time came home, with her Child
in her arms, a lusty Boy, frolick and lively.

This *Indian* dwelling near the Sea-coast, upon the Main, an *English*
ship put in to a Bay, and sent some of her men a shoar, to try what
victuals or water they could find, for in some distress they were: But
the *Indians* perceiving them to go up so far into the Country, as they
were sure they could not make a safe retreat, intercepted them in their
return, and fell upon them, chasing them into a Wood, and being disper-
sed there, some were taken, and some kill'd: but a young man amongst
them stragling from the rest, was met by this *Indian* Maid, who upon
the first sight fell in love with him, and hid him close from her Country-
men (the *Indians*) in a Cave, and there fed him, till they could safely
go down to the shoar, where the ship lay at anchor, expecting the return
of their friends. But at last, seeing them upon the shoar, sent the long-
Boat for them, took them aboard, and brought them away. But the
youth, when he came ashoar in the *Barbadoes*, forgot the kindness of
the poor maid, that had ventured her life for his safety, and sold her
for a slave, who was as free born as he: And so poor *Tarico* for her love,
lost her liberty.

Now for the Masters, I have yet said but little, nor am able to say
half of what they deserve. They are men of great abilities and parts,
otherwise they could not go through, with such great works as they
undertake; the managing of one of their Plantations, being a work
of such a latitude, as will require a very good head-peece, to put in
order, and continue it so.

I can name a Planter there, that feeds daily two hundred mouths,
and keeps them in such order, as there are no mutinies amongst them;
and yet of several nations. All these are to be employed in their several abilities, so as no one be idle. The first work to be considered, is
Weeding, for unless that be done, all else (and the Planter too) will
be undone, and if that be neglected but a little time, it will be a hard
matter to recover it again, so fast will the weeds grow there. But the
ground being kept clean, 'tis fit to bear any thing that Country will
afford. After weeding comes Planting, and they account two seasons
in the year best, and that is, *May* and *November*; but Canes are to be
planted at all times, that they may come in, one field after another;
otherwise, the work will stand still. And commonly they have in a
field that is planted together, at one time, ten or a dozen acres. This
work of planting and weeding, the Master himself is to see done;
unless he have a very trusty and able Overseer; and without such a
one, he will have too much to do. The next thing he is to consider,
is the Ingenio, and what belongs to that; as, the Ingenio it self,
which is the *Primum Mobile* of the whole work, the Boyling-house,
with the Coppers and Furnaces, the Filling room, the Still-house,
and

and Cureing-house; and in all these, there are great casualties. If any thing in the Rollers, as the Goudges, Sockets, Sweeps, Cogs, or Bray-trees, be at fault, the whole work stands still; or in the Boyling-house, if the Frame which holds the Coppers, (and is made of Clinkers, fastned with plaister of *Paris*) if by the violence of the heat from the Furnaces, these Frames crack or break, there is a stop in the work, till that be mended. Or if any of the Coppers have a mischance, and be burnt, a new one must presently be had, or there is a stay in the work. Or if the mouths of the Furnaces, (which are made of a sort of stone, which we have from *England*, and we call it there, high gate stone) if that, by the violence of the fire, be softned, that it moulder away, there must new be provided, and laid in with much art, or it will not be. Or if the bars of Iron, which are in the floor of the Furnace, when they are red hot (as continually they are) the fire-man, throw great shides of wood in the mouths of the Furnaces, hard and care-lesly, the weight of those logs, will bend or break those bars, (though strongly made) and there is no repairing them, without the work stand still; for all these depend upon one another, as wheels in a Clock. Or if the Stills be at fault, the *kill-devil* cannot be made. But the main impediment and stop of all, is the loss of our Cattle, and amongst them, there are such diseases, as I have known in one Plantation, thirty that have dyed in two dayes. And I have heard, that a Planter, an eminent man there, that clear'd a dozen acres of ground, and rail'd it about for pasture, with intention, as soon as the grass was grown to a great height, to put in his working Oxen; which accordingly he did, and in one night fifty of them dyed; so that such a loss as this, is able to undo a Planter, that is not very well grounded. What it is that breeds these diseases, we cannot find, unless some of the Plants have a poysonous quality; nor have we yet found out cures for these diseases; Chickens guts being the best remedy was then known, and those being chop'd or minc'd, and given them in a horn, with some liquor mixt to moisten it, was thought the best remedy: yet it recovered very few. Our Horses too have killing diseases amongst them, and some of them have been recovered by Glisters, which we give them in pipes, or large Seringes made of wood, for the same purpose. For, the common diseases, both of Cattle and Horses, are obstructions and bindings in their bowels; and so lingring a disease it is, to those that recover, as they are almost worn to nothing before they get well. So that if any of these stops continue long, or the Cattle cannot be recruited in a reasonable time, the work is at a stand; and by that means, the Canes grow over ripe, and will in a very short time have their juice dryed up, and will not be worth the grinding.

Now to recruit these Cattle, Horses, Camels, and Assinigos, who are all liable to these mischances and decayes, Merchants must be consulted, ships provided, and a competent Cargo of goods adventured, to make new voyages to forraign parts, to supply those losses; and when that is done, the casualties at Sea are to be considered, and those happen several wayes, either by shipwrack, piracy, or fire. A Master of a ship, and a man accounted both able, stout, and honest, having

transpor-

tranfported goods of feveral kinds, from *England* to a part of *Africa*, the River of *Gambra*, and had there exchanged his Commodities for *Negroes*, which was that he intended to make his voyage of, caufed them all to be fhip'd, and did not, as the manner is, fhakle one to another, and make them fure; but having an opinion of their honefty and faithfulnefs to him, as they had promifed; and he being a credulous man, and himfelf good natur'd and merciful, fuffered them to go loofe, and they being double the number of thofe in the Ship, found their advantages, got weapons in their hands, and fell upon the Saylers, knocking them on the heads, and cutting their throats fo faft, as the Mafter found they were all loft, out of any poffibility of faving; and fo went down into the Hold, and blew all up with himfelf; and this was before they got out of the River. Thefe, and feveral other wayes there will happen, that extreamly retard the work of Sugarmaking.

Now let us confider how many things there are to be thought on, that go to the actuating this great work, and how many cares to prevent the mifchances, that are incident to the retarding, if not the fruftrating of the whole work; and you will find them wife and provident men, that go on and profper in a work, that depends upon fo many contingents.

This I fay, to ftop thofe mens mouths, that lye here at home, and expect great profit in their adventures, and never confider, through what difficulty, induftry and pains it is acquired. And thus much I thought good to fay, of the abilities of the Planters.

The next thing is, of their natures and difpofitions, which I found compliable in a high degree to all vertues, that thofe of the beft fort of Gentlemen call Excellent; as, Civilly intreating of Strangers, with communicating to them any thing within the compafs of their knowledge, that might be beneficial to them, in any undertaking amongft them, and affifting them in it, giving them harbour for themfelves and fervants. And if their intentions were to buy Plantations, to make diligent enquiries for fuch as they defired, and to drive the bargain as near the wind for their advantages, as poffibly they could, and to put themfelves in fome travels, in fetling the bufinefs: Or, if that could not do them fervice, ro recommend them to any friend they had, that lay more fit and convenient for their purpofe. Loving, friendly, and hofpitable one to another; and though they are of feveral Perfwafions, yet, their difcretions ordered every thing fo well, as there never were any fallings out between them: which to prevent, fome of them of the better fort, made a Law amongft themfelves, that whofoever nam'd the word *Roundhead* or *Cavalier*, fhould give to all thofe that heard him, a Shot and a Turky, to be eaten at his houfe that made the forfeiture; which fometimes was done purpofely, that they might enjoy the company of one another; and fometimes this Shot and this Turky would draw on a dozen difhes more, if company were accordingly. So frank, fo loving, and fo good natur'd were thefe Gentlemen one to another; and to exprefs their affections yet higher, they had particular names one to another, as, Neighbour, Friend, Brother, Sifter: So that I perceived nothing wanting, that might make

up

up a firm and lafting friendfhip amongft them; though after I came away, it was otherwife.

Sports and exercifes they never us'd any, as Bowling, Shooting, Hunting, or Hawking; for indeed there are no places fit for the two firft exercifes, the Countrey being fo Rocky, uneven and full of ftumps of trees: and for the other two, they want game; for there are no kind of wild beafts in the Ifland, nor any foul fit to hawk at; befides the Country is fo woody, as there is no Champian to fly in; Pheafants, Partridges, Heathpoults, Quailes, or Rayles, never fet foot upon this ground, unlefs they were brought there; and if fo, they never liv'd: and for Hawkes, I never faw but two, and thofe the merrieft ftirrers that ever I faw fly; the one of them was in an evening juft at Sun fetting, which is the time the Bats rife, and fo are to a good height; and at a downcome, this *Barbary* Faulcon took one of them and carried it away.

Tame beafts that are living on the Ifland. Camels.

If I fhall begin with the largeft, firft I muft name Camels, and thefe are very ufeful beafts, but very few will live upon the Ifland: divers have had them brought over, but few know how to dyet them. Captain *Higginbotham* had four or five, which were of excellent ufe, not only for carrying down fugar to the bridge, but of bringing from thence hogfheads of Wine, Beer, or Vinegar, which horfes cannot do, nor can Carts pafs for Gullies, and *Negroes* cannot carry it, for the reafons afore-mentioned; a good Camel will carry 1600 l. weight, and go the fureft of any beaft.

Horfes.

We have from feveral parts of the world, *England, Holland, Bonavifta,* the Ifles of *Cape Verd, Virginia, New England,* and fome from one of the *Leward Iflands* in the *Carribbies* call'd *Curriffa,* befides fome we breed, and very ftrong and good mettled, bold and fit to charge on: thefe horfes we ufe either for the Ingenio, or the Saddle, feldom or never for carrying fugar, the gullies being fo fteep.

Oxen, Bulls, and Cowes.

We have from the feveral places I have nam'd, but chiefly Bulls, from the Ifle of *May,* and *Bonavifta;* vvhich are Cattle, being well taught, will work the orderlieft that I have feen any. With thefe, we have Cows, and fome of them vve ufe for the Payle, and fome for the Ingenio, fome vve breed, and have fpeedier increafe than in *Europe,* for here a Calf vvill bring a Calf in fourteen months; and if it vvere not for the difeafes that take avvay our Cattle, vve fhould not need to fetch any from forraign parts.

Affinigoes.

Are here of exceeding great ufe in the Ifland, in carrying our fugar, down to the bridge, which by reafon of the gullies, the Horfes cannot do: befides when the great rains fall, the wayes are fo deep, and full of roots, as when a horfe puts in his leg between two roots, he can hardly pull it out again, having a great weight on his back; and if he fall, 'tis hard lifting him up. Whereas the Affinigoes pick and choofe their way, and fometimes choofe out little wayes in the wood, fuch as they know are fit for them to pafs, which horfes cannot do, becaufe the wayes are now to narrow for them, or if they were not, they would want much the wit of the Affinigoes, to pick and choofe their way. And if by chance the Affinigoes fall, two *Negroes* are able to help him up, and we feldom ufe more than two, for affiftance to the

Chriftian

Chriſtian that has the charge of the carriages. One of theſe Aſſini-goes will carry 150 weight of ſugar; ſome of the ſtrongeſt 200 weight; our Planters have been very deſirous if it were poſſible to get Mules there, for they would be of excellent uſe, in carrying their ſugars, and working in the Ingenio; but they had got none when I was there, but they were making tryals, either to get ſome of thoſe, or ſome large Horſe Aſſinigoes, to breed with the Mares of that Coun-trey.

Hogs.
We have here in abundance, but not wild or looſe, for if they were they would do more harm than their bodies are worth; they are en-clos'd, and every man knows his own: thoſe that rear them to ſell, do commonly ſell them for a groat a pound, weighing them alive; ſometimes ſix pence if fleſh be dear. There was a Planter in the Iſland, that came to his neighbour, and ſaid to him, Neighbour I hear you have lately bought good ſtore of ſervants, out of the laſt ſhip that came from *England*, and I hear withall, that you want proviſions, I have great want of a woman ſervant; and would be glad to make an exchange; If you will let me have ſome of your womans fleſh, you ſhall have ſome of my hogs fleſh; ſo the price was ſet a groat a pound for the hogs fleſh, and ſix-pence for the Womans fleſh. The ſcales were ſet up, and the Planter had a Maid that was extream fat, laſie, and good for nothing, her name was *Honor*; The man brought a great fat ſow, and put it in one ſcale, and *Honor* was put in the other; but when he ſaw how much the Maid outweighed his Sow, he broke off the bargain, and would not go on: though ſuch a caſe as this, may ſeldom happen, yet 'tis an ordinary thing there, to ſell their ſervants to one another for the time they have to ſerve; and in exchange, re-ceive any commodities that are in the Iſland; I have ſaid as much al-ready of the largeneſs weight and goodneſs of theſe hogs as is needful, and therefore I ſhall need no more.

Sheep.
We have here, but very few; and thoſe do not like well the paſture, being very unfit for them; a ſoure tough and ſapleſs graſs, and ſome poyſonous plant they find, which breeds diſeaſes amongſt them, and ſo they dye away, they never are fat, and we thought a while the rea-ſon had been, their too much heat with their wool, and ſo got them often ſhorn; but that would not cure them: yet the Ews bear alwayes two Lambs: their fleſh when we tryed any of them, had a very faint taſte, ſo that I do not think they are fit to be bred or kept in that Countrey: other ſheep we have there, which are brought from *Guinny* and *Binny*, and thoſe have hair growing on them, inſtead of wool; and liker Goats than Sheep, yet their fleſh is taſted more like Mutton than the other.

Goats.
We have in greater plenty, and they proſper far better than the Sheep, and I find little difference in the taſte of their fleſh, and the Goats here; they live for the moſt part in the woods, ſometimes in the paſture, but are alwayes inclos'd in a fence, that they do not treſpaſs upon their neighbours ground; for whoſoever finds Hog or Goat of his neighbours, either in his Canes, Corn, Potatoes, Bonaviſt, or Plan-tines, may by the lawes of the Iſland ſhoot him through with a Gun, and kill him; but then he muſt preſently ſend to the owner, to let him know where he is.   The

Birds.

The Birds of this place (setting two aside) are hardly worth the pains of describing; yet, in order, as I did the Beasts, I will set them down. The biggest is a direct Buffard, but somewhat less than our grey Buffards in *England*, somewhat swifter of wing; and the only good they do, is, sometimes to kill the Rats. The next to him in bigness, is the larger Turtle Dove, and of them, there is great store in the Island: 'tis a much handsomer bird, both in shape and colour, than ours in *England*, and is very good meat. Next to her is the lesser Turtle, a far finer bird than she, but of a contrary shape; for this is of the shape of a Partridge, but her plumidge gray, and a red brown under the wings; a pretier bird I do not know, of so few glorious colours, her tune like the other. The next is a bird like a Thrush, of a melancholly look, her feathers never smooth, but always ruffled, as if she were mewing, her head down, her shoulders up, as if her neck were broke. This bird has for three or four notes, the loudest and sweetest, that ever I heard; if she had variety, certainly no bird could go beyond her; she looks always, as if she were sick or melancholly.

Another there is, not much unlike a Wren, but big as a Thrush; and this is as merry and jolly, as the other is sad; and as she sits on a stick, jets, and lifts up her train, looking with so earnest and merry a countenance, as if she would invite you to come to her, and will sit till you come very near her. This bird I never heard sing. The next is a Black-bird, with white eyes, and that so ill becomes her, as she is accounted an unhandsome bird; her voice harsh, somewhat like our Jay in *England*; they go in great flocks, and are harmful birds, for they are great devourers of corn, and blossoms of trees, and the Planters wish them destroyed, though they know not which way. They are a kind of Stares, for they walk, and do not hop as other birds. One thing I observe in these birds, which I never saw in any but them, and that is, when they fly, they put their train into several postures; one while they keep it straight, as other birds; sometimes they turn it edge-wayes, as the tail of a fish, and by and by put it three square, with the covering feather a top, and the sides downwards. The next is of the colour of a Feldefare, but the head seems too big for her body, and for that reason they call her a Counsellor; her flying is extream wanton; and for her tune, 'tis such as I have not heard any like her, not for the sweetness, but the strangeness of it, for she performs that with her voice, that no instrument can play, nor no voice sing, but hers; and that is, quarter notes, her song being composed of five tones, and every one a quarter of a note higher than other. Mr. *John Coprario*, a rare composer of Musick, and my dear friend, told me once, that he was studying a curiosity in musick, that no man had ever attempted to do; and that was, of quarter notes; but he not being able to go through with it, gave it over: But if he had liv'd to have gone with me to the *Barbadoes*, this Bird should have taught him. Under this size there are none considerable; Sparrowes, Hayfocks, Finches, Yellow Hamers, Titmice, and divers others of that sort, for which I have no names. But the last and strangest of all, is, that which we call the humming bird, much less than a Wren, not

much

much bigger than an humble Bee, her body long, her wings small and sharp, of a sullen sad green, no pleasant colours on her; her manner of feeding is, just as a Bee, putting her bill into a blossom or a flower, tastes as lightly as a Bee, never sitting, but purring with her wings, all the time she stayes with the flower; and the motion of her wings are as nimble and swift, as a Bee : We have no way to take her, but by shooting sand out of a Gun at her, which mazes her for the present, that you may take her up; but there is no way to keep her alive, her feeding being such, as none can give her but her self. Now for the Birds that live upon the outward verge of the Island, I have not much to say. Sometimes Teals come to our Ponds, three or four couple together, but never go away; for when we see them, we take a gun, and coming near, shoot them, and the report of the gun frights, and makes those that are alive fly away, and fetch one turn, and come back to see their fellows dead, and alight to them, and so we shoot and shoot again till all be kill'd; for they will alwayes come back to see their dead friends. The like we do with those birds we call Oxen and Kine, which come to us in like manner. Small Swallows we have now and then, but somewhat different from ours in colour.

But there is a Bird they call, a Man of war, and he is much bigger than a Heron, and flies out to Sea upon discoveries, (for they never light upon the Sea) to see what ships are coming to the Island; and when they return, the Islanders look out, and say, a ship is coming, and find it true. I have seen one of them, as high as I could look, to meet us twenty leagues from land; and some others, almost as big as Ducks, that in an evening came in a flock of twenty, or there about, and they made divers turns about the ship, a little before Sun-setting; and when it grew dark, they lighted upon the ribs of the ship, and with little nooses of packthred, the Saylers caught them; they were very fat and good.

Though the Bat be no Bird, yet she flyes with wings, and alwayes a little before Sun-setting, at which time they come out of holes, chimneys, and hollow trees, and will raise them to a great height, feeding themselves with flyes that they find in the air, at that time of the evening.

Having done with Beasts and Birds, we will enquire what other lesser Animals or Insects there are upon the Island, of which, Snakes are the chief, because the largest; and I have seen some of those a yard and a half long. The only harm they do, is to our Pigeon-houses, and milk-pans; so that if we leave any hole in the bottom of the house, where they can come in, they will get to the nests, and devour the young Pigeons, if they be not over big. And yet 'tis strange to see, what great morsels they will swallow; slide they will up against a wall, if it be but perpendicular; but if it be declining outward, they cannot get up, but will fall back ten foot high, if they be hindred by any stooping of the wall; for which reason vve make jetties, near the top of such rooms, as vve vvill keep them out of; they have climbed six foot high upon the outside of a vvall, come in at a vvindovv, dovvn on the inside, skim our milk pans, and avvay again : Till vve took one of them there, vve knevv not by vvhat means our pans vvere thus

Of lesser Animals and Insects.

skim'd,

skim'd. They never sting any body, nor is there any venomous beast in the Island. The next to these are Scorpions, of which, some of them are as big as Rats, smooth, and coloured like a Snake, somewhat blewer, their bellies inclining to yellow, very nimble and quick to avoid their pursuers : yet, the Snakes will now and then take them, between whom there is a great conflict, before the quarrel be decided ; for the Scorpions that are large, are very strong, and will maintain the fight sometimes half an hour; I have seen them wrestle together a good part of that time : But in conclusion, the Snakes get the better, and devour the other. These Scorpions were never known to hurt man or beast. Toads or Frogs we have none.

Lizards we had in great plenty, but the Cats kill them so fast in the houses, as they are much lessened in their number. This little Animal loves much to be where men are, and are delighted to stand and gaze in their faces, and hearken to their discourse. These with us, I think, are different from those of *Europe* ; the bodies of ours are about four inches long, the tail near as much, headed not much unlike a Snake ; their colour, when they are pleased, a pure grass-green on the back, blewish toward the side, and yellowish on the belly ; four legs, and those very nimble : When they see at distance some of their own kind, that they are angry with, they swell a little bigger, and change their colour, from green to russet or hair-colour, which abates much of their beauty, for their green is very pleasant and beautiful : Cold they are as Frogs. Next to these are Cockroches, a creature of the big-ness and shape of a Beetle ; but of a pure hair-colour, which would set him off the better, if he had not an ugly wabling gate, but that makes him unhandsome. He appears in the evening when 'tis dark, and will, when he pleases, fly to your bed, when he finds you sleep-ing, and bite your skin, till he fetch blood, if you do not wake ; and if you take a Candle to search for him, he shifts away and hides him-self, as the Purneses do in *Italy*. The Negroes, who have thick skins, and by reason of their hard labour, sleep soundly at night, are bitten so, as far as the breadth of both your hands together, their skins are rac'd, as if it were done with a curry-comb. Next to these tormen-tors, are Musketos, who bite and sting worse than the Gnats and Stouts, that sting Cattle in *England*, (and are commonly felt in marish ground). And next to them Meriwings, and they are of so small a size, and so thin and aereall, as you can hardly discern them, but by the noise of their wings, which is like a small bugle horn, at a great di-stance : Where they sting, there will rise a little knob, as big as a pease, and last so a whole day ; the mark will not be gone in twenty four hours. Caterpillars we have sometimes in abundance, and they do very great harm ; for, they light upon the leaves of our Potatoes, which we call Slips, and eat them all away, and come so low, as to eat of the Root too : And the onely remedy we have, is, to drive a flock of Turkies into the place where they are, and they will devour them. The harms these vermine do us, is double ; first, in the slips, which is the food we give our Horses, and is cast into the rack ; and in our Potatoes, being the root of these slips, which we our selves feed upon.

                                                                        Flyes

Flyes we have of so many kinds, (from two inches long with the great horns, which we keep in boxes, and are shewed by *John Tredescan* amongst his rarities) to the least Atome, as it would be a weary work to set them down; as also the sudden production of them, from Nothing to Maggets, from Maggets to Flyes; and there is not only a race of all these kinds, that go in a generation, but upon new occasions, new kinds; as, after a great downfall of rain, when the ground has been extreamly moistned, and softned with the water, I have walk'd out upon a dry walk (which I made my self) in an evening, and there came about me an army of such flyes, as I had never seen before, nor after; and they rose, as I conceived, out of the earth : They were as big bodied as Bees, but far larger wings, harm they did us none, but only lighted on us; their colour between ash-colour and purple.

The next of these moving little Animals, are Ants, or Pismires, and those are but of a small size, but great in industry; and that which gives them means to attain to their ends, is, they have all one soul. If I should say, they are here or there, I should do them wrong; for they are every where, under ground, where any hollow or loose earth is, amongst the roots of trees, upon the bodies, branches, leaves, and fruit of all trees, in all places, without the houses and within, upon the sides, walls, windows, and roofs without; and on the floors, side-walls, sealings, and windows within; tables, cupbords, beds, stools, all are covered with them, so that they are a kind of Ubiquitaries. The Cockroaches are their mortal enemies, and though they are not able to do them any mischief, being living, (by reason they are far stronger and mightier than a hundred of them, and if they should force any one of them with multitudes, he has the liberty of his wings to make his escape) yet, when they find him dead, they will divide him amongst them into Atomes; and to that purpose, they carry him home to their houses or nests. We sometimes kill a Cockroach, and throw him on the ground, and mark what they will do with him; his body is bigger than a hundred of them, and yet they will find the means to take hold of him, and lift him up; and having him above ground, away they carry him, and some go by as ready assistants, if any be weary; and some are the Officers that lead and shew the way to the hole into which he must pass; and if the Vancurriers perceive, that the body of the Cockroach lies cross, and will not pass through the hole, or arch, through which they mean to carry him, order is given, and the body turned endwise, and this done a foot before they come to the hole, and that without any stop or stay; and this is observable, that they never pull contrary wayes.

Those that are curious, and will prevent their coming on their Tables, Cupbords, or Beds, have little hollows of timber, fill'd with water, for the feet of these to stand in; but all this vvill not serve their turn; for they will some of them, go up to the seiling, and let themselves fall upon the teasters of the Beds, Cupbords, and Tables.

To prevent them from coming on our shelves where our meat
is

is kept, we hang them to the roof by ropes, and tar those ropes, and the roofs over them, as also the strings of our Hamocks, for which reason we avoid them better in Hamocks than in beds.

Sometimes when we try conclusions upon them; we take the Carpet off the Table, and shake it, so that all the Ants drop off, and rub down the legs and feet of those tables, (which stood not in water)and having done so : we lay on the Carpet again, and set upon it a Sallet dish, or Trencher, with sugar in it, which some of them in the room will presently smell, and make towards it as fast as they can, which is a long journey, for he must begin at the foot of the table, and come as high as the inside of the Carpet, and so go down to the bottom and up of the outside of the Carpet, before he gets on the table, and then to the sugar, which he smels to; and having found it, returns again the same way, without taking any for his pains, and informs all his friends of this booty; who come in thousands, and ten thousands, and in an instant, fetch it all away; and when they are thickest upon the table, clap a large book (or any thing fit for that purpose) upon them, so hard as to kill all that are under it, and when you have done so, take away the book, and leave them to themselves, but a quarter of an hour, and when you come again, you shall find all those bodies carried away.   Other tryals we make of their Ingenuity, as this.   Take a Pewter dish, and fill it half full of water, into which put a little Gally pot fill'd with Sugar, and the Ants will presently find it, and come upon the Table; but when they perceive it inviron'd with water, they try about the brims of the dish, where the Gally pot is nearest, and there the most venturous amongst them, commits himself to the water, though he be conscious how ill a swimmer he is, and is drown'd in the adventure : the next is not warn'd by his example, but ventures too; and is alike drown'd, and many more, so that there is a small foundation of their bodies to venture on; and then they come faster than ever, and so make a bridge of their own bodies, for their friends to pass on ; neglecting their lives for the good of the publique; for before they make an end, they will make way for the rest, and become Masters of the Prize. I had a little white sugar which I desired to keep from them, and was devising which way to do it, and I knockt a Nail in the beam of the room, and fastned to it a brown thread, at the lower end of which thread, I tyed a large shell of a fish, which being hollow, I put the sugar in, and lockt the door, thinking it safe; but when I returned, I found three quarters of my sugar gone, and the Ants in abundance, ascending and descending, like the Angels on *Jacob*'s Ladder, as I have seen it painted, so that I found no place safe, from these more than busie Creatures.

Another sort of Ants there are, but nothing so numerous or harmful as the other, but larger by far ; these build great nests, as big as Bee hives, against a wall, or a tree, of Clay and Lome, sometimes within doors, and in it several little Mansions, such as Bees make for themselves, but nothing so curious ; these the Cockroaches and Lizards meet withall, way-laying them near their nests, and feed upon them: which to prevent, they make from thence many and several

galleries

galleries that reach fome of them fix or feven yards feveral wayes, of the fame earth they do their nefts ; fo that for fuch a diftance as that, they are not to be perceiv'd, by any of their enemies, and commonly, their Avenues go out amongft leaves, or mofs, or fome other Covert, that they may not be perceiv'd ; but the moft of thefe are in the woods; for we have deftroyed their nefts, and their galleries within doors fo often, as they are weary of building, and fo quit the houfe : I can fay nothing of thefe, but that they are the quickeft at their work of building, of any little Creatures that ever I faw. Spiders we have, the beautifulleft and largeft that I have feen, and the moft curious in their webs ; they are not at all Poyfonous.

One fort more of thefe harmful Animals there are, which we call Chegoes ; and thefe are fo little that you would hardly think them able to do any harm at all, and yet thefe will do more mifchief than the Ants, and if they were as numerous as harmful, there were no induring of them ; they are of a fhape, not much unlike a Loufe, but no bigger than a mite that breeds in cheefe, his colour blewifh : an *Indian* has laid one of them, on a fheet of white paper, and with my fpectacles on I could hardly difcern him ; yet this very little Enemy, can and will do much mifchief to mankind. This vermine will get thorough your Stocken, and in a pore of your skin, in fome part of your feet, commonly under the nail of your toes, and there make a habitation to lay his offfpring, as big as a fmall Tare, or the bag of a Bee, which will caufe you to go very lame, and put you to much fmarting pain. The *Indian* women have the beft skill to take them out, which they do by putting in a fmall pointed pin or Needle, at the hole where he came in, and winding the point about the bag, loofen him from the flefh, and fo take him out. He is of a blewifh colour, and is feen through the skin, but the *Negroes* whofe skins are of that colour (or near it) are in ill cafe, for they cannot find where they are ; by which means they are many of them very lame : fome of thefe Chegoes are poyfonous, and after they are taken out, the Orifice in which they lay, will fefter and rankle for a fortnight after they are gone. I have had ten taken out of my feet in a morning, by the moft unfortunate *Yarico*, an *Indian* woman.

Some kind of Animals more there are in the woods, which becaufe I never faw, I cannot fpeak their forms : fome of them I guefs are no bigger than Crickets, they lye all day in holes and hollow trees, and as foon as the Sun is down, they begin their tunes, which are neither finging nor crying, but the fhrilleft voyces that ever I heard : nothing can be fo nearly refembl'd to it, as the mouths of a pack of fmall beagles at a diftance ; and fo lively, and chirping the noife is, as nothing can be more delightful to the ears, if there were not too much of it, for the mufick hath no intermiffion till morning, and then all is hufht.

I had forgotten amongft my fifhes to mention Crabs ; but becaufe this kind of them live upon the land, I might very well overflip them, and now bring them in, amongft thefe Animals : they are fmall Crabs, fuch as women fell by dozens in baskets in the ftreets, and of that colour raw and alive, as thefe are boyl'd, which are of a reddifh colour.

Thefe

Theſe Crabs are coming from the Sea all the year long, (except in *March*) they hide themſelves in holes, and in houſes, and ſometimes in hollow trees ; and into every part of the Iſland they come, ſome-times we meet them going up ſtairs in the night, ſometimes in our low rooms, ſometimes in our Gardens, where they eat the herbs. We hold them not good meat : But the Negroes will often upon *Sun-dayes* go a Crabbing, and think them very great dainties when they are boyled. Theſe Crabs in *March* come all out of their holes, and march down towards the Sea in ſuch multitudes, as to cover a great part of the ground where they go, and no hedge, wall, or houſe can ſtop them, but they will over. As we ride, our Horſes tread on them, they are ſo thick on the ground. And they have this ſenſe, to go the neareſt way to the Sea, from the place where they are, and nothing can ſtop or ſtay them, but death : 'Tis the time I gueſs they go to breed.

Having paſt through all the reaſonable and ſenſitives Creatures of this Iſland, I come now to ſay ſomewhat of the Vegetables, as of Trees : and of thoſe there are ſuch infinite varieties, as to mention all, were to looſe my ſelf in a wood ; for, it were impoſſible for any one in the time I ſtayed there, (though he ſtudied nothing elſe) to give an account of the particulars. And therefore I will onely mention ſuch, as for beauty or uſe, are of moſt and greateſt eſteem in the Iſland.

And for that there is none of more uſe than the *Phyſick-Nut*, I will begin firſt with that, which though the name ſeem to promiſe health, yet it has poyſon lodg'd ſecretly within, and that poyſon may bring health, being phyſically applyed, and in fit times and ſeaſons. The reaſon why I think it poyſonous, is, becauſe Cattle will not brouſe, nor feed on the leaves, nor willingly come near the ſhade. This tree will grow to be eighteen foot high, but we have a way to employ it ; as for beauty and uſe, there are none ſuch in the Iſland. This tree (*which is of the height as I have told you*) has many ſprigs, of four, five, and ſix foot long ; we lop them one after another, and as we take off the bran-ches, cut ſtakes of them, about four foot and a half long, and ſtick them in the ground an inch deep, and no more, cloſe to one another, in the manner of Paliſſadoes ; and ſo, with a rail of either ſide, to keep them even, and here and there a ſpur or braket on either ſide, to keep them ſteddy for a month ; by which time, they will not only ga-ther roots to ſtrengthen them, and hold them up, but leaves to cover their tops, and ſo even and ſmooth they fall, as to cover the tops of themſelves, at leaſt two foot and a half downward ; and will in a month more, be ſo firmly rooted in the earth, as you may remove your rails and brakets, to aſſiſt thoſe that are planted after them, in other places. Theſe leaves being large, ſmooth, and beautifully ſhap'd, and of a full green, appear to your eyes like ſo much green Sattin, hang'd on a rail or line, ſo even and ſo ſmooth they hang natu-rally.

The ſtems will grow apace, but more in their bigneſs than their height, (for you may if you pleaſe, keep them at this height, by cut-ting off the tops) and in a while they will not only touch, but imbody

them-

themselves one into another; and then they become as strong and useful a fence, as any can be made, so close, as to keep in Conies, and keep out Rats; for, neither Cattle nor Vermine love to come near it. And as it is a beautiful and useful fence, for Gardens and Orchards, and to keep in Conies, Turkies, *Muscovia* Ducks, and Dung-hill fowl, that cannot fly over, (having one wing clipt) so it serves us for singular use, in fencing about all our Pastures, or what other ground we would enclose : For, our fences being all made of faln trees, with the ends laid cross one upon another, and many of those trees such wood, as were apt to rot and decay, by extream moisture, and violent heat; and the Planters having found the most of them were rotten and decayed, and to make new fences of that kind unpossible, by reason the timbers and trees that grew very near that place, were imployed in making those fences, (for as they made them, the timber stood in their way, and no more ado but cut them down, and lay them in their places without further removing) and removes of so great trees as they were, not to be done with few and weak hands : So that they were come to a great strait, and knew not which way, nor how to renew these fences; some of the Pastures having no less than three thousand two hundred sixty eight trees to encompass them. At last, they thought upon this way, of making new fences, which is the most commodious that can be imagined. And so they gather'd all the Physick-nuts they could, and sowed them, and made large Nurseries of them, which as soon as they grew to any strength, they remov'd, and planted them so, as making a sleight hedge between the old fence and the Pasture, that Cattle might not tread them down, being young and tender, they planted them between; and in four years time they grew so strong, as they were of sufficient ability to defend themselves, and became a very sufficient fence to keep in or out the strongest Bulls in the Pasture. And then, all the wood of the old fence being dry, and fit for the Furnaces, was cut in short pieces, cleft, and sent home by the Assinigoes; and part was gathered together, and made into Charcoals, for fewel at home, and for the Smiths Forge, for we have there no Sea-coals. Besides this, there is another use of this Plant, and that is Physical : Take five of the kernels, and eat them in a morning fasting, and they are a Vomit and Purge; but the body must be strong that takes so many : three will serve a body that is easie to work on : I my self took five of them, and they gave me twelve vomits, and above twenty stools, which was too great an evacuation in a hot Countrey, where the body is weak, and the spirits exhausted by continual sweating.

But I saw a stronger man there take them before me, and they wrought moderately with him; but, finding a weaker constitution to work on, they had the more powerful operation.

This Nut, as it grows on the tree, is like a white Pear-plumb, and of a yellowish colour, with a pulp on it, as much as a Plumb; but that being taken off, there remains a stone, of a blackish colour, and within that, a kernel, and in that kernel, in the parting it in two halves, as our Hazle-nuts in *England*, will part in the middle long-wise, you shall find a thin film, which looks of a faint Carnation,

which

which colour is eafily difcerned , the reft of the kernel being fo per-fectly white; Take out that film , and you may eat the nut fafely , without any operation at all, and 'tis as fweet, as a *Jordan*-Almond. This film is perfectly difcern'd, when the nut is new gathered; but I have look'd on them which have been longer kept , after I brought them into *England*, and I find the Carnation colour quite gone, but the kernel retains ftill his operation, both in Vomit and Purge.

The leaves are fhap'd not much unlike a Vine leaf, but thrice as big, and much thicker, and fuller green.

Poyfon tree.   The poyfoned tree , though I cannot commend for her vertues, yet for her beauties I can. She is almoft as large every way as the Lo-cuft, but not of that manner of growing ; her leaves full out as large and beautiful, as the Lawrels, and fo like , as not to be known afun-der. The people that have lived long there, fay, 'tis not wholfom to be under the fhade of this tree. The fellers, as they cut them down, are very careful of their eyes ; and thofe that have Cipers, put it over their faces; for if any of the fap fly into their eyes, they become blind for a month. A Negro had two Horfes to walk, which were left with him by two Gentlemen ; and the Horfes beginning to fight , the Negro was afraid, and let them go ; and they running into the wood toge-ther, ftruck at one another, and their heels hitting fome young trees of this kind, ftruck the poyfonous juice into one anothers eyes, and fo their blindnefs parted the fray, and they were both led home ftone blind, and continued fo a month, all the hair and skin pilling off their faces. Yet, of this timber we make all, or the moft part, of the Pots we cure our Sugar in; for, being fawed, and the boards dryed in the Sun, the poyfon vapours out.

Caffavie.   And as this tree's poyfon in her fap, fo the Mantionell's is in her fruit, which they account as high a poyfon, as that of the Caffavie. The fruit is like an apple *John*, and 'tis faid to be one of thofe poyfons, where-with the *Indian* Caniballs invenome their Arrows.

And now I have nam'd the Caffavie, 'tis fit it come in the rank of poyfons, though with good ordering it makes bread. 'Tis rather a fhrub than a tree, the fprigs, few of them bigger than a broom-ftaff, crooked and ill fhap'd ; but no matter for that, for the leaves are fo thick as to cover them ; and they grow in tufts or bunches, and ever an odd one, as, 5. 7. 9. or 11. every leaf an inch broad, and fix or feven inches long; dark green, and turning backward from the forefide. Their Roots I have fet down already, their bignefs, and manner of growth, with the ufe of them.

Coloquinti-   Coloquintida is as beautiful a fruit, as any you can fee, of the big-
da.   nefs of an Oftraches egg; a fruit of fo ill a tafte, as a fpoonful of the liquor mars a whole pot of pottage ; the rind fmooth , with various greens, interlac'd with murries, yellows, and faint Carnations.

Caffia-fiftu-   Next to this fhall be the Caffia fiftula, which is a tree that will grow
la.   the moft, in the leaft time, of any that ever I knew : I fet one of the feeds, (which is but a fmall feed) and in a years time, it grew to be eight foot high, and as large and big in the ftem , as an ordinary Rat-toon you walk withall : The leaf of this tree is like that of an Afh, but much longer, and of a darker colour; the fruit, when 'tis ripe, juft of
the

the colour of a black pudding, and shap'd as like, but longer. I have seen of them above 16 inches long; the pulp of it is purgative, and a great cooler of the reins.

Now becaufe we will have all , or as many of the poyfonous and Phyfical trees and plants together as we can, that they may not trouble another leaf, we will put in a plant amongft the trees, and that is fo like a fugar Cane as hardly to be difcern'd , the one from the other : and this Plant hath this quality, that whofoever chews it, and fucks in any of the juyce, will have his tongue, mouth, and throat, fo fwell'd as to take away the faculty of fpeech for two dayes, and no remedy that I know but patience. *The poyfo-ned Cane.*

Tamarine-trees were but newly planted in the Ifland, at the time I came away, and the Palm tree (fo much admir'd for her two rare vertues of Oyle and Wine) was newly begun to be planted, the plant being brought ns from the *Eaft-Indies* , but the Wine fhe brings may rather be called a pleafant drink , than to affume the name of Wine: 'tis thus gather'd, they cut the bark in fuch a part of the tree, where a bottle may fitly be plac'd, and the liquor being received into this bottle, it will keep very good for a day and no longer, but is a very delicious kind of liquor. *Tamarine.*

The poyfonous trees and plants being paft over : 'tis now fit to mention fuch as will make amends, and put our mouths in tafte , but not too fuddenly to fall upon the beft, I will begin with the moft con-temptible fruits which are in the Ifland, the Fig tree and Cherry-tree, which have favory names, but in their natures neither ufeful, nor well tafted.   The Fig tree being very large, but bears a fmall fruit, and thofe of fo mean a condition, as I never faw any one eat of them, and the leaves not at all of the fhape of our Fig leaves, nor the fifth part fo large, the body of the tree I have feen as large as an ordinary Elme here in *England.* *Fruit trees.* *Fig-tree.*

The Cherry tree is not altogether fo large , the fruit as ufelefs and infipid : but the colour fomething refembling a Cherry , and the fhape not much unlike; which caufed the planters to call it by that name. *Cherrytree.*

The next to thefe fhall be fruits, rather for fauce than meat, to whet our appetites to thofe that follow after; and thefe are the Citrons, Oranges, Lemons, Lime.

The Citron is a fmall tree, though fhe bear a great fruit ; and fo ill matcht they are, as the fruit pulls it down to the ground, and moft of the fruit touches, and bears upon the ground ; the ftalk of a dark co-lour, the leaf fhap'd like that of the Lemon, but of a very dark green : thefe fruits we had in great abundance, when firft we came there, but were all caft away, by reafon we had none but Mufcavado fugar , and that is not fit to preferve with ; befides there were very few then that had the skill to do them.

The Orange trees do not profper here, nor are the fruits fo kindly as thofe of *Bermudos*: large they are and full of juice, but not fo delicious as thofe of that Ifland ; befides they are very full of feeds , and their rinds neither fo deep, and pure an Orange Tawny, nor fo thick, and therefore not fo fit to preferve : the trees feldom laft above feven years in their prime, and then decay.   The *Orange.*

Lemon.

The Lemon tree is much better ſhap'd and larger, but this fruit is but here and there, ſtragling in the Iſland. I have ſeen ſome of the fruit large, and very full of juice, with a fragrant ſmell: the leaves both of theſe and the Orange trees, I ſhall not need to mention being ſo well known in *England*.

Lime-tree.

The Lime tree is like a thick Hollybuſh in *England*, and as full of prickles: if you make a hedge of them, about your houſe, 'tis ſufficient proof againſt the *Negroes* ; whoſe naked bodies cannot poſſible enter it, and it is an extraordinary ſure fence againſt Cattle ; it commonly grows ſeven or eight foot high, extreamly thick of leaves and fruit, and of prickles ; the leaves not unlike thoſe of a Lemon tree, the fruit ſo like as not to be diſcerned, at the diſtance of three yards, but only that 'tis leſs, but in the taſte of the rind and juice, extreamly different, much fitter for ſauce than the Lemon, but not ſo good to eat alone.

Prickled apple.

The Prickled apple, grows on a tree extreamly thick leav'd, and thoſe leaves large, and of a deep green, ſhap'd not much unlike the leaf of a Wallnut tree in *England*: this fruit is ſhap'd like the heart of an Oxe, and much about that bigneſs ; a faint green on the outſide, with many prickles on it, the taſte very like a muſtie Lemon.

Prickled Pear.

The next in order, ſhall be the prickled pear, much purer in taſte and better form'd ; the fruit being not unlike in ſhape to a Greenfield-pear, and of a faint green, intermixt with ſome yellow near the ſtalk ; but the body of a mixt red, partly Crimſon, partly Stammell, with prickled ſpots of yellow, the end of it growing ſomewhat larger than the middle, at which end, is a round ſpot of a murrey colour, the bredth of an inch, and circular with a Centre in the middle, and a ſmall circle about it, and from that circle within, lines drawn to the utmoſt extent of that round Murrey ſpot, with faint circles between the ſmall circle and the largeſt, upon that Murrey ſpot.

Theſe lines and circles, of a colour no more different in lightneſs from the murrey, than only to be diſcerned, and a little yellower colour.

Pomegra-nate.

The Pomegranate is a beautiful tree the leaves ſmall, with a green mixt with Olive colour, the bloſſom large, well ſhap'd, and of a pure Scarlet colour ; the fruit not ſo large there, as thoſe we have from *Spain*. The young trees being ſet in rows, and planted thick make a very good hedge, being clipt even a top with Garden ſhears. The fruit is very well known to you, and therefore I ſhall need ſay nothing of that, and theſe are all the remarkable fruits that grow on trees, and are proper to this Iſland, that I can remember, though I believe there are many more.

Papa.

The Papa is but a ſmall tree, her bark of a faint willow colour, her leaves large, and of the ſhape of the Phyſick nut tree, but of the colour of her own bark, the branches grow out four or five of one height, and ſpread almoſt level, from the place where they bud out ; to the ends of the branches, and about two foot higher, ſuch other branches ſpreading in the ſame manner, and if the tree grow to a greater height than ordinary, a ſtory or two more of theſe bows : the top handſomely

form'd

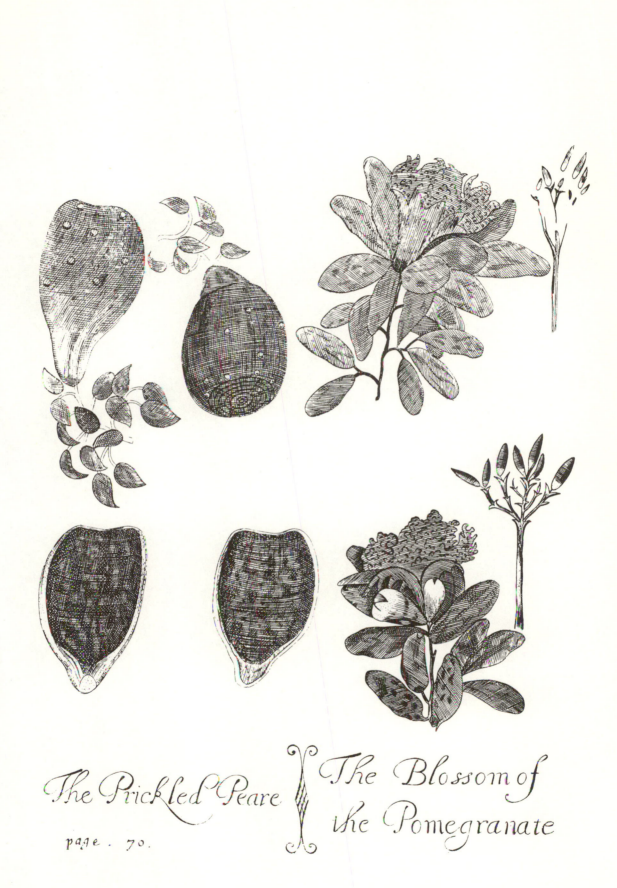

The Prickled Peare

The Blossom of the Pomegranate

form'd to the branches, the fruit fomewhat bigger than Turnips, growing clofe to the body of the tree, where the branches grow, and are fomewhat a fainter Willow, then either the body, branches, or leaves. The tree, though it may be accounted wood, yet the fofteft that yet I ever faw; for, with my knife, I can cut down a tree as big as a mans leg at one chop. The fruit we boyl, and ferve it up with powdred pork, as we do turnips in *England*; but the turnip is far the more favoury fruit.

The Guaver grows on a Tree, bodied and leav'd like a Cherry-tree, but the leaves fomewhat larger and ftiffer; the fruit of the big-nefs of a fmall Lemon, and near that colour, onely the upper end fomewhat blunter than the Lemon; the rind about the thicknefs of the rind of a Lemon, but foft, and of a delicate tafte; it holds within a pulpy fubftance, full of fmall feeds, like a fig, fome of them white within, and fome of a ftammel colour. Thefe feeds have this property, that when they have paft through the body, wherefoever they are laid down, they grow. A Planter, and an eminent man in the Ifland, feeing his Daughter by chance about her natural bufinefs, call'd to her : *Plant even, Daughter, Plant even.* She anfwered : *If you do not like 'em, remove 'em, Father, remove 'em.* Thefe fruits have different taftes, fome rank, fome fweet; fo that one would give a reafon of this variety, which was, according to the feveral conftitutions they had paft through, fome ha-ving a milder, fome a ftronger favour. *Gnaver.*

This tree doth much harm in our Plantations; for the Cattle eating of them, let fall their loads every where, and fo they grow in abun-dance, and do much harm to the Paftures, and much pains and labour is taken to deftroy them. They are the beft fruits preferv'd of any, the feeds being taken out, and the rind only preferved.

I have been told by fome Planters in the Ifland, that Coco-trees grow there, and they are fuch men as I give credit to, but I never faw any, yet, I may venture to tell what fhapes they bear, having been well acquainted with them at the Ifland of St. *Jago,* where there grew very many of them. They feldom are above 80 or 90 foot high, fome a 100. The branches of thefe come out in feveral parts of the tree, leaving fpaces between the heights; but the greateft quantity is at top, and that top alwayes ftoops a little; but the Nuts grow where the lower boughs break out. *Coco.*

Thefe Nuts are of feveral fizes, the moft of them as big as a large foot-ball, with a green skin without, and between that and the fhell, a pulpy fubftance, which when it is dry, is like the rind of the Man-grave tree, of which they make roaps, or (to bring the refemblance a little nearer) like hemp hurds. This Nut-fhell is near half an inch thick, which we commonly cut at one end, a hole as big as a thirty fhilling piece, and we find the fhell full of a clear and pure tafted li-quor, very delicious, but not very wholfome. This fhell is lin'd within with a fubftance as thick as it felf, a white colour, and taftes fweeter than the beft *French* Walnut, and of that foftnefs. The colour of the leaves of this tree, are like the Olive leaves.

The Cuftard apple grows on a tree full of branches and large leaves, and is a lively and lufty tree to look on; the fruit, when 'tis ripe, *Cuftard-apple.*

ripe, as big as the largeſt Pomewater, but juſt of the colour of a Warden. When 'tis ripe, we gather it, and keep it one day, and then it is fit to be eaten. We cut a hole at the leſſer end, (that it may ſtand the firmer in the diſh) ſo big, as that a ſpoon may go in with eaſe, and with the ſpoon eat it. Never was excellent Cuſtard more like it ſelf, than this to it; only this addition, which makes it tranſcend all Cuſtards that art can make, though of natural ingredients; and that is, a fruity taſte, which makes it ſtrange and admirable. Many ſeeds there are in it, but ſo ſmooth, as you may put them out of your mouth with ſome pleaſure.

Anchovie-Pear.

'Twas never my luck to ſee any of thoſe trees, that bear the Anchovie-Pears, nor to taſte of the fruit, and therefore can give you no account of that tree; only to let you know, that there is ſuch a tree in the Iſland.

Trees of mixt kinds. Macow.

The Macow is one of the ſtrangeſt trees, the Iſland affords; the body and branches being ſtuck all over with prickles, of the fineſt forms that I have ſeen.

They are black as jet, or Ebony poliſh'd; the ſizes, from one to ſeven inches long, ſharp at the point, with proportionable increaſings, from that part where it grows to the tree or bough, and wav'd, as I have ſeen ſome ſwords, from the point to the hilts, the fineſt natural pick-tooths that can grow. I brought a large bundle with me, but had them pickt out of my Box by the way. This tree is about the largeneſs of an ordinary Willow, the leaves of that colour and ſhape, but extreamly ſtiff and hard.

It bears at top a large tuff of fruit, which we call Apples, but they are not a fruit to be eaten; their colour as their leaves, willow-green, and juſt ſuch for ſhape as the Cyprus tree bears. Sure, Nature form'd this tree to ſome great purpoſe, ſhe is ſo arm'd; for neither man nor beaſt can touch her, without being wounded. She is well ſhap'd, her body ſtrait, her branches well proportion'd, her top round.

Date tree.

Next to this in colour are Date-trees, but the leaves ſomewhat longer. The ſhape of this tree I cannot give you, having never ſeen any old enough to bear the name of a tree, but ſprigs riſing from the root, at leaſt ten foot high.

Mangrave.

The Mangrave is a tree of ſuch note, as ſhe muſt not be forgotten; for, though ſhe be not of the tall and luſty ſort of trees, yet, ſhe is of great extent; for, there drops from her limbs a kind of Gum, which hangs together one drop after another, till it touch the ground, and then takes root, and makes an addition to the tree. So that if all theſe may be ſaid to be one and the ſame tree, we may ſay, that a Mangrave tree may very well hide a troop of Horſe. The bark of this tree being well ordered, will make very ſtrong ropes, and the *Indians* make it as fine as flax, and ſpin it into fine thred, whereof they make Hamocks, and divers other things they wear: and I have heard, the linnen they wear is made of this bark, as alſo their chairs and ſtooles.

Calibaſh.

The Calibaſh tree bears leaves of the fulleſt and richeſt green, of any that I know, and the greateſt plenty of leaves; her fruit not for food, it is for the moſt part as big as that of the Coco, round as a ball,

green

green as the leaves of the fame tree, fmooth and fhining, and their manner of growing is fo clofe to the body, and the largeft of the boughs, as to touch them fo, that till it be pull'd or cut off, we cannot perceive any ftalk it has. Of this round ball, we make difhes, bowls and cups; for, being hollow within, as the Coco-nut, we employ them for feveral ufes, as they are of different fizes; fome for difhes, fome for cups, fome for bafons, and fome of the largeft to carry water in, as we do Goards, with handles a top, as that of a kettle, for they are fmoother, and much ftronger than they. Thefe look very beautifully on the tree, and to me the more beautiful, by how much they were the more ftrange; for, by their firm and clofe touching the trees, without any appearance of ftalks, they feem to cleave, rather than grow to the trees.

One, and but one tree in this Ifland have I feen, that bears an *Englifh* name, and that is the Bay tree, whofe leaves are fo aromatick, as three or four of them will amply fupply the place of Cloves, Mace, and Cinamon, in dreffing any difh of meat where that is required. It differs nothing in fhape or colour from ours in *England*. *Bay tree.*

The Cedar is without queftion the moft ufeful timber in the Ifland; for being ftrong, lafting, and not very heavy, 'tis good for building, but by reafon of the fmoothnefs and fairnefs of the grain, there is much of it us'd in Wainfcots, Chairs, Stools, and other Utenfils within dores; but, as they grow, I never faw any of them beautifully fhap'd, the leaves juft like thofe of the Afh in *England*, but fomewhat bigger. *Timber trees.*

The Maftick is a tree very tall, but the body flender, and therefore Nature hath provided means to fupport her; for, fhe has fpurs or brackets above feven foot from the ground, which are fixt or engrafted in the body; and fome of the fpurs reach out from the tree to the root, fo broad, as that tables have been made of a round form, above three foot and a half diameter. Some trees have two, fome three of thefe fpurs. This tree has commonly a double top, one fide being fomewhat higher than the other. The fruit is like none of the reft, 'tis of a ftammel colour, and has neither skin nor ftone; but it is more like a Cancre than a Fruit, and is accounted unwholfom, and therefore no man taftes it: 'tis, I believe, the feed of the tree, for we fee none other. The leaves of this tree grow of fuch a height, as till they fall down, we can give no judgment of them. The timber of this tree is rank'd amongft the fourth fort, three being better than it. I have feen the bodies of thefe trees near fixty foot high. *Maftick.*

The Bully tree is lefs than the Maftick, and bears a fruit like a Bullis in *England*; her body ftrait, and well fhap'd, her branches proportionable, her timber excellent and lafting. *Bully.*

Redwood is a handfome tree, but not fo lofty as the Maftick, excellent timber to work, for it is not fo hard as fome others, which is the caufe they feldom break their tooles in working it, and that is the reafon the work-men commend it above others. 'Tis a midling tree for fize, the body about two foot and a half diameter. *Redwood.*

This is accounted as good as the Red-wood in all refpects, and is *Prickled yellow-wood.*

is a strong and lasting timber, good for building, and for all uses within doors.

Iron wood.

Iron wood is called so, for the extream hardness; and with that hardness it has such a heaviness, as they seldom use it in building; besides, the workmen complain that it breaks all their tools. 'Tis good for any use without doors, for neither Sun nor rain can any wayes mollifie it. 'Tis much used for Coggs to the Rollers.

Lignum vitæ.

Lignum vitæ they use now and then for the same purpose, when the other is away; but having no bowling in that Countrey, little is used: They send it commonly for *England*, where we employ it to several uses; as, for making Bowles, Cabinets, Tables, and Tablemen.

Locust.

The Locust is a tree, not unfitly to be resembled to a Tuscan Pillar, plain, massie, and rurall, like a well limb'd labourer; for, the burden it bears being heavy and ponderous, ought to have a body proportionably built, to bear so great a weight. That rare Architect, *Vicruvius*, taking a pattern from Trees, to make his most exact Pillars, rejects the wreathed, vined, and figured Columns; and that *Columna Atticurges*, mentioned by himself, to have been a squared Pillar; and those that are swell'd in the middle, as if sick of a Tympany or Dropsie; and chuses rather the straightest, most exact, and best siz'd, to bear the burthen that lyes on them. So, looking on these trees, and finding them so exactly to answer in proportion to the Tuscan Pillars, I could not but make the resemblance the other way: For, Pillars cannot be more like Trees, than these Trees are like Tuscan Pillars, as he describes them. I have seen a Locust (and not one, but many) that hath been four foot diameter in the body, near the root, and for fifty foot high has lessened so proportionably, as if it had taken pattern by the ancient Remainders, which *Philander* was so precise in measuring, which is a third part of the whole shaft upward, and is accounted as the most graceful diminution. The head to this body is so proportionable, as you cannot say, 'tis too heavy or too light; the branches large, the sprigs, leaves, and nuts so thick, as to stop all eye-sight from passing through, and so even at top, as you would think you might walk upon it, and not sink in. The nuts are for the most part three inches and a half long, and about two inches broad, and somewhat more than an inch thick; the shell somewhat thicker than a half crown piece, of a russet Umbre, or hair colour; the leaves bigger than those that grow upon the Ash in *England*: I shall not mention the timber, having given it in my Buildings. The Kernels are three or four in every nut, and between those, a kind of light pulpy substance, such as is in a Hazle-nut, before the kernel be grown to the full bigness: In times of great famine there, the poor people have eaten them for sustenance: But of all tastes, I do not like them.

Bastard Locust.

Another Locust there is, which they call the bastard-Locust. This looks fair, but will not last.

Palmeto the less.

There is a tree called the *Palmeto*, growing near the Sea-coast, which being a sandy light ground, does not afford that substance of mould, to make a large tree; nor shall you find in that low part of the Island, any considerable trees fit for building, which is a main want and hinderance to them that would build there; for, there is no means to

transport

transport any from the high lands, by reason of the unpassableness of the wayes; the body of this tree I have seen about 45 or 50 foot high, the Diameter seldom above 15 or 16 inches, the rind of a pure ash colour, full of wrinkles, the leaves about two foot and a half long, in bunches, just as if you took twenty large flags, with their flat sides together, and tyed them at the broader ends. With these bunches they thatch houses, laying every bunch by himself on the lathes, somewhat to overhang one another, as tiles do. This is a very close kind of thatch, keeps dry and is very lasting, and looking up to them on the inside of the room, they are the prettiest becomming figures that I have seen of that kind, these leaves grow out no where but at the tops of the trees.

Another kind of Palmeto there is, which as it hath an addition to the name, hath likewise an addition to the nature: for I believe there is not a more Royal or Magnificent tree growing on the earth, for beauty and largeness, not to be paralell'd; and excells, so abundantly in those two properties and perfections, all the rest, as if you had ever seen her, you could not but have fallen in love with her; I'm sure I was extreamly much, and upon good and antique Authority: For if *Xerxes* strange *Lydian* love the Plantane tree, was lov'd for her age, why may not I love this for her largeness? I believe here are more women lov'd for their largeness than their age, if they have beauty for an addition, as this hath; and therefore I am resolved in that poynt, to go along with the multitude, who run very much that way: but how to set her out in her true shape and colour, without a Pencil, would ask a better pen than mine; yet I will deliver her dimensions as near truth as I can, and for her beauty much will arise out of that. But first I will beg leave of you to shew her in her infancy, which is about ten or twelve years old, at which time she is about seaventeen foot high, her body, and her branches, and that part which touches the ground, not unlike an Inkhorne, which I have seen turn'd in Ivory, round at the bottome, and bellied at that part which holds the Inke; and the stem or body of the tree, growing less, as that part which holds the Pens, but turn'd by a more skilful workman; and some of this body, part tawny, part purple, with Rings of white and green mixt, that go about her; and these Rings at six Inches distance. This stem, to be about six foot and a half high, upon which growes the bottome of the stalks, thin as leaves of parchment, enwrapping one another so close as to make a continued stem, of the same bigness, or two foot and a half above the other, every stone of those filmes or skins, bearing a stalk, which lessens so insensibly, from the skin to the poynt, as none but the great former of all beauty can make the like.

Palmeto Royal.

These stalks or branches, are of several lengths, those that are the most inward, are the highest, and every one of those stalks adorn'd with leaves, beginning a little from the filmes to the poynt, and all these Leaves like Cylinders, sharp at either end, and biggest in the middle: that part of the stem which is the enwrappings of the filmes of a pure grasse green, shining as parchment dyed green, and slickt with a slick-stone, and all the branches with the leaves, of a full grass green spreading every way, and the highest of them eight foot above the

the green stem, the other in order to make a well shap'd Top, to so beautiful a stem. The branches sprout forth from the middle, or intrinsick part of the tree, one at once ; and that wrapt up so close as 'tis rather like a Pike than a branch with leaves , and that Pike alwayes bends towards the East ; but being opened by the Suns heat spreads the leaves abroad , at which time the outmost or eldest branch or sprig below withers and hangs down, and pulls with it the film that bears it, and so both it and the film which holds it up turn of a russet colour and hang down like a dead leaf, till the wind blows them off ; by which time the Pike above is become a branch, with all its leaves opened ; then comes forth another Pike, and then the next outmost branch and film below, falls away as the former, and so the tree grows so much higher, as that branch took room, and so a pike and a dead leaf , a pike and a dead leaf, till she be advanc'd to her full height, which will not be till 100 years be accomplished : about thirty or forty years old, she will bear fruit, but long before that time, changes her shape, her belly being lessened partly by the multiplicity of roots, she shoots down into the earth (nature foreseeing how great a weight they were to bear, and how great a stress they were to suffer, when the winds take hold of so large a head, as they were to be crown'd with) and partly by thrusting out sustenance and substance, to raise and advance the stem or body (for out of this belly which is the store-house of all this good it comes) so that now she becomes taper, with no more lessening than a well shap'd arrow, and full out as strait, her body then being of a bright Ash colour, with some dapples of green, the films a top retaining their smoothness and greenness,only a little variation in the shape,and that is a little swelling near the place that touches the stem or body, not much unlike an Urinal, so that the swelling that was in the body, is now raised up to the films or skins above. But at this age , the branches stand not so upright, as when the tree was in her minority, but has as great beauty in the stooping and declension, as she had in the rising of her branches, when her youth thrusts them forth with greater violence and vigour , and yet they had then some little stooping near the points. And now there is an addition to her beauty by two green studds, or supporters, that rise out of her sides, near the place where the films joyn to the tree, and they are about three foot long, small at the place from whence they grow, but bigger upwards, purely green, and not unlike the Iron that Glasiers use to melt their Sawder with.

One grows on one side of the tree, the other on the other side, and between these two of the same height, on either side the tree, a bush upon which the fruit grows, which are of the bigness of large *French* grapes, some green, some yellow, some purple, and when they come to be purple, they are ripe,and in a while fall down, and then the yellow becomes purple, and the green yellow ; and so take their turns, till the tree gives over bearing. These fruits we can hardly come by being of so great a height, nor is it any great matter : for the taste is not pleasant ; but the Hogs find them very agreeable to their palats for those that eat of them grow suddenly fat. I have seen an *Negro* with two short ropes clime the tree , and gather the fruit , about this
time,

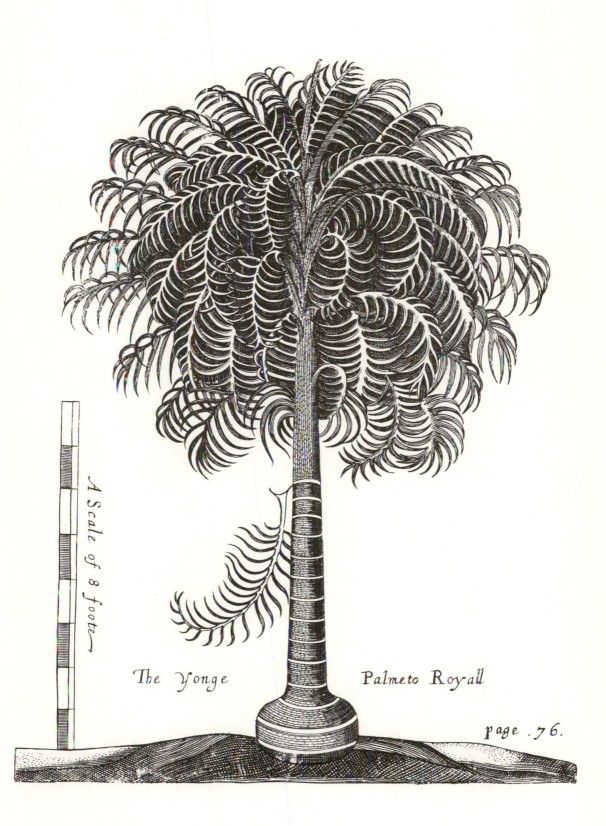

A Scale of 8 foote

The Yonge   Palmeto Royall

page .76.

time, fhe is 80 foot high, and continues that form, without variation; only as fhe growes older, fo taller and larger; and has alwayes green, yellow, and purple fruit, fucceeding one another; whether there be bloffomes, I know not, for I never went fo high as to look. This fort of trees I have feen of all fifes, from ten, to two hundred foot high; and I have been told by fome of the antient Planters, that when they came firft upon the Ifland, they have feen fome of them three hundred foot high: And fome reafons I have to perfwade me to believe it; for, amongft thofe that I have feen growing, which I have gueft to be two hundred foot high, the bodies of which I meafured, and found to be but fixteen inches diameter. And I once found in a wood, a tree lying, which feemed to have been long fallen; for, the young wood was fo grown about her, as ftanding at one end, I could not fee the other: But, having a couple of Negros with me, that were axe-men, I caufed them to cut away the wood that grew about the tree, that I might come to the other end, which I thought would never be done, fhe was fo long, and yet a great part of her cut off, and carried away. I meafured the diameter of her ftem, and found it to be 25 inches.

Now if we go by the rule of Three, and fay, if 16 inches diameter make 200 foot high, what fhall 25 inches? And by this rule we fhall prove her to be 312 foot high. But the branches of this tree were all carried away, fo that I could fee none of them. But I have meafured a branch of one of thofe trees of 200 foot high, and found it 25 foot

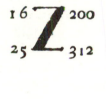

$$16 \diagup 200$$
$$25 \diagdown 312$$

$$200 \diagup 25$$
$$312 \diagdown 39$$

long. So then, by the fame Rule? If 200 foot high bear a branch of 25 foot long, what fhall a Tree of 312 foot high do? And I fee by the fame Rule, it appears to be 39 foot long. And one of thefe trees, after fhe comes to bear fruit, will have no lefs than 20 branches at once, (but many more in her nonage) and halfe of them hold this length. I have feen a branch of one of thefe fmall tree of 200 foot high, fallen down, and blown from the tree in the falling, twenty paces off, which has made me admire from whence it fhould come: For the tree being of fo great a height, the branches lofe much of their bignefs and length by their diftance: But, lying on the ground, where we can take the juft meafure, we find what they are. And it is an admirable thing, to fee the form of this fprig or branch, which is not above two inches broad where it joynes to the film, and is leffening of the breadth from that end to the point, which is twenty five foot long, fo infenfible, as it is not poffible to difcern where the diminution is. So fmooth, fo even, fo firme and tough, as though it were not wood, 'tis much ftronger, and abler to endure the weather, or any kind of bending. The leaves that grow upon this ftalk, are all of

them

them (unless towards the points) two foot long, that part which touches the stalk, small, but strong enough to bear the leafe, aud hath a little short stalk, to which the leafe growes, which leafe is as exactly form'd as the stalk, growing by degrees, to make two inches broad in the middle, and losing that breadth insensibly to the poynt.   These leaves are thin, but tough enough to indure the strongest wind that blowes, without being broken, and not above four inches distant one from another , which multiplicity of leaves, makes the beauty of the tree the fuller. About the time this tree parts with her belly,& growes to a slender kind of shape,she drawes up amongst her roots some of the soyle that bred her, about two foot higher than the levell of ground that is near it; and by reason it is held in by an infinity of small Roots, that come from the body, it there remains firm, and falls not down; the outside of this earth is about a foot round about, broader than the Diameter of the Tree ; so that if the Diameter of the Tree be a foot,the Diameter of this earth is three foot at top, but somwhat more below ; for the sides are not so steep as to hold one breadth above and below. If this earth were beautiful, smooth, and large enough, it might be called the Pedestal to that Corinthian Pillar, the Palmeto Royal. But what is wanting in the Pedestal, is supplyed in the dimensions of the Pillar ; for, the Corinthian Pillar is allowed for length but nine of her own Diameters, and this will not aske leave to take 150. which makes her the more beautiful , since the strength she hath, is able to support the weight she bears : And for the Architrave, Frize,and Cornice, they are not to be compar'd to the beauty of the head of this Pillar, together with the fruit and supporters. And I believe,if *Vetruvius* himself had ever been where this Pillar grew,he would have chang'd all his deckings and garnishings of Pillars, according to the form of this. And though the Corinthian Pillar be a Column lasciviously deckt, like a Curtesan , and therein participating (as all inventions do) of the place where they were first born ; (*Corinth* having been without controversie, one of the wantonnest Towns in the world) yet, this wants nothing of her beauty, and yet is chast, which makes her the more admirable, and the more worthy to be prized. One thing more I have to say of this Tree, which is not only the Root that brings forth all this beauty, but the root of much admiration and wonder; that, being a tree of that height, bearing a top of so vast an extent, as from the poynt of the branches on one side, to the poynt of the stalk on the other side, to be 78 foot, upon which the winde cannot but have a main power and force, yet, I never saw any of them blown down, nor any root of this Tree bigger than a Swans quill : but there are many of them, and they fasten themselves in the Rocks, which hold them very firm.   The wood of this Tree is so extream hard, and tough withall, as most of the axes that are imployed to fell them, are broken in the work , and they are well enough served for cutting down such beauty.   The use our Planters made of them at first coming, before they knew how to make shingles,was,to saw the bodies of these trees to such length, as might reach to the ridge pole, to the Eves of the house ; for they were hollow, and then sawing them long wise, there were two concaves, which they laid together, setting the hollow sides

up-

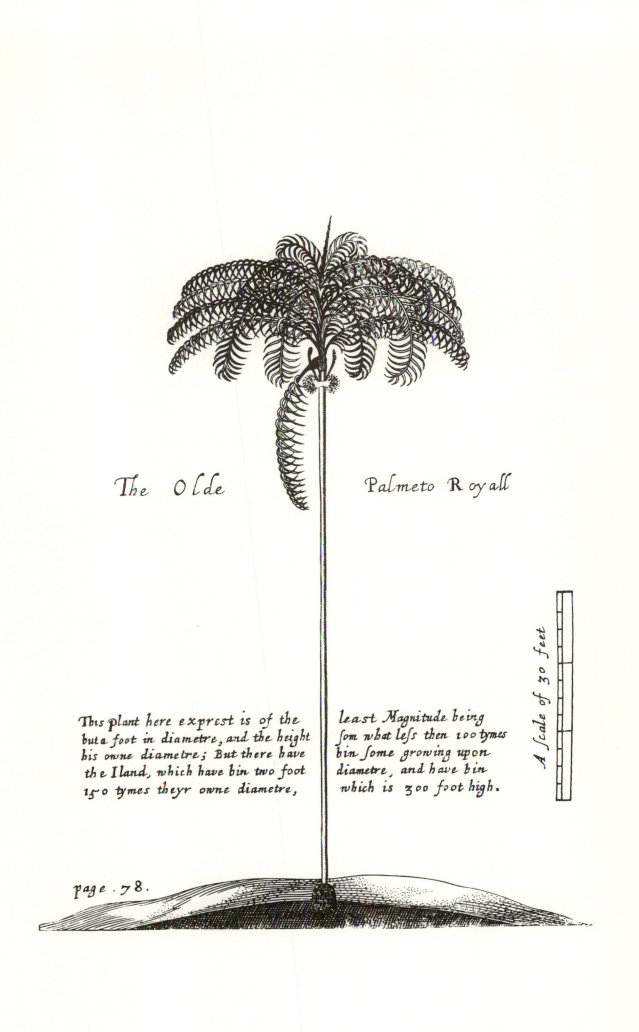

The Olde   Palmeto Royall

This plant here exprest is of the least Magnitude being but a foot in diametre, and the height som what less then 100 tymes his owne diametre; But there have bin some growing upon the Iland, which have bin two foot diametre, and have bin 150 tymes theyr owne diametre, which is 300 foot high.

A Scale of 30 feet

upward ; and where they close, one to cover them, with the hollow side downward, and so the whole house over.   And this was the use they made of the bodies of these Trees, for which, very many of them were destroyed.

But, I doubt, I have tir'd you with naming so many Trees, and therefore I will give over ; but with this rule, that which way soever I have travelled (from the place I dwelt) either East, West, North, or South, (but four miles distant) I have still found trees, such as I had never seen before, and not one of those I have named, and many of them extreamly large and beautiful.   And the nearer the middle of the Island, the larger the trees, and the leaves ; so that from trees of a hundred foot high, to a diminution of twenty; and from leaves of eighteen inches long, with a proportionable breadth to that length, to the small ones of half an inch, which most of the trees bear that are near the Bridge, and, I think, near the Sea, every where you shall find many, and the most such.   And the reason I have given before ; the land in the highest part of the Island being very rich mould, and that near the Sea being a sandy light earth.   And in the partings or twists of the branches of those trees, (which I have not named) such excrescences grow out, as are strange for their formes, and no doubt medicinable in their natures ; such as is our *Misleto*, or *Polypodium*; and much larger, and more frequent ; but we want skilfull men to find out their vertues.

There are (besides the Bay-leaves, which, as I told you, might serve for Cloves, Mace, and Cinamon) two sorts of Spices, Ginger, and red-Pepper: The Ginger being a root which brings forth blades, not unlike in shape to the blades of Wheat, but broader and thicker, for they cover the ground so, as you cannot see any part of it.   They are of a Popinjay colour, the blossome a pure Scarlet.   When 'tis ripe, we dig up the roots, (cutting off the blades) and put them into the hands of an Overseer, who sets many of the young Negroes to scrape them with little knives, or small Iron spuds, ground to an edge.   They are to scrape all the outward skin off, to kill the spirit ; for, without that, it will perpetually grow. Those that have Ginger, and not hands to dress it thus, are compelled to scald it, to kill the spirit ; and that Ginger is nothing so good as the other, for it will be hard as wood, and black, whereas the scrapt Ginger is white and soft, and hath a cleaner and quicker taste.

Plants that bear fruit. Ginger.

There is of this kind two sorts ; the one so like a childs Coral, as not to be discerned at the distance of two paces ; a crimson and scarlet mixt, the fruit about two inches long, and shines more than the best polisht Coral.   The other of the same colour, and glistering as much, but shap't like a large Button of a Cloak ; both of one and the same quality ; both so violently strong, as when we break but the skin, it sends out such a vapour into our Lungs, as we fall all a Coughing, which lasts a quarter of an hour after the fruit is removed ; but, as long as we are garbling it, we never give over. This Spice the Spaniards love, and will have it in all their meat, that they intend to have picant, for a greater *Hough goe* is not in the world.   Garlick is faint and cool to it.   It growes on a little shrub, no bigger than a Goosberry bush.   Having

Red Pepper.

Cucumber. Having inflam'd this leafe with a burning heat, it is fit to apply a Cooler, left it fall on fire; and that is fuch a one, as is cold in the third degree, a Cucumber; of which kind we have excellent good, from the beginning of *November*, to the end of *February*, but after that, the weather growes too hot. They ferve as Sallets cold, with Oyle, Vinegar, and Pepper; and hot, being ftewed, or fryed, of which we make Sawce for Mutton, Pork, Turkeys, or Mufcovia Ducks. Geefe I never faw but two in the Ifland, and thofe were at the Governours houfe.

Mellons. Millons we have likewife for thofe four months; but before or after, the weather is too hot. They are for the moft part larger than here in *England*. I have feen them cut four inches thick; they eat moifter then here they do, which makes them the lefs wholfome. We take no other care (after the feeds are put into the ground) but to weed them. I have feen of them fixteen inches long.

Water-Mil-lon. The Water Millon there, is one of the goodlieft fruits that growes. I have feen of them, big as a Cloakbag, vvith a fuit of cloaths in it; purely green, engrayl'd with ftraw colour; And fo wanton Nature is, in difpofing thofe figures, as though they be upon all parts of the fruit; yet, they vary and flow fo infinitely, and no inch of fquare or circle is to be found upon the rinde, that is like one another, and the whole rinde as fmooth as polifht glafs. Where they put out upon the ground, there they lie; for the Vine they grow by, has not ftrength to remove them. This fruit within is not unlike an Apple for colour; but for tafte, not like any fruit I know in *England*, waterifh, and wallowifh; yet the people there eat ftrange quantities of it, two or three pieces, big, as if cut round about a twelve-penny loafe, an inch thick: They hold it rarely cooling to the body, and excellent for the ftone. The feeds are of themfelves fo ftrong a Purple, as to dye that part of the fruit it touches, of the fame colour; and till they do fo, the fruit is not full ripe: They account the largeft, beft. Extreamly full of feeds they are, which in the eating flip out with fuch eafe, as they are not at all troublefome.

Grapes. Grapes we have in the Ifland, and they are indifferently well tafted, but they are never ripe together; fome may be pickt out to make Wine, but it will be fo fmall a quantity, as it will not be worth the while. There is alwaies fome green, fome ripe, fome rotten grapes in the bunch.

Plantine. Though the Plantine bear not the moft delicious fruit that growes on this Ifland; yet, for that fhe is of great ufe, and beauty too, and for many other rarities that fhe excels other Plants in, I fhall endeavour to do her right in my defcription. And firft, for the manner of planting; we put a root into the ground, fix inches deep, and in a very fhort time, there will come forth three or four fprouts, whereof one has the precedence, and holds that advantage, (as the prime Hawke does in an Ayery.) And as this fp'out growes, it fprings from the intrinfick part of the ftem, and the out-leaves hang down and rot; but ftill new ones come within, as rife up as the Palmeto does, like a pike, which opened with the Sun, becomes a leafe; and about the time it comes to be eight or ten foot high, the pikes, (and confequently the

A Scale of :8: foote

The Plantine Blossomd

page 80

the leaves) will be of their full bigneſs, and ſo (as others grow) continue that bigneſs, till the laſt ſprout come forth ; which is the ſoul of the Plant, and will never be a leaf, but is the ſtem upon which the fruit muſt grow. About the time the leaves come to their full bigneſs, they rot no more, but continue in their full beauty ; a rich green, with ſtripes of yellow ſo intermixt, as hardly to be diſcerned where they are. Theſe leaves are the moſt of them above ſix foot long, and two foot broad ; ſmooth, ſhining, and ſtiffe as a Lawrel leaf; and from the middle of the leaf to the end, ſuch a fall, as a father has, in a well ſhap't plume. But, as all theſe leaves came out in a pike, ſo that pike ever bends a little towards the Eaſt, though as ſoon as it becomes a a leaf, chooſes any point of the Compaſs to lean to ; and ſo in a due proportion hangs round about the ſtem. At the time it comes to be of the full height, the uppermoſt leaves will be fifteen or ſixteen foot high, and then you ſhall perceive the ſtem upon which the fruit muſt grow, more than a foot higher than the reſt, with a green bunch at top; which bunch has ſuch a weight, as to make it ſtoop by degrees, till it be but ſeven foot from the ground ; and then the green leaves which held the bloſſome in, open, and ſhew the bloſſome it ſelf, which is of a pure purple, and as big as the heart of a Stagg, and of that ſhape, with the point downwards, and ſo continues, without opening the leaves, till it be ready to fall off ; and when it falls, pulls with it above a foot of the ſtalk that held it, which is covered with yellow bloſſomes. This purple bloſſome, when it fell, I gueſs to be a pound weight, beſides the ſtalk it took along with it. After this is fallen, the fruit grows out from that end which remained ; and as it growes, turnes up towards the ſtalk that bears it, much like a Grapple that holds the long-Boat of a Ship ; or, as a dozen large fiſh-hooks tied together, turning up ſeveral waies ; each turning up of that fruit being ſeven or eight inches long, and as big as a large Battoon you walk with. In ſix months, this Plant will be grown, and this fruit ripe, which is a pleaſant, wholſome, and nouriſhing fruit, yellow, when 'tis ripe : But the Negroes chuſe to have it green, for they eat it boyl'd, and it is the only food they live upon. Our manner of eating it, is, when it is full ripe, take off the skin, which will come off with much eaſe, and then the fruit looks yellow, with a froth upon it, but the fruit firme. When it is gathered, we cut down the Plant, and give it to the Hoggs, for it will never bear more. The body of this plant is ſoft, skin within skin, like an Onyon, and between the skins, water iſſues forth as you cut it. In three months, another ſprout will come to bear, and ſo another, and another, for ever ; for we never plant twice. Groves we make of theſe plants, of twenty acres of ground, and plant them at ſuch diſtances, and in ſuch rows, as you do Cherry-trees in *Kent*, ſo that we walk under the leaves, as under the Arches in St. *Faith's* Church under St. *Pauls*, free from ſun and rain.

The wilde Plantine grows much as the others does, but the leaves not ſo broad, and more upright, the fruit not to be eaten ; of a ſcarlet colour, and almoſt three ſquare. I know no uſe of this fruit or leaves, but to look on. *Wild Plantine.*

The Bonano differs nothing from the Plantine in the body and leaves, *Bonano.*

leaves, but only this, that the leaves are ſomewhat leſs, and the bodie has here and there ſome blackiſh ſpots, the bloſſome no bigger then a large bud of a Roſe ; of a faint purple, and Aſh-colour mixt, the ſtalk that bears it, adorn'd with ſmall bloſſomes, of ſeveral colours; when they fall off, there comes out the fruit, which does not turn back as the Plantines do, but ſtand outright like a bunch of puddings, all neer of a length, and each of them between four and five inches long.   This fruit is of a ſweeter taſte then the Plantine ; and for that reaſon the *Negroes* will not meddle with them, nor with any fruit that has a ſweet taſte; but we find them as good to ſtew, or preſerve, as the Plantine, and will look and taſte more like Quince.   This tree wants little of the beauty of the Plantine, as ſhe appears upon the ground, in her full growth ; and though her fruit be not ſo uſeful a food for the belly, as that of the Plantine, yet ſhe has ſomewhat to delight the eyes, which the other wants, and that is the picture of Chriſt upon the Croſs ; ſo lively expreſt, as no Limner can do it (with one colour) more exactly ; and this is ſeen, when you cut the fruit juſt croſs as you do the root of Ferne, to find a ſpread Eagle : but this is much more perfect, the head hanging down, the armes extended to the full length, with ſome little elevation ; and the feet croſs one upon a-nother.

This I will ſpeak as an Artiſt ; let a very excellent Limner, paint a Crucifix, only with one colour, in limning ; and let his touches be as ſharp, and as maſterly as he pleaſes, the figure no bigger then this which is about an inch long, and remove that picture at ſuch a diſtance from the eye, as to loſe ſome of the Curioſity, and dainty touches of the work, ſo as the outmoſt ſtels, or profile of the figure may be perfectly diſcern'd, and at ſuch a diſtance ; the figure in the fruit of the Bonano, ſhall ſeem as perfect as it : much may be ſaid upon this ſubject by better wits, and abler ſouls then mine : My contemplation being only this, that ſince thoſe men dwelling in that place profeſſing the names of Chriſtians, and denying to preach to thoſe poor ignorant harmleſs ſouls the *Negroes*, the doctrine of Chriſt Crucified, which might convert many of them to his worſhip, he himſelf has ſet up his own Croſs, to reproach theſe men, who rather then they will loſe the hold they have of them as ſlaves, will deny them the benefit and bleſſing of being Chriſtians.   Otherwiſe, why is this figure ſet up for theſe to look on, that never heard of Chriſt, and God never made any thing uſeleſs, or in vain.

Pine.   Now to cloſe up all that can be ſaid of fruits, I muſt name the Pine, for in that ſingle name, all that is excellent in a ſuperlative degree, for beauty and taſte, is totally and ſummarily included : and if it were here to ſpeak for it ſelf, it would ſave me much labour, and do it ſelf much right,   Tis true, that it takes up double the time the Plantine does, in bringing forth the fruit; for 'tis a full year before it be ripe; but when it comes to be eaten, nothing of rare taſte can be thought on that is not there ; nor is it imaginable, that ſo full a Harmony of taſtes can be raiſed out of ſo many parts, and all diſtinguiſhable. But before I come to ſay any thing of that, I will give you ſome little hints of her ſhape and manner of growth, which though I muſt acknowledge

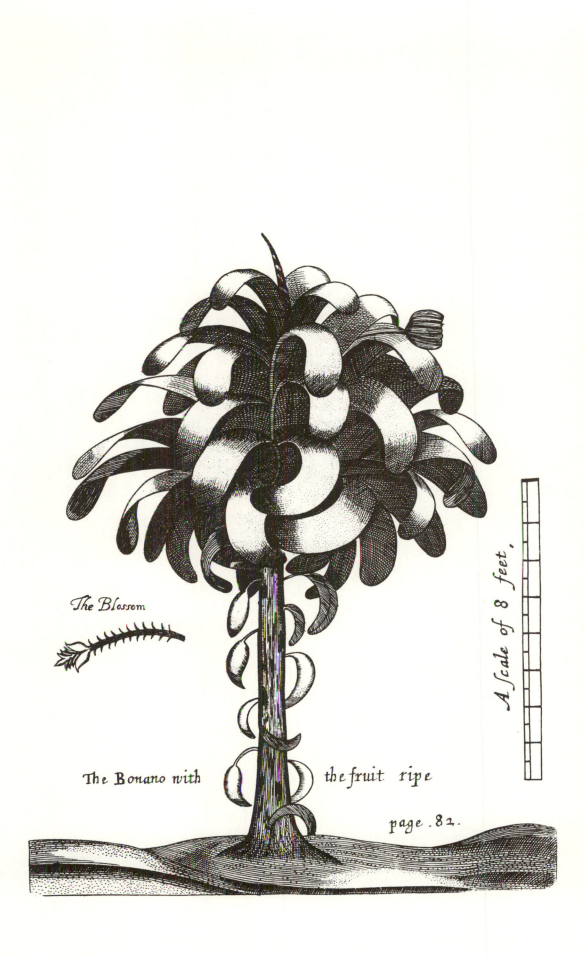

The Blossom

The Bonano with   the fruit ripe

page . 82 .

A Scale of 8 feet.

ledg my felf to be down-right lame, in the expreffion ; yet rather
then you fhall lofe all, I will indeavour to reprefent fome of her beauties, in fuch faint expreffions as I have. A Slip taken from the body of
this plant, and fet in the ground, will not prefently take root, but the
Crown that growes upon the fruit it felf will fooner come to perfection then it ; and will have much more beauty all the time of
growing. In a quarter of a year, it will be a foot high, and then the
leaves will be about 7 or 8 inches long, which appear to your eyes
like Semi-Circles: the middle being a little hollow, fo as I have feen
a french fword, that is made for lightnefs and ftrength. The colour
for the moft part, froft upon green, intermixt with Carnation, and
upon edges of the leaves, teeth like thofe upon Sawes , and thefe
are pure incarnadine. The leaves fall over one another, as they are
plac't higher on the ftem ; the points of the loweft, touching the
ground ; in a quarter of a year more, you fhall perceive on the top
of the ftem a Bloffome, as large as the largeft Carnation, but of different colours, very fmall flakes, Carnation, Crimfon and Scarlet intermixt, fome yellow, fome blew leaves, and fome Peach Colour,
intermixt with purple, Sky colour, and Orange tawny, Gridaline, and
Gingeline, white and Philyamort. So that the Bloffome may be
faid to reprefent many of the varieties to the fight, which the fruit
does to the tafte, thefe colours will continue a week or ten dayes,
and then wither and fall away, under which there will appear a little
bunch of the bignefs of a Walnut which has in it all thefe colours
mixt, which in the bloffome were difperft; and fo grows bigger for two
months more, before it fhews the perfect fhape, which is fomewhat of
an Oval form, but blunt at either end ; and at the upper end, growes
out a Crown of leaves, much like thofe below for colour, but more
beautiful ; fome of the leaves of this Crown, fix inches long ; the out
leaves, fhorter by degrees. This fruit is inclos'd with a rind, which
begins with a fcrew at the ftalk, and fo it goes round till it comes to the
top or Crown, gently rifing, which fcrew is about ¾ of an inch
broad ; and the figures that are imbroydred upon that fcrew neer of
that dimenfion, and divifions between. And it falls out fo, as thofe
divifions are never over one another in the fcrew, but are alwayes
under the middle of the figures above, thofe figures do vary fo in the
colouring, as if you fee an hundred Pines they are not one like another,
and every one of thofe figures has a little tuft or beard, fome of green,
fome yellow, fome Afh colour, fome Carnation : There are two forts
of pines, the King and Qeen Pine : The Queen is far more delicate,
and has her colours of all greens, with their fhadowes intermixt, with
faint Carnations, but moft of all froft upon green, and Sea greens. The
King Pine, has, for the moft part, all forts of yellows, with their fhadowes intermixt with grafs greens, and is commonly the larger Pine.
I have feen fome of them 14 inches long, and fix inches in the diametre ; they never grow to be above four foot high, but the moft of them
having heavy bodies, and flender ftalks, lean dovvn and reft upon the
ground. Some there are, that ftand upright, and have coming
out of the ftem, belovv, fome fprouts of their own kind, that bear
fruits which jett out from the ftem a little, and then rife upright, I
have

have ſeen a dozen of theſe round about the prime fruit, but not ſo high as the bottom of that, and the whole Plant together, ſhews like a Father in the middle, and a dozen Children round about him : and all thoſe will take their turnes to be ripe, and all very good. When this fruit is grown to a ripeneſs, you ſhall perceive it by the ſmell, which is asfar beyond the ſmell of our choiceſt fruits o *Europe,* as the taſte is beyond theirs. When we gather them, we leave ſome of the ſtalk to take hold by ; and when vve come to eat them, vve firſt cut off the crovvn, and ſend that out to be planted ; and then vvith a knife, pare off the rinde, vvhich is ſo beautiful, as it grieves us to rob the fruit of ſuch an ornament ; nor vvould we do it, but to enjoy the precious ſubſtance it contains ; like a Thief, that breakes a beautiful Cabinet, which we would forbear to do, but for the treaſure he expects to find within.   The rinde being taken off, vve lay the fruit in a diſh, and cut it in ſlices, half an inch thick ; and as the knife goes in, there iſſues out of the pores of the fruit, a liquor, cleer as Rock-vvater, neer about ſix ſpoonfulls, vvhith is eaten whith a ſpoon ; and as you taſte it, you find it in a high degree delicious, but ſo milde, as you can diſtinguiſh no taſte at all ; but when you bite a piece of the fruit, it is ſo violently ſharp, as you vvould think it vvould fetch all the skin off your mouth ; but, before your tongue have made a ſecond trial upon your palat, you ſhall perceive ſuch a ſvveetneſs to follovv, as perfectly to cure that vigorous ſharpneſs ; and betvveen theſe tvvo extreames, of ſharp and ſvveet, lies the reliſh and flavor of all fruits that are excellent ; and thoſe taſtes will change and flow ſo faſt upon your palate, as your fancy can hardly keep way with them, to diſtinguiſh the one from the other : and this at leaſt to a tenth examination, for ſo long the Eccho will laſt. This fruit within, is neer of the colour of an Abricot not full ripe, and eates criſpe and ſhort as that does ; but it is full of pores, and thoſe of ſuch formes and colours, as 'tis a very beautiful ſight to look on, and invites the appetite beyond meaſure.   Of this fruit you may eat plentifully, without any danger of ſurfeting.   I have had many thoughts which way this fruit might be brought into *England,* but cannot ſatisfie my ſelf in any ; preſevr'd it cannot be, whole ; for, the rinde is is ſo firm and tough, as no Sugar can enter in ; and if you divide it in peices, (the fruit being full of pores) all the pure taſte will boyle out.   'Tis true, that the *Dutch* preſerve them at *Fernambock,* and ſend them home ; but they are ſuch as are young, and their rinde ſoft and tender : But thoſe never came to their full taſte, nor can we know by the taſte of them, what the others are. From the *Bermudoes,* ſome have been brought hither in their full ripeneſs and perfection, where there has been a quick paſſage, and the fruites taken in the nick of time ; but, that happens very ſeldom. But, that they ſhould be brought from the *Barbadoes,* is impoſſible, by reaſon of the ſeveral Climates between. We brought in the ſhip ſeventeen of ſeveral growths, but all rotten, before we came halfe the way.

Sugar Canes, with the manner of planting ; of their growth, time of ripeneſs, with the whole proceſs of Sugar-making.   Though I have ſaid as much as is fit, and no more then truth, of the beauty and taſte of theſe formentioned Trees and Plants, beyond which, the Sun with his maſculine force cannot beget, nor the teeming Earth bear ; all which are proper and peculiar to the Iland ; for

they

The superfities or Plott forme of the Ingenio that grinds or
squitses the canes which make the suger

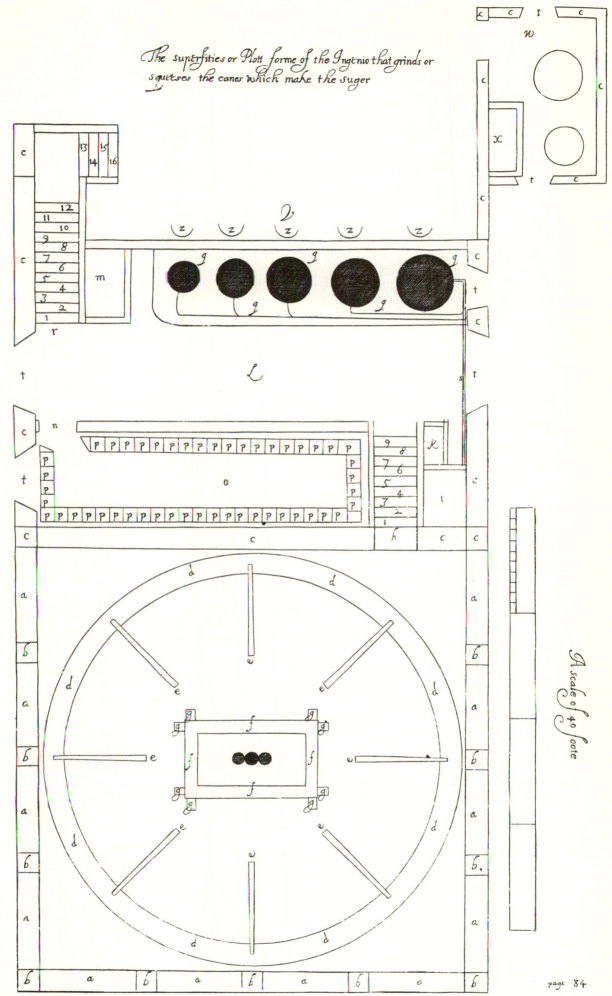

A scale of 40 foote

page 84

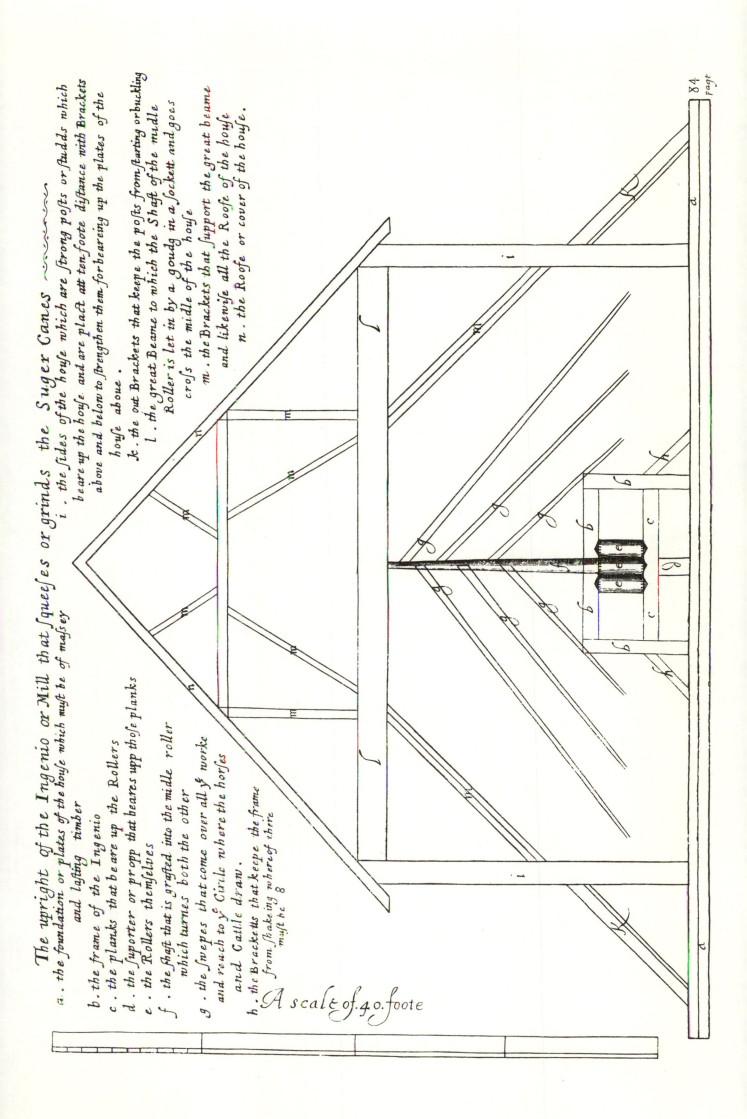

The upright of the Ingenio or Mill that squeeses or grinds the Suger Canes

a. the foundation or plates of the house which must be of massey and lasting timber
b. the frame of the Ingenio
c. the planks that beare up the Rollers
d. the supporter or propp that beares upp those planks
e. the Rollers themselves
f. the shaft that is grafted into the midle roller which turnes both the other
g. the sweepes that come over all ye worke and reach to ye Cirle where the horses and Cattle draw.
h. the Bracketts that keepe the frame from shaking whereof there must be 8

i. the sides of the house which are strong posts or studds which beare up the house, and are plact att ten foote distance with Brackets above and belon to strengthen them for bearing up the plates of the house above.
k. the out Brackets that keepe the posts from starting or buckling
l. the great Beame to which the Shaft of the midle Roller is let in by a goudg in a sockett and goes cross the midle of the house.
m. the Brackets that support the great beame and likewise all the Roofe of the house
n. the Roofe or cover of the house.

A scale of 40. foote

The first Storie of the Cureing house where the potts stand which hold the Suger and is 8. foote 2 inches from the ground haveing 14. steps to rise of. 7. inches to a stepp.

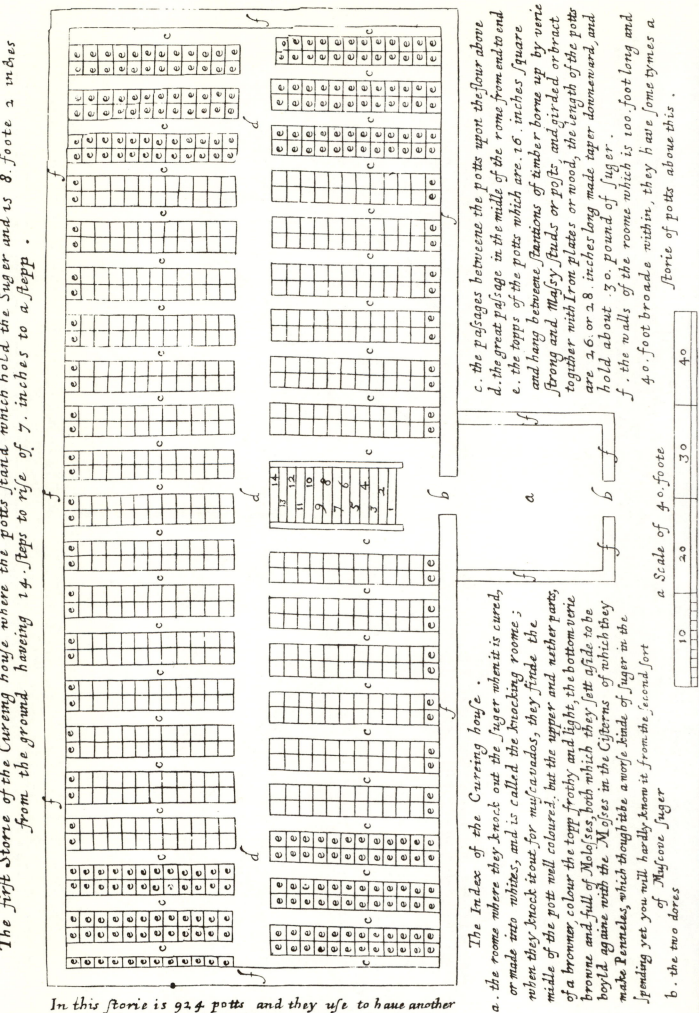

The Index of the Cureing house.
a. the roome where they knock out the suger when it is cured, or made into whites, and is called the knocking roome; when they knock it out for muscavados, they finde the midle of the pott well coloured. but the upper and nether parts, of a browner colour the topp frothy and light, the bottom verie browne and full of Molosses, both which they sett aside to be boyld againe with the Molosses in the Cisterns of which they make Penneles, which though it be a worse kinde of suger in the spending yet you will hardly know it from the second sort of Muscove suger
b. the two dores

c. the passages betweene the potts upon the flour above
d. the great passage in the midle of the roome from end to end
e. the topps of the potts which are. 16. inches square and hang betweene stantions of timber borne up by verie strong and massy studs or posts, and girded or brac't together with Iron plates or wood, the length of the potts are. 26. or 28. inches long made taper downeward, and hold about. 30. pound of suger.
f. the walls of the roome which is 100. foot long and 40. foot broade within, they have some tymes a storie of potts aboue this.

a Scale of 40. foote

10   20   30   40

In this storie is 924 potts and they use to have another storie above this which will hold above 600. potts more

The ground roome of the Curing house of the place where the gutters by w.ch convey y.e Molosses to y.e Cisterns

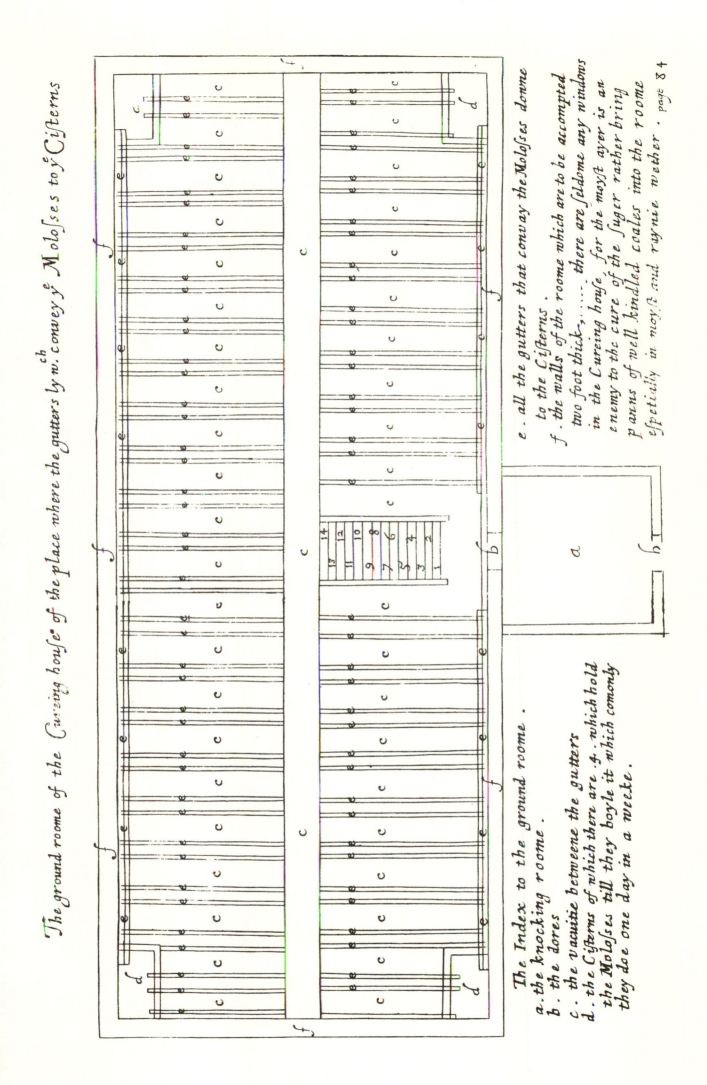

The Index to the ground roome.
a. the knocking roome.
b. the dores.
c. the vacuitie betweene the gutters
d. the Cisterns of which there are .4. which hold
the Molosses till they boyle it which comonly
they doe one day in a weeke.

e. all the gutters that convay the Molosses donne
to the Cisterns.
f. the walls of the roome which are to be accompted
two foot thick ..... there are seldome any windows
in the Cureing house, for the moyst ayer is an
enemy to the cure of the Suger rather bring
pannes of well kindled coales into the roome
espetially in moyst and raynie wether. page 84

An Index *to the* Platforme *or* Superficies *of an* Ingenio, *that grinds or squeezes the Sugar.*

A. THe ground-plat , upon which the Posts or Pillars stand , that bear up the house, or the Intercolumniation between those Pillars.

B The Pillars or Posts themselves.

C The wall between the Mill-house and Boyling-house.

D The Circle or Circumference, where the Horses and Cattle go, which draw the Rollers about.

E The Sweeps, to which the Horses and Cattle are fastned , that draw about the Rollers.

F The Frame of the *Ingenio.*

G The Brackets or Butteresses , that support that Frame.

H The Dore, that goes down stairs to the Boyling-house.

I The Cistern, into which the Liquor runs from the Ingenio, immediately after it is ground, and is carried in a Pipe under ground to this Cistern, where it remains not above a day at most.

K The Cistern that holds the Temper, which is a Liquor made with ashes, steept in water, and is no other than the Lye we wash withall in *England.* This temper , we straw in the three last Coppers , as the Sugar boyles, without which, it would never Corn, or be any thing but a Syrope; but the salt and tartarousness of this Temper, causes it to turn, as Milk does, when any soure or sharp liquor is put into it; and a very small quantity does the work.

L The Boyling-house.

The five black Rounds are the Coppers, in which the Sugar is boyled , of which the largest is called the clarifying Copper, and the least, the Tatch.

M The cooling Cistern, which the Sugar is put into, presently after it is taken off the fire, and there kept till it be Milk-warm ; and then it is to be put into Pots made of boards, sixteen inches square above, and so grow taper to a point downward; the Pot is commonly about thirty inches long , and will hold thirty or thirty five pounds of Sugar.

N The Dore of the Filling-room.

O The Room it self, into which the Pots are set, being fill'd, till the Sugar grow cold and hard, which willbe in two dayes & two nights, & then they are carried away to the Cureing-house.

P The tops of the Pots, of sixteen inches square, and stand between two stantions of timber , which are girded together in several places ,

with wood or Iron , and are thirteen or fourteen inches assunder; so that the tops of the Pots being sixteen inches, cannot slip between, but are held up four foot from the ground.

Q. The Frame where the Coppers stand, which is raised above the flowre or level of the room, about a foot and a half, and is made of Dutch Bricks , which they call Klinkers, and plaister of *Paris.* And besides the Coppers , there are made small Gutters, which convey the skimmings of the three lesser Coppers, down to the Still-house , whereof the strong Spirit is made, which they call *kill-devil,* and the skimmings of the two greater Coppers are conveyed another way, as worthless and good for nothing.

R The Dore that goes down the stairs to the fire-room , where the Furnaces are , which cause the Coppers to boyl; and though they cannot be exprest here, by reason they are under the Coppers ; yet, I have made small semi-circles , to let you see where they are , behind the partition-wall, which divides the fire-room from the boyling-house ; which wall goes to the top of the house, and is mark'd with the Letter (*c*) as the other walls are.

S A little Gutter made in the wall , from the Cistern that holds the first Liquor, to the clarifying Copper, and from thence is conveyed to the other Coppers , with Ladles that hold a gallon a piece, by the hands of Negres that attend that work day and night, shifting both Negres and Cattle every four hours, who also convey the skimmings of the three lesser Coppers down to the Stillhouse, there to be twice distill'd; the first time it comes over the helme, it is but small, and is called Low-wines; but the second time, it comes off the strongest Spirit or Liquor that is potable.

T All Windowes.

U The Fire-room, where the Furnaces are , that make the Coppers boyl.

W The Still-house.

X The Cistern that holds the skimmings, till it begin to be soure, 'till when, it will not come over the helme.

Y The two Stills in the Still-house.

Z The Semi-circles, that shew where about the Furnaces stand.

The Queen Pine.

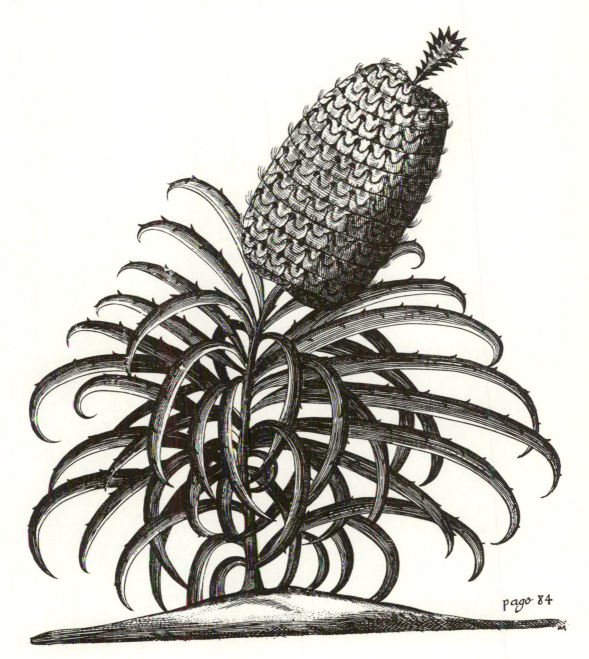

pago 84

they were planted there by the great Gardiner of the World. Yet, there is one brought thither as a stranger, from beyond the Line, which has a property beyond them all; and that is the Sugar-Cane, which though it has but one single taste, yet, that full sweetness has such a benign faculty, as to preserve all the rest from corruption, which, without it, would taint and become rotten; and not only the fruits of this Island, but of the world, which is a special preheminence due to this Plant, above all others, that the earth or world can boast of. And that I may the more fully and amply set her off, I will give you all the observations I made, from my first arrival on the Island, when planting there, was but in its infancy, and but faintly understood, to the time I left the place, when it was grown to a high perfection.

At the time we landed on this Island, which was in the beginning of *September*, 1647. we were informed, partly by those Planters we found there, and partly by our own observations, that the great work of Sugar-making, was but newly practised by the inhabitants there. Some of the most industrious men, having gotten Plants from *Fernambock*, a place in *Brasil*, and made tryal of them at the *Barbadoes*; and finding them to grow, they planted more and more, as they grew and multiplyed on the place, till they had such a considerable number, as they were worth the while to set up a very small Ingenio, and so make tryal what Sugar could be made upon that soyl. But, the secrets of the work being not well understood, the Sugars they made were very inconsiderable, and little worth, for two or three years. But they finding their errours by their daily practice, began a little to mend; and, by new directions from *Brasil*, sometimes by strangers, and now and then by their own people, (who being covetous of the knowledge of a thing, which so much concerned them in their particulars, and for the general good of the whole Island) were content sometimes to make a voyage thither, to improve their knowledge in a thing they so much desired. Being now made much abler to make their queries, of the secrets of that mystery, by how much their often failings, had put them to often stops and nonplusses in the work. And so teturning with most Plants, and better Knowledge, they went on upon fresh hopes, but still short, of what they should be more skilful in: for, at our arrival there, we found them ignorant in three main points, that much conduced to the work; *viz*. The manner of Planting, the time of Gathering, and the right placing of their Coppers in their Furnaces; as also, the true way of covering their Rollers, with plates or Bars of Iron: All which being rightly done, advance much in the performance of the main work. At the time of our arrival there, we found many Sugar-works set up, and at work; but yet the Sugars they made, were but bare Muscavadoes, and few of them Merchantable commodities; so moist, and full of molosses, and so ill cur'd, as they were hardly worth the bringing home for *England*. But about the time I left the Island, which was in 1650. they were much better'd; for then they had the skill to know when the Canes were ripe, which was not, till they were fifteen months old; and before, they gathered them at twelve, which was a main disadvantage to the making
king

king good Sugar; for, the liquor wanting of the fweetnefs it ought
to have, caufed the Sugars to be lean, and unfit to keep. Befides,
they were grown greater proficients, both in boyling and curing them,
and had learnt the knowledge of making them white, fuch as you
call Lump Sugars here in *England*; but not fo excellent as thofe they
make in *Brafil*, nor is there any likelyhood they can ever make fuch:
the land there being better, and lying in a Continent, muft needs have
conftanter and fteadier weather, and the Aire much drier and purer,
than it can be in fo fmall an Iland, and that of *Barbadoes*. And now,
feeing this commodity, Sugar, hath gotten fo much the ftart of all the
reft of thofe, that were held the ftaple Commodities of the Iland, and
fo much over-top't them, as they are for the moft part flighted and
neglected. And, for that few in *England* know the trouble and care of
making it, I think it convenient, in the firft place, to acquaint you, as
far as my memory will ferve, with the whole procefs of the work of
Sugar-making, which is now grown the foul of Trade in this Iland.
And leaving to trouble you and my felf, with relating the errours our
Predeceffors fo long wandred in, I will in brief fet down the right
and beft way they practifed, when I left the Ifland, which, I think, will
admit of no greater or farther improvement.

But, before I will begin with that, I will let you fee, how much the
land there hath been advanc'd in the profit, fince the work of Sugar
began, to the time of our landing there, which was not above five or
fix years: For, before the work began, this Plantation of Major *Hilli-
ards*, of five hundred acres, could have been purchafed for four hundred pound fterling; and now the halfe this Plantation, with the
hafte of the Stock upon it, was fold for feven thoufand pound fterling.
And it is evident, that all the land there, which has been imployed to
that work, hath found the like improvement. And I believe, when
the fmall Plantations in poor mens hands, of ten, twenty, or thirty
acres, which are too fmall to lay to that work, be bought up by great
men, and put together, into Plantations of five, fix, or feven hundred
acres, that two thirds of the Iland will be fit for Plantations of Sugar,
which will make it one of the richeft Spots of earth under the
Sun.

And now, fince I have put my felf upon this Difcovery, I think it
fit to let you know the nature of the Plant, the right way of Planting
it, the manner of growth, the time of growing to ripenefs, the manner
of cutting, bringing home, the place where to lay them, being brought
home, the time they may lye there, without fpoyl, the manner of
grinding or fqueezing them, the conveyance of the liquor to the Cifterns, how long it may ftay there without harme, the manner of boyling and skimming, with the conveyance of the skimmings into the
Cifterns, in the Still-houfe, the manner of diftilling it, which makes
the ftrongeft Spirits that men can drink, with the temper to be put in;
what the temper is, the time of cooling the Sugar before it be put into
the Pots; the time it ftaies in the Cureing houfe, before it be good
Mufcavado Sugar. And laft, the making of it into Whites, which we
call Lump-Sugar.

Firft then, it is fit to fet down, what manner of place is to be cho-
fen,

sen , to set this Sugar-work, or Ingenio, upon; and it must be the brow of a small hill, that hath within the compass of eighty foot, twelve foot descent, *viz.* from the grinding place, which is the highest ground, and stands upon a flat, to the Still-house, and that by these descents: From the grinding place to the boyling house, four foot and a half, from thence to the fire-room, seven foot and a half; and some little descent to the Still-house. And the reason of these descents are these; the top of the Cistern, into which the first liquor runs, is, and must be somewhat lower than the Pipe that convaies it, and that is a little under ground. Then the liquor which runs from that Cistern must vent it self at the bottom, otherwise it cannot run all out; and that Cistern is two foot and a half deep: and so, running upon a little descent, to the clarifying Copper, which is a foot and a half above the flowre of the Boyling house, (and so is the whole Frame, where all the Coppers stand); it must of necessity fall out, that the flowre of the Boyling-house must be below the flowre of the Mill-house, four foot and a half. Then admit the largest Copper be a foot and a half deep, the bottom of the Copper will be lower then the flowre of the Boyling-house, by a foot; the botton of the Furnaces must be three foot below the Coppers; and the holes under the Furnaces, into which the ashes fall, is three foot below the bottom of the Furnaces : A little more fall is required to the Still-house, and so the account is made up. Upon what place the Sugar-work is to be set, I have drawn two Plots, that express more than language can do, to which I refer you. And so I have done with the Ingenio, and now to the work I promised, which I shall be brief in.

When I first arrived upon the Iland, it was in my purpose, to observe their several manners of planting and husbandry there; and because this Plant was of greatest value and esteem, I desired first the knowledge of it. I saw by the growth, as well as by what I had been told, that it was a strong and lusty Plant, and so vigorous, as where it grew, to forbid all Weeds to grow very neer it ; so thirstily it suck't the earth for nourishment , to maintain its own health and gallantry.

But the Planters, though they know this to be true, yet, by their manner of Planting , did not rightly pursue their own knowledge; for their manner was, to dig small holes, at three foot distance, or there about , and put in the Plants endwise, with a little stooping, so that each Plant brought not forth above three or four sprouts at the most , and they being all fastned to one root, when they grew large, tall, and heavy, and stormes of wind and rain came, (and those raines there, fall with much violence and weight) the roots were loosened, and the Canes lodged, and so became rotten, and unfit for service in making good Sugar. And besides, the roots being far asunder, weeds grew up betvveen, and vvorse then all weeds, Withs, vvhich are of a stronger grouth then the Canes, and do much mischiefe vvhere they are; for, they vvinde about them, and pull them dovvn to the ground, as disdaining to see a prouder Plant than themselves. But experience taught us, that this vvay of planting vvas most pernicious, and therefore vvere resolved to try another, vvhich is, vvithout question, the best; and that

is,

is, by digging a small trench of six inches broad, and as much deep, in a straight line, the vvhole length of the land you mean to plant, laying the earth on one side the trench as you make it; then lay tvvo Canes along the bottom of the trench, one by another, and so concinue them the vvhole length of the trench, to the lands end, and cover them vvith the earth you laid by; and at tvvo foot distance, another of the same, and so a third and fourth, till you have finish'd all the land you intend to plant at that time: For, you must not plant too much at once, but have it to grovv ripe successively, that your vvork may come in order, to keep you still doing; for, if it should be ripe all together, you are not able to vvork it so; and then for vvant of cutting, they vvould rot, and grovv to loss: By planting it thus along, tvvo together, every knot vvill have a sprout, and so a particular root, and by the means of that, be the more firmer fixt in the ground, and the better able to endure the vvind and vveather, and by their thick grovving together, be the stronger to support one another. By that time they have been in the ground a month, you shall perceive them to appear, like a land of green Wheat in *England*, that is high enough to hide a Hare; and in a month more, tvvo foot high at least. But upon the first months grovvth, those that are careful, and the best husbands, command their Overseers to search, if any vveeds have taken root, and destroy them, or if any of the Plants fail, and supply them; for vvhere the Plants are vvanting, vveeds vvill grovv; for, the ground is too vertuous to be idle. Or, if any Withs grovv in those vacant places, they vvill spread very far, and do much harm, pulling dovvn all the Canes they can reach to. If this husbandry be not used vvhen the Canes are young, it vvill be too late to find a remedy; for, vvhen they are grovvn to a height, the blades vvill become rough and sharp in the sides, and so cut the skins of the Negres, as the blood vvill follovv; for their bodies, leggs, and feet, being uncloathed and bare, cannot enter the Canes vvithout smart and loss of blood, vvhich they vvill not endure. Besides, if the Overseers stay too long, before they repair these void places, by new Plants, they will never be ripe together, which is a very great harm to the whole field, for which there is but one remedy, and that almost as ill as the disease, which is, by burning the whole field, by which they lose all the time they have grown: But the roots continuing secure from the fire, there arises a new spring all together; so that to repair this loss of time, they have onely this recompence, which is, by burning an army of the main enemies to their profit, Rats, which do infinite harm in the Island, by gnawing the Canes, which presently after will rot, and become unserviceable in the work of Sugar. And that they may do this justice the more severely, they begin to make their fire at the out-sides of that land of Canes they mean to burn, and so drive them to the middle, where at last the fire comes, and burns them all; and this great execution they put often in practice, without Assises or Sessions; for, there are not so great enemies to the Canes, as these Vermine; as also to the Houses, where they lay up their stores of Corn and other provisions; and likewise in dwelling houses for their victuals. For, when the great down-falls of rain come, which is in *November* and *December*, and in the time of the *Turnado*,

nado, they leave the field, and shelter themselves in the dwelling houses, where they do much mischief.

The Canes with their tops or blades, do commonly grow to be eight foot high; the Canes themselves are commonly five or six foot, (I have seen some double that length, but 'tis but seldome) the bodies of them, about an inch diametre, the knots above five or six inches distant one to another, many times three or four inches, some more, some lesse, for there is no certain rule for that; the colour of the blades, and tops, pure grass green; but the Canes themselves, when they are ripe of a deep Popinjay; and then they yeeld the greater quantity, and fuller and sweeter juyce. The manner of cutting them is with little hand bills, about six inches from the ground; at which time they divide the tops from the Canes, which they do with the same bills, at one stroak; and then holding the Canes by the upper end, they strip off all the blades that grow by the sides of the Canes, which tops and blades are bound up in faggots, and put into Carts, to carry home; for without these, our Horses and Cattle are not able to work, the pasture being so extream harsh and saplesse, but with these they are very well nourisht and kept in heart. The Canes we likewise bind up in faggots, at the same time, and those are commonly brought home upon the backs of *Assinigoes*, and we use the fashion of *Devon-shire* in that kind of Husbandry, (for there we learnt it) which is small pack-saddles, and crooks which serve our purposes very fitly, laying upon each Crook a faggot, and one a top, so that each Assinigo carries his three faggots; and being accustomed to go between the field and the place where they are to unload, will of themselves make their returnes without a guide; So understanding this little beast in performing his duty. The place where they unload, is a little platform of ground, which is contiguous to the Mill-house, which they call a *Barbycu*; about 30 foot long and 10 foot broad; done about with a double rayle to keep the Canes from falling out of that room; where one, or two, or more, (who have other work to do in the Mill-house,) when they see the *Assinigoes* coming, and make a stop there, are ready to unload them, and so turning them back again, they go immediately to the field, there to take in fresh loading; so that they may not unfitly be compar'd to Bees; the one fetching home Hony, the other Sugar: being laid on the *Barbyon*, we work them out clean, and leave none to grow stale, for if they should be more then two dayes old, the juyce will grow sour, and then they will not be fit to work, for their sournesse will infect the rest; The longest time they stay, after they are cut, to the time of grinding, is from Saturday evening to Munday morning at one or two a clock; and the necessity of Sunday coming between, (upon which we do not work) causes us to stay so long, which otherwise we would not do. The manner of grinding them, is this, the Horses and Cattle being put to their tackle, they go about, and by their force turne (by the sweeps) the middle roller; which being Cog'd to the other two, at both ends, turne them about; and they are three, turning upon their Centres, which are of Brass and Steel, going very easily of themselves, and so easie as a mans taking hold of one of the sweeps with his hand will turne all the rollers about with much ease. But when the Canes are put in between

tween the rollers, it is a good draught for five Oxen or Horses; a *Negro* puts in the Canes of one side, and the rollers draw them through to the other side, where another *Negre* stands, and receives them; and returns them back on the other side of the middle roller, which draws the other way. So that having past twice through, that is forth and back, it is conceived all the juyce is prest out; yet the Spaniards have a press, after both the former grindings, to press out the remainder of the liquor but they having but small works in *Spain*, make the most of it, whilst we having far greater quantities, are loath to be at that trouble. The Canes having past to and again, there are young *Negre* Girles, that carry them away, and lay them on a heap, at the distance of six score paces or thereabout; where they make a large hill, if the work have continued long: under the rollers, there is a receiver, as big as a large Tray; into which the liquor falls, and stays not there, but runs under ground in a Pipe or gutter of lead, cover'd over close, which pipe or gutter, carries it into the Cistern, which is fixt neer the staires, as you go down from the Mill-house to the boyling house. But it must not remain in that Cisterne above one day, lest it grow sowr; from thence it is to passe through a gutter, (fixt to the wall) to the Clarifying Copper, as there is occasion to use it, and as the work goes on, and as it Clarifies in the first Copper, and the skumme rises, it is conveyed away by a passage, or gutter for that purpose; as also of the second Copper, both which skimmings, are not esteem'd worth the labour of stilling; because the skum is dirtie and gross: But the skimmings of the other three Coppers, are conveyed down to the Still-house, there to remain in the Cisterns, till it be a little sowr, for till then it will not come over the helme. This liquor is remov'd, as it is refin'd, from one Copper to another; and the more Coppers it passeth through, the finer and purer it is, being continually drawn up, and keel'd by ladles, and skim'd by skimmers, in the Negres hands, till at last it comes to the tach, where it must have much labour, in keeling and stirring; and as it boyles, there is thrown into the four last Coppers, a liquor made of water and ashes which they call Temper, without which, the Sugar would continue a Clammy substance and never kerne. The quantities they put in are small, but being of a tart quality it turnes the ropiness and clamminess of the Sugar to cruddle and separate: which you will find, by taking out some drops of it, to Candy, and suddenly to grow hard; and then it has enough of the fire. Upon which Essay they presently poure two spoonfuls of Sallet Oyle into the tach, and then immediately it gives over to bubble or rise. So after much keeling, they take it out of the tach, by the ladles they use there, and put it into ladles that are of greater receipt, with two handles, and by them remove it into the cooling Cistern, neer the stayers that goes to the fire room: But as they remove the last part of the liquor out of the tach, they do it with all the celerity they can; and suddenly cast in cold water, to cool the Copper from burning, for the fire in the furnace, continues still in the same heat: and so when that water is removed out again by the Ladles, they are in the same degree careful, and quick, as soon as the last Ladle full is taken out, to throw in some of the

liquor

liquor of the next Copper, to keep the tach from burning, and so fill it up out of the next, and that out of the third, and that out of the fourth, and that out of the Clarifying Copper, and so from the Cistern, and so from the Mill-house or Ingenio. And so the work goes on, from Munday morning at one a clock, till Saturday night, (at which time the fire in the Furnaces are put out) all houres of the day and night, with fresh supplies of Men, Horses, and Cattle. The Liquor being come to such a coolness, as it is fit to be put into the Pots, they bring them neer the Cooler, and stopping first the sharp end of the Pot (which is the bottom) with Plantine leaves, (and the passage there no bigger then a mans finger will go in at) they fill the Pot, and set it between the stantions, in the filling room, where it staies till it be thorough cold, which will be in two dayes and two nights; and then if the Sugar be good, knock upon it with the knuckle of your finger, as you would do upon an earthen pot, to try whether it be whole, and it will give a sound; but if the Sugar be very ill, it will neither be very hard, nor give any sound. It is then to be removed into the Cureing house, and set between stantions there: But first, the stopples are to be pull'd out of the bottom of the pots, that the Molosses may vent it self at that hole, and so drop drown upon a gutter of board, hollowed in the the middle, which conveyeth the Molosses from one to another, till it be come into the Cisterns, of which there is commonly four, at either corner one; and there remains, till it rise to a good quantity, and then they boyl it again, and of that they make Peneles, a kind of Sugar somewhat inferiour to the Muscavado; but yet will sweeten indifferently well, and some of it very well coloured. The pots being thus opened at the bottoms, the Molosses drops out, but so slowly, as hardly to vent it selfe in a month, in which time, the Sugar ought to be well cur'd; and therefore they thought fit, to thrust a spike of wood in at the bottom, that should reach to the top, hoping by that means, to make way for the Molosses to have the speedier passage: But they found little amendment in the purging, and the reason was this, the spike as it went in, prest the Sugar so hard, as it stopt all pores of passage for the Molosses. So finding no good to come of this, they devis'd another way, and that was, by making an augure of Iron, which instrument cuts his way, without pressing the Sugar, and by that means the Molosses had a free passage, without any obstruction at all. And so the Sugar was well cur'd in a month. As for the manner of using it, after it is cur'd, you shall find it set down in my Index, to the plot of the Cureing house. And this is the whole process of making the Muscavado Sugar, whereof some is better, and some worse, as the Canes are; for, ill Canes can never make good Sugar.

I call those ill, that are gathered either before or after the time of such ripeness, or are eaten by Rats, and so consequently rotten, or pull'd down by Withes, or lodg'd by foule weather, either of which, will serve to spoil such Sugar as is made of them. At the time they expect it should be well cur'd, they take the pots from the stantions in the Curing-house, and bring them to the knocking room, which you shall find upon the plot of the cureing house; and turning it up-

side

side down, they knock the pot hard againſt the ground, and the Sugar comes whole out, as a bullet out of a mold; and when it is out, you may perceive three ſorts of colours in the pot, the tops ſomevvhat browniſh, and of a frothy light ſubſtance; the bottom of a much darker colour, but heavy, groſs, moiſt, and full of Moloſſes; both which they cut away, and reſerve to be boyl'd again, with the Moloſſes for peneles: The middle part, which is more then two thirds of the whole pot, and looks of a bright colour, dry and ſweet, they lay by it ſelf, and ſend it down daily upon the backs of Aſſinigoes and Camells, in leather baggs, with a Tarr'd cloth over, to their Store-houſes at the *Bridge*, there to be put in Caskes and Cheſts, to be ſhipt away for *England*, or any other parts of the World, where the beſt market is. Though this care be taken, and this courſe uſed, by the beſt huſbands, and thoſe that reſpect their credits, as Collonel *James Drax*, Collonel *Walrond*, Mr. *Raynes*, and ſome others that I know there; yet, the greater number, when they knock out their Sugars, let all go together, both bottom and top, and ſo let the better bare out the worſe. But, when they come to the Merchant to be ſold, they will not give above 3li. 10s. for the one; and for the other, about 6li. 4s. And thoſe that uſe this care, have ſuch credit with the Buyer, as they ſcarce open the Cask to make a tryal; ſo well they are aſſured of the goodneſs of the Sugars they make; as of Collonel *James Drax*, Collonel *Walrond*, Mr. *Raines*, and ſome others in the Iſland that I know.

I have yet ſaid nothing of making white Sugars, but that is much quicker ſaid than done: For, though the Muſcavado Sugar, require but a months time to make it ſo, after it is boyl'd; yet the Whites require four months, and it is only this. Take clay, and temper it with water, to the thickneſs of Frumenty, or Peaſe pottage, and poure it on the top of the Muſcavado Sugar, as it ſtands in the pot, in the Curing-houſe, and there let it remain four months; and if the clay crack and open, that the aire come in, cloſe it up with ſome of the ſame, either with your hand, or a ſmall Trowell. And when you knock open theſe pots, you ſhall find a difference, both in the colour and goodneſs, of the top and bottom, being but to ſuch a degree, as may be rank'd with Muſcavadoes; but the middle perfect White, and excellent Lump-Sugar, the beſt of which will ſell in *London* for 20d. a pound.

I do not remember I have left unſaid any thing, that conduces to the work of Sugar-making, unleſs it be, ſometimes after great rains, (which moiſten the aire more then ordinary) to lay it out upon fair daies in the Sun, upon cloaths, or in the knocking room, and ſometimes to bring in pans of coals, well kindled, into the Cureing-houſe. If I have omitted any thing here, you ſhall find it ſupplyed in the Indexes of my Plots.

As for diſtilling the skimmings, which run down to the Still-houſe, from the three leſſer Coppers, it is only this: After it has remained in the Ciſterns, which my plot ſhews you in the Still-houſe, till it be a little ſoure, (for till then, the Spirits will not riſe in the Still) the firſt Spirit that comes off, is a ſmall Liquor, which we call

Low-

low-wines, which Liquor we put into the Still, and draw it off a-gain ; and of that comes so strong a Spirit, as a candle being brought to a near distance, to the bung of a Hogshead or But, where it is kept, the Spirits will flie to it, and taking hold of it, bring the fire down to the vessell, and set all a fire, which immediately breakes the vessell, and becomes a flame, burning all about it that is combustible matter.

We lost an excellent Negro by such an accident, who bringing a Jar of this Spirit, from the Still-house, to the Drink-room, in the night, not knowing the force of the liquor he carried, brought the candle somewhat neerer than he ought, that he might the better see how to put it into the Funnel, which conveyed it into the Butt. But the Spirit being stirr'd by that motion, flew out, and got hold of the flame of the Candle, and so set all on fire, and burnt the poor Negro to death, who was an excellent servant. And if he had in the instant of firing, clapt his hand on the bung, all had been saved ; but he that knew not that cure, lost the whole vessel of Spirits, and his life to boot. So that upon that misadventure, a strict command was given, that none of those Spirits should be brought to the Drink-room ever after in the night, nor no fire or Candle ever to come in there.

This drink, though it had the ill hap to kill one Negro, yet it has had the vertue to cure many ; for when they are ill, with taking cold, (which often they are) and very well they may, having nothing un-der them in the night but a board, upon which they lie, nor any thing to cover them : And though the daies be hot, the nights are cold, and that change cannot but work upon their bodies, though they be hardy people. Besides, coming home hot and sweating in the evening, sit-ting or lying down, must needs be the occasion of taking cold, and sometimes breeds sicknesses amongst them, which when they feel, they complain to the Apothecary of the Plantation, which we call *Doctor*, and he gives to every one a dram cup of this Spirit, and that is a present cure. And as this drink is of great use, to cure and refresh the poor Negroes , whom we ought to have a special care of, by the la-bour of whose hands, our profit is brought in ; so is it helpful to our Christian Servants too ; for, when their spirits are exhausted, by their hard labour, and sweating in the Sun, ten hours every day, they find their stomacks debilitated, and much weakned in their vigour every way, a dram or two of this Spirit, is a great comfort and refreshing to them. This drink is also a commodity of good value in the Planta-tion ; for we send it down to the *Bridge*, and there put it off to those that retail it. Some they sell to the Ships, and is transported into for-raign parts, and drunk by the way. Some they sell to such Planters, as have no Sugar-works of their own, yet drink excessively of it, for they buy it at easie rates ; half a crown a gallon was the price, the time that I was there ; but they were then purposing to raise the price to a deerer rate. They make weekly, as long as they work, of such a Plantation as this 30 l sterling, besides what is drunk by their servants and slaves.

And now for a close of this work of Sugar, I will let you see, by way of

of eſtimate, to what a Revenue this Iſland is raiſed; and, in my opinion, not improbable. If you will be pleaſed to look back to the extent
of the Iſland , you ſhall find , by taking a medium of the length and
breadth of it, that there is contained in the Iſland 392 ſquare miles,

$$
\begin{array}{r}
28 \\
14 \\
\hline
112 \\
28 \\
\hline
392
\end{array}
$$

out of which we will ſubſtract a third part, which is the moſt remote
part of the Iland from the *Bridge*, where all, or the moſt part of Trade
is, which by many deep and ſteep Gullies interpoſing , the paſſage is
in a manner ſtop'd : beſides, the Land there is not ſo rich and fit to
bear Canes as the other ; but may be very uſefull for planting proviſions of Corn, Yeams, Bonaviſta, Caſſavie, Potatoes; and likewiſe of
Fruits, as Oranges, Limons, Lymes, Plantines, Bonanoes; as alſo, for
breeding Hoggs, Sheep, Goats, Cattle, and Poultry, to furniſh the reſt
of the Iſland, that want thoſe Commodities. For which reaſons , we
will ſubſtract a third part from 392. and that is 130. and ſo the re-

$$
\begin{array}{ll}
392\ (130\tfrac{2}{3} & \quad 392 \\
333 & \quad 130 \\
& \quad \overline{262}
\end{array}
$$

maining ⅔ is 262 ſquare miles; the greateſt part of which may be
laid to Sugar-works, and ſome to be allowed and ſet out for ſmall
Plantations, which are not able to raiſe a Sugar-work or ſet up an Ingenio, by reaſon of the paucity of acres, being not above twenty, thirty, or forty acres in a Plantation; but theſe will be fit to bear Tobacco,
Ginger, Cotten-wool, Maies, Yeames, and Potatoes, as alſo for breeding Hoggs.   But moſt of theſe will in ſhort time, be bought up by
great men, and laid together, into Plantations of five, ſix, and ſeven
hundred acres.   And then we may make our computation thus, *viz.*
A mile ſquare will contain 640 acres of land, and here we ſee is 262
acres, being ⅔ of the Iſland. So then, we multiply 262 by 640. and the
product will amount unto 167680.   Now we will put the caſe, that
ſome of thoſe men that have ſmall Plantations, will not ſell them, but
keep them for proviſions , which they may live plentifully upon ;
for thoſe proviſions they raiſe, will ſell at good rates; for which uſe,
we will ſet out thirty thouſand acres. So then we ſubſtract 30000
acres from 167680, and there will remain 137680 acres , to be for
Sugar-works; out of which, ⅔ may be planted with Canes, the other
⅓ for Wood, Paſture, and Proviſions, which muſt ſupport the Plantations, according to the ſcale of Collonel *Modiford*'s Plantation, as I
                                                                    ſaid

of the Ifland of Barbadoes. 95

```
      640
      262
     ————
     1280
     3840        ꝛꝛꝛꝛ
     1280      ꭓꝛꝛ68ꝺ  (27536
     ————     ꝸꝸꝸꝸ  ⟨27536
    167680         ————
     30000         55072
    ————
    137680
```

faid before. Now thefe two fifts are, as you fee 55072 acres, and an
acre of good Canes will yield 4000 pound weight of Sugar, and none
will yield lefs then 2000 weight; but we will take a *Medium*, and reft
upon 3000 weight, upon which we will make our computation, and
fet our price upon the Sugar, according to the loweft rates, which
fhall be 3 d. per pound, as it is Mufcavado, to be fold upon the Ifland,
at the *Bridge*. In fifteen months the Canes will be ripe, and in a month
more, they will be well cur'd, and ready to be caft up, and ftowed in
the Ware-houfe. So here, we make our computation upon the place,
and fay, 3000 threepences is 37 l. 10 s. ten acres of which is 375 l.
fterling. So then we fay, if 10 acres of Canes will produce 375 l. what
fhall 55072. which is the number of acres contained upon the ⅔ of the
land, alotted for Sugar Plantations, upon which the Canes muft grow:
and by the Rule of 3. we find, that it amounts to 2065200. in fixteen
months: Now add four months more to the time of cureing, and

```
                              55072
                               375
                             ————
                             275360
                             385504
                             165216
       10 ⟍ 375ˡ.            ————
     55072  Z                2065200 ⌊0
          ⟍ 2065200 l.      2065200
                             ————
                             4130400
                             1032600
                             ————
                             3097800
                             3097800
                             ————
                             6195600
```

making it into whites, which is that we call Lump-Sugar in *England*,
and then the price will be doubled to 4130400. out of which we will
abate ¼ for wafte, and what is cut off from the tops and bottoms of
the pots, which will be good Mufcavadoes; but we will abate for that,
and wafte ¼ which is 1032600. and that we will fubftract from
4130400. and there remains 3097800. which is the totall of the revenue

venue of Sugars, that grow on the *Barbadoes* for twenty months, and accounted there, upon the Iland, at the Bridge. But if you will run the Hazards of the Sea, as all Marchants doe, and bring it for England, it will fell in London, for 12 d. the pound, and so 'tis doubled again; and then it will amount to 6195600. and in two months time more it will be in England. Now you fee what a vaft Revenew this little fpot of ground can produce in 22 months time; And so I have done with this plant, onely one touch more, to conclude with all; as Mufitians, that firft play a Preludium, next a Leffon, and then a Saraband; which is the life and fpirit of all the reft. So having played you a fhort Preludium, to this long and tedious leffon of Sugar and Sugar-making, I do think fit to give you a Saraband, with my beft Touches at laft; which fhall be only this, that as this plant has a faculty, to preferve all fruits, that grow in the world, from corruption and putrifaction; So it has a vertue, being rightly applyed, to preferve us men in our healths and fortunes too. Doctor *Butler* one of the moft learned and famous Phyfitians that this Nation, or the world ever bred, was wont to fay that,

> *If Sugar can preferve both Peares and Plumbs,*
> *Why can it not preferve as well our Lungs ?*

And that it might work the fame effect on himfelf, he alwayes drank in his Claret wine, great ftore of the beft refin'd Sugar, and alfo prefcribed it feveral wayes to his Patients, for Colds, Coughs, and Catarrs; which are difeafes, that reign much in cold Climates, efpecially in Ilands, where the Ayre is moyfter then in Continents; and so much for our Health.

Now for our fortunes, they are not onely preferv'd, but made by the powerful operation of this plant.

Colonel *James Drax*, whofe beginning upon that Iland, was founded upon a ftock not exceeding 300 l. fterling, has raifed his fortune to fuch a height, as I have heard him fay, that he would not look towards England, with a purpofe to remain there, the reft of his life, till he were able to purchafe an eftate of ten thoufand pound land yearly; which he hop'd in few years to accomplifh, with what he was then owner of; and all by this plant of Sugar. Colonel *Thomas Modiford*, has often told me, that he had taken a Refolution to himfelf, not to fet his face for England, til he had made his voyage, and imployment there, worth him an hundred thoufand pounds fterling; and all by this Sugar plant. And thefe, were men of as percing fights, and profound judgments, as any I have known in that way of management. Now if fuch Eftates as thefe, may be raifed, by the well ordering this plant, by Induftrious and painful men, why may not fuch eftates, by careful keeping, and orderly and moderate expending, be preferv'd, in their pofterities, to the tenth Generation, and by all the fweet Negotiation of Sugar ?

One Vegetable we have on the Iland, which will neither become the name of a Tree, or a plant; and that is a Withe; which is in some refpect, the harmfulleft weed that can grow; for it pulls down all that it can reach to, Canes, and all other fmall plants, it makes nothing of.

of; if it be ſuffer'd to look up in a Garden, it vvill vvind about all Herbs and Plants that have ſtalks, pull them dovvn and deſtroy them; or if it find the vvay into any Orchard, it vvill clime up by the bodies of the trees into the branches, and there invvrap them ſo, as to draw them (as it were) into a purſe, (for out of the main ſtalk, hundreds of ſmall ſprigs will grow;) and if any other tree be ſo neer as to touch it, it will find the way to it, and pull the tops of them together, and utterly disfigure the trees, and hinder the growth of the fruit; and if you cut the main ſtalk below, neer the root, in hope to kill it, the moyſture a-bove in the branches, will thruſt down a Vine into the ground, and get a new root: Nay, this is not all the miſchief, for it will reach the higheſt timber, and involve and enwrap ſo the branches, as to hinder their growths, and many times faſten one tree to another, that one ſhall hinder the growth of another. A couple of Colonel *Draxes* Axemen were felling a tree, and about the time it began to bend, that they perceiv'd which way it would fall, got clear on the other ſide, and thought themſelves ſafe: But this being faſtned to another by ſtrong Withes, pull'd a great branch of that tree after it, which fell upon the fellers, and bruiſed them ſo as they hardly ſcap'd with their lives. Cleere a paſſage of ten foot broad, that goes between a wood and a land of Canes overnight, and come next morning, and you ſhall find the way croſt all over with Withs, and got neer the Canes; So that if you had left your viſit till the next day, they had gotten into the Canes, and then it would be too late to help: for when they are mixt with them you cannot deſtroy the one without the other, for where-ſoever they touch ground they get new roots, and ſo creep into every place, and as they go pull down all. Theſe harmeful Withes, have with all theſe vices ſome virtues. They ſerve for all uſes where roaps or cords are required, as for binding our Wood and Canes into faggots, or what elſe roapes are needful for; and without them we were in ill condition, for we have not any wood fit to make hoops for hogſheads, barrels, rubbs, or what not; and we can have them of what length and bigneſs we pleaſe, and they are for that uſe very good.

Several kinds of theſe Withes there are, ſome that bear fruit, ſomewhat bigger then the Cod of a Bean, which being divided long-wiſe with a ſharp knife, you ſhall perceive the moſt various and beauti-fulleſt Colours that can be, and ſo well matcht, as to make up a very great beauty.

Fell a doſen acres of wood, going on in a ſtraight line, and when the ground is cleered, the ſide of that wood you left ſtanding will be likewiſe in the ſame ſtrait line, and in a few years theſe Withes will mount to the tops of the Trees, which are for the moſt part, eighty or 100 foot high, and from that top to the ground, on the outſide of the wood, all will be cover'd with leaves, and thoſe are broad, green, and ſhining, ſo that if you be abſent from the place two or three years, and look to find a wood, you find a fair green Curtain, 300 paces long, and 80 foot high, which is as pretty a *deceptio viſus*, as you can find any where, and this is one of the pleaſanteſt Viſtos in the Iſland: the ſame things are done in the mouths or entrances of Caves, where
you

you shall find a Cave large enough to hold 500 men, and the mouth of it cover'd with a green curtain, 40 foot high, and 200 foot long; and so close a Curtaine it is (the vines being wrapt and interwove one into another) as without putting it aside, you can hardly have light to read by.

These Caves are very frequent in the Island, and of several dimensions, some small, others extreamly large and Capacious: The runaway Negres, often shelter themselves in these Coverts, for a long time, and in the night range abroad the Countrey, and steale Pigs, Plantins, Potatoes, and Pullin, and bring it there; and feast all day, upon what they stole the night before; and the nights being dark, and their bodies black, they scape undiscern'd.

There is nothing in that Countrey so useful as Liam Hounds, to find out these Thieves. I have gone into divers of those Caves, to try what kind of ayre is to be found there; and have felt it so close, and moyst withall, as my breath was neer stopt; and I do believe, if I should remain there but one night, I should never come out again.

I have often wondred, why such vast Caves and Rocks should not afford some springs of water, the ayre which touches them, being so very moyst; for we see in *England*, where Rocks are, Springs of water issue out; and sometimes (when wet weather is) the moysture hangs upon the Rocks in drops, and so runs down, and finds a way to vent it self into small bibling Springs; but here it does not so, though the Ayre be much moyster than in *England*: But certainly the reason is, the extraordinary drines, and spungines of the Stone, which sucks up all moysture that touches it, and yet it is never satisfied.

I had it in my thoughts, to make an Essay, what Sir *Francis Bacons* experiment solitarie, touching the making of Artificial Springs would do; but troughs of that stone, being of so dry and spungy a quality, would never have been fit for it; besides, we have no brakes growing there, which is one of the materials us'd in that experiment.

Another sort of Withs we have, but they are made of the gum of trees, which falls from the boughs drop after drop, one hanging by another, till they touch ground; from whence they receive some nourishment, which gives them power to grow larger: and if it happen that three or four of them come down so neer one another as to touch, and the wind twist them together, they appear so like ropes, as they cannot be discern'd five paces off, whether it be a rope or a Withe. I have seen of these of several sizes, from the smallest whipcord to the greatest Cable of the Soveraine; and the most of those timber trees I have named, has them; some four, some five, some half a dozen, hanging down like Bell-ropes, from the branches to the ground, which was a sight of much rarity to me at first coming.

Aloes. *Aloes* we have growing here, very good, and 'tis a beautiful plant; the leaves four inches broad, $\frac{1}{4}$ of an inch thick, and about a foot and an half long, with prickles of each side; and the last sprout which rises up in the middle, bears yellow flowers, one above another, and those flowers are higher than any of the leaves by two foot. These thick

leaves

leaves we take, and cut them through, and out of them issue the A-loes, which we set in the Sun, and that will rarifie it, and make it fit to keep. But it is the first coming which we save; for if we let it run too long, the second running will be much worse; but before that comes, we throw away the leaf. The leaves of this Plant, (which we call *semper vivens* in *England*, and growes neer the fire in Kitchins, hung up to a beam with an oyl'd clout about the root) with the inner bark of *Elder*, and some other ingredients, boyl'd in Sallet-oyle, is the best medicine in the world for a burn or a Scald, being presently applyed; and for that the medicine is beyond all that ever was, for that cure, I will set it down, and 'tis this.

Take *Semper vivens*, Plantine leaves, and the green rinde of *Elder*, of each a like quantity, and boyl them in Sallet-oyle, so much as will draw out all that tincture by boyling; then strain the Oyle well out, and put it on the fire again, and put to it a small quantity of spirit of Wine, and so much yellow Wax, as will bring it to the consistence of a Liniment.

One other Plant we have, and that is the Sensible plant, which closes the leaves upon any touch with your hand, or that end of your staff by which you hold, and in a little time will open again.

Flowers.

There are very few Flowers in the Island, and none of them sweet; as the white Lilly, which grows in the woods, and is much a fairer flower than ours; as also a red Lilly of the same bignes, but neither of them sweet. The St. *Jago* flower is very beautiful, but of a nauseous savour. One more we have, and that must not be forgotten for the rarity, because it opens, when all else close, when the Sun goes down; and for that reason we call it, the flower of the Moon: It growes in great tuffs, the leaves almost in the form of a Heart, the point turning back, the flower somewhat bigger than a Primrose, but of the purest purple that ever I beheld. When this flower falls off, the seed appears, which is black, with an eye of purple; shap'd, and of the size of a small button, so finely wrought, and tough withall, as it might serve very well to trim a suit of apparel.

I know no herbs naturally growing in the Island, that have not been brought thither from other parts, but Purcelane; and that growes so universally, as the over-much plenty makes it disesteemed; and we destroy it as a Weed that cumbers the ground.

English Herbs and Roots.

Rosemary, Time, Winter-savory, sweet Marjerom, pot Marjerom, Parsley, Penniroyal, Camomile, Sage, Tansie, Lavender, Lavender-Cotten, Garlick, Onyons, Colworts, Cabbage, Turnips, Redishes, Marigolds, Lettice, Taragon, Southernwood. All these I carried with me in seeds, and all grew and prospered well. Leek-Seed I had, which appeared to me very fresh and good; but it never came up. Rose trees we have, but they never bear flowers.

There is a Root, of which some of the Negroes brought the Seeds, and planted there, and they grew: 'Tis a very large Root, drie, and well tasted; the manner of planting it, is, to make little hills as big as Mole-hills, and plant the seed a top, and as soon as it puts forth the stalks, they turn down to the ground on either side, and then as they touch it, they thrust up a stalk, not unlike an Asparagus, but of a

purple

purple colour. Thefe being gathered, and eaten as a Sallet, with oyle, vinegar, and falt, will ferve an ordinary pallet, where no better is to be had: But the root truly is very good meat, boyl'd with powdred pork, and eaten with butter, vinegar, and pepper. Moft of thefe roots are as large, as three of the biggeft Turnips we have in *England.* We carried divers of them to Sea, for our provifion, which ftood us in good ftead, and would have ferv'd us plentifully in our great want of Victuals; but the Rats (of which we had infinite numbers aboard) rob'd us of the moft part.

Strength of the Iſland by Nature to Seaward.

That part of the Iſland which lies to the windeward, and is part Eaft, part North, the ftormes and ftiffe windes coming from thofe points, have fo wafh'd away all earthly fubftance, as there remaines nothing but fteep Rocks; and the Sea being very deep on that fide, the Anchors will hardly touch the bottom, though the Cables be long; fo that what Ship foever rides on that fide, comes at her own peril. Contrarily, if any Ship be under Sail, on the Leeward fide, and goes but fo far out, as to lofe the fhelter of the Iſland, it is certain to be carried away dovvn to the leeward Iſlands, and then it will be a very hard work to beat it up again, without putting out into the main. So that there can hardly be any fafe landing, but vvhere the Harbours and Baies are, vvhich lie to the Southvveft; and thofe places are fo defenfible by Nature, as vvith fmall cofts, they may be very ftrongly fortified. But they have *been much neglected by the Proprietor,* for vvhich reafon, (and fome others) the Planters refufed to call him by that name.

Captain Burrows.

There vvas a Gentleman in the Iſland, vvho pretended to be a Souldier, and an Ingeneer, that undertook to fortifie all the landing places, and to furnifh them vvith fuch ftore of Artillery, as fhould be fufficient to defend them; provided, he might have the Excife paid to him for feven years, vvhich vvas promifed by the Governours and Affembly. Whereupon he vvent to vvork, and made fuch a Fort, as vvhen abler Ingeneers came upon the Iſland, they found to be moft pernicious; for, commanding all the Harbour, and not of ftrength to defend it felf, if it vvere taken by an enemy, might do much harm to the land-vvard. So that at my coming from thence, they vvere pulling it dovvn, and inftead of it, to make Trenches, and Rampiers, vvith Pallifadoes, Horn-vvorks, Curtains, and Counter-fcarfes; and having left a very good Fortification of ftanding vvood round about the Iſland near the Sea, thefe vvere thought as much as needed for their defence, againft the landing of any forraign Forces, and for their ftrength vvithin.

Strength of the Iſland within land.

They built three Forts, one for a Magazine to lay their Ammunition and Povvder in, the other tvvo to make their retreats upon all occafions. At my coming from thence, they vvere able to mufter ten thoufand Foot, as good men, and as refolute as any in the vvorld, and a thoufand good Horfe; and this vvas the ftrength of the Iſland about the time I came avvay.

How Governed and how Divided.

They Govern the e by the Lavves of *England,* for all Criminal, Civil, Martial, Ecclefiaftical, and Maritime affairs.

This Lavv is adminiftred by a Governour, and ten of his Council, four Courts of ordinary Juftice, in Civil caufes, vvhich divide the land

land in four Circuits ;   Juftices of Peace, Conftables, Churchwardens, and Tithing-men : five Seffions in the year, for tryal of Criminal caufes, and all Appeals from inferiour Courts, in Civil caufes. And when the Governour pleafes to call an Affembly, for the fupream Court of all, for the laft Appeals, for making new Laws and abolifhing old, according to occafion, in nature of the Parliament of *England*, and accordingly confifts of the Governour, as Supream, his Council, in nature of the Peers, and two Burgeffes chofen by every Parifh for the reft. The Ifland is divided into eleven Parifhe, no Tith es paid to the Minifter, but a yearly allowance of a pound of Tobacco, upon an acre of every mans land, befides certain Church-duties, of Marriages, Chriftenings, and Burials.

A ftanding Commiffion there was alfo, for punifhing Adultery and Fornication, though rarely put in execution.

Something would be faid concerning the feafons of the year; but it is little, and therefore will be the leaft troublefome. Four months in the year, the weather is colder then the other eight, and thofe are *November, December, January* and *February*; yet they are hotter then with us in *May.*   There is no general Fall of the leaf, every Tree having a particular fall to himfelf; as if two Locufts ftands at the diftance of a ftones caft, they have not their falls at one time; one Locuft will let fall the leaves in *January*, another in *March*, a third in *July*, a fourth in *September*; and fo all months one kind of Trees having their feveral times of falling: But if any months falls more leaves then other, 'tis *February*; for fo in my niceft obfervation I found it. The leaves we find fallen under the trees, being the moft of them large and ftiffe, when they were growing, and having many veines, which go from the middle ftalk, to the uppermoft extent of the leaf, when the thin part of the leaf is rotten and confum'd, thofe veins appear like Anatomies, with the ftrangeft works and beautifulleft forms that I have feen, fit to keep as a rarity in the Cabinets of the greateft Princes. As alfo the Negres heads, which we find in the Sands, and they are about two inches long, with a forehead, eyes, nofe, mouth, chin, and part of the neck; I cannot perceive any root by which they grow, but find them alwayes loofe in the fand; nor is it a fruit that falls from any tree, for then we fhould find it growing; black it is as jet, but from whence it comes, no man knows.

Mines there are none in this Ifland, not fo much as of Coal, for which reafon, we preferve our Woods as much as we can.   *Mines.*

We find flowing out of a Rock in one part of the Ifland, an unctuous fubftance, fomewhat like Tarre, which is thought to have many vertues yet unknown; but is already difcovered to be excellent good to ftop a flux, by drinking it, but by annointing for all aches and bruifes, and fo fubtle it is, as being put into the palm of the hand, and rub'd there, it will work through the back.

Another gummy fubftance there is, black, and hard as pitch, and is ufed as pitch; 'tis called Mountjack.

Having given you in my Bills of Fare, a particular of fuch Viands, as this Ifland afforded, for fupportation of life, and fomewhat for delight too, as far as concerns the Table; yet, what are you the better for

[Most of
this Para-
graph is
mentioned
before.]

for all this, when you must be fcorch't up from morning till night
with the torrid heat of the Sun ; So as in that twelve hours, you
hardly can find two, in which you can enjoy your felf with contentment. Or how can you expect to find heat, or warmth in your fto-
mack, to digeft that meat, when the Sun hath exhaufted your heat
and fpirits fo to your outer parts, as you are chill'd and numb'd
within ? For which reafon you are compell'd to take fuch remedies,
as are almoft as ill as the difeafe ; liquors fo ftrong, as to take a-
way the breath as it goes dovvn, and red pepper for fpice, vvhich
vvants little of the heat of a fire-coale; and all thefe vvill hardly dravv
in the heat, which the Sun dravvs out; and part of this deficiency
is occafioned by the improvidence, or inconfideration of the Inhabitants, vvho build their dvvellings, rather like ftoves then houfes; for
the moft of them are made of timber, lovv rooft keeping out the vvind,
letting in the Sun, vvhen they have means to have it othervvife ; for
I vvill undertake to contrive a houfe fo, as no one fhall have juft
caufe to complain of any exceffive heat; and that vvhich gives this
great remedy, fhall bring vvith it the greateft beauty that can be
look't on.   The Palmetoes, vvhich being plac't (as I vvill give you
directions in my plot) in convenient order, fhall interpofe fo betvveen
the Sun and houfe, as to keep it continually in the fhade; and to have
that fhade at fuch a diftance, as very little heat fhall be felt in any
time of the day : For fhades that are made by the higheft trees, are
undoubtedly the cooleft, and frefheft, by reafon it keeps the heat
fartheft off. Befides this, there are many advantages to be made,
in the contrivance of the houfe ; for I fee the Planters there, never
confider vvhich vvay they build their houfes, fo they get them up;
vvhich is the caufe that many of them, are fo infufferably hot, as neither themfelves nor any other can remain in them vvithout fvvel-
tring.

Firft then, vve vvill confider vvhat the errours are in their contrivances, that vve may be the better able to fhevv the beft vvay to mend
them; A fingle houfe that is built long-vvife, and upon a North and
South line, has thefe difadvantages: the Sun fhines upon the Eaftfide-
vvalls from fix a clock till eight, fo as the beams reft flat upon that fide,
for tvvo hours. And the beams refting upon a flat or oblique line (as
that is,) gives a greater heat then upon a diagonal, vvhich glaunces
the beams afide. As a tennis ball, ftrook againft the fide walls of the
Court, glauncing, hits with lefs force then when it feels the full refi-
ftance of the end wall, where 'tis met with a flat oblique line : So the
Sun beams, the more directly they are oppos'd by any flat body, the
more violently they burne. This fide-wall being warm'd; the Sun
gets higher, and fhines hotter, and then the rafters become the oblique
line, which is thinner, and lefs able to refift the beams ; and the covering being fhingles, receives the heat quicker, and retains it longer,
than tiles would do, fo that for the whole forenoon, that fide of the
roofe, receives as much heat, as the Sun can give, and fo paffes over
to the other fide, giving it fo much the more in the afternoon, as is
increaft by warming the houfe and Aire all the morning before, and fo
the Oven being heat on both fides, what can you expect, but that thofe
within,

within, should be sufficiently bakt: and so much the more, for that the wind is kept out, that should come to cool it, by shutting up all passages, that may let it in, which they alwayes doe, for fear the raine come with it; and letting in the Sun at the West end, where and when it shines hottest. Therefore this kind of building is most pernicious to those that love their health, which is the comfort of their lives: but you will say, that a double house will lessen much of this heat, by reason that the West side is not visited by the sun in the morning, nor the East in the afternoon; I do confess that to be some little remedy, but not much, for the double roofs being open to the Sun, in oblique lines, a great part of the forenoon; and being reflected from one side to another, when it comes to the Meridian (and before and after, at least two hours,) with the scorching heat it gives to the gutter, which is between them, and is in the middle of the house from end to end, will so warm the East-side of the House, as all the shade it has in the afternoon will not cool it, nor make it habitable; and then you may guess in what a temper the West side is.

Whereas, if you build your house upon an East and West line, you have these advantages, that in the morning the Sun never shines in or neer an oblique line, (which is upon the East end of your house,) above two hours, and that is from six to eight a clock, and as much in the afternoon, and not all that time neither; and upon the roof it can never shine in an oblique line, but glancing on both sides, cast off the heat very much; I do confess that I love a double house, much better then a single, but if it have a double cover, that is, two gable ends, and a gutter between, though it be built up an East and West line: yet the Sun (which must lye upon it all the heat of the day) will so multiply the heat, by reflecting the beams from inside to inside, and so violently upon the gutter, from both, which you know must be in the middle of the house, from end to end, as you shall feel that heat above, too sensibly in the ground stories below, though your fieling be a foot thick, and your stories sixteen foot high. Therefore if I build a double house, I must order it so, as to have the division between either room of a strong wall, or of Dorique Pillers Archt from one to another, and in each intercolumniation a square stud of stone for the better strengthning and supporting of the Arches above; for I would have the rooms Archt over with stone, and the innermost poynts of the Arches, to rest upon the Pillars, and the whole house to be coverd with Couples and Rafters, and upon that shingles, the Ridge Pole of the house running along over the Pillars, so that the covering is to serve both Arches, that covers your rooms: by which means there is but one Gable end, which will glaunce off the scorching beams of the Sun of either side, as, with the help of the Arches underneath, there will be little heat felt in the rooms below. But then a main care must be had to the side walls, that the girders be strong, and very well Dove-tayld, one into another, upon the Dorique pillars, or partition walls; and well crampt with Iron, or else the rafters being of that length, will thrust out the side walls by reason the Arches will hinder the Couplets from coming so low as to keep the rafters steady from opening at the bottom. For prevention

vention of this great mifchief, it will be very needful to have ftrong Buttereffes without, and thofe being plac't juft againft the Couples, will be of main concern to the fide-walls. If you make the breadth of your houfe fifty foot, allowing two foot to the partition, and two foot to either of the fide-walls above, (but more below) which is fix foot in all, you will have remaining forty four foot, which being equally divided will afford twenty two foot for the breadth of either room, you may for the length allow what you pleafe. But this I fpeak by per-miffion, and not by direction. But I will fend you a Plot with this, and an Index annexed to it, of fuch a houfe as I would build for plea-fure and convenience, if I were to live there, and had mony enough to beftow; and I believe, with fuch conveniences and advantages for fhade and coolnefs, as few people in thofe Weftern parts have ftudied, or ever thought on.

And now I have as neer as I can, delivered the fum of all I know of the Ifland of *Barbadoes*, both for Pleafures and Profits, Commodities and Incommodities, Sickneffes and Healthfulnefs. So that it may be expected what I can fay to perfwade or diffwade any that have a defire to go and live there. But before I give a full anfwer to that, I muft enquire and be enformed of what difpofition the party is that hath this defign; If it be fuch a one as loves the pleafures of *Europe*, (or particularly of *England*) and the great varieties of thofe, let him never come there, for they are things he fhall be fure to mifs. But, if he can find in himfelf a willingnefs to change the pleafures which he enjoyed in a Temperate, for fuch as he fhall find in a Torrid Zone, he may light upon fome that will give him an exchange, with fome advantage.

And for the pleafures of *England*, let us confider what they are, that we may be the better able to judge how far they are confiftent with the Climate of *Barbadoes*, and what gainers or lofers they will be by the exchange, that makes the adventure; and by the knowledge and well weighing of that, invite or deter thofe, that are the great lovers and admirers of thofe delights, to come there, or ftay away.

And amongft the fports and recreations that the people of *England* exercife moft for their healths without dores, they are Courfing, Hun-ting and Hawking.

And for the Greyhound, though he be compleat in all his fhapes that are accounted excellent, headed like a Snake, neckt like a Drake, back't like a Beam, fided like a Breme, tail'd like a Rat, footed like a Cat, deep breafted with large phillets and gaskins, excellently win-ded, with all elfe may ftyle him perfect, and of a right race: Yet, what of all this, if the Country afford no Game to courfe at; or if there were, that would amount to nothing; for, in the running of twelve fcore yards, they will either bruife their bodies againft ftumps of trees, or break their necks down the fteep falls of Gullies which are there too common.

And for the Huntfman and his Hounds they will find themfelves at a dead fault, before they begin, for upon this foyle no Stag with his lofty well fhap't head, and active body, has ever fet his nimble feet; and Herds of Vallow Deer, were never put to make a ftand upon

this

this ground; the nimble Roe-Buck, nor the subtle Fox, the Badger, Otter, or the fearfull Hare, have ever run their Mases in these Woods. And then, what use of Hounds?

Onely one kind are useful here, and those are Liam Hounds, to guide us to the run away Negreos, who, as I told you, harbour themselves in Woods and Caves, living upon pillage for many months together.

And for the Faulconer, though his Hawk have reach'd such excellencies, as may exalt her praise as high, as her wings can raise her body; yet, she must be taken down to a bare Lure. And the painfull and skilfull Faulconer, who has applyed himself solely to the humour of the brave Bird he carries, who must be courted as a Mistress, be she never so froward, and like a coy Mistress, will take check at any thing, when her liberty gives her license; and though by a painfull and studied diligence, he have reclaimed her so, as to flie at what, and when, and where, and how she is directed; and she, by her own practice and observation, has learnt to know, which Spaniel lies, and which tells truth, that accordingly she may sleight the one, and regard the other, and with this, has all other qualities that are excellent, in so noble and heroick a Bird: Yet, this painful diligence in the Faulconer, this rare perfection in the Hawk, will be of little use, where there is neither Champion to fly in, Brooks to flie over, nor Game to flie at. No mountie at a Hieron, to cause the lusty Jerfaulcon to raise her to a losse of her self, from the eyes of her Keeper, till by many dangerous thorows, she binde with her Qnarrie, and both come tumbling down together. No teem of Ducks, or bunch of Teales, to cause the high flying Haggard make her stooping, and strike her Quarrie dead. And for the Ostringer, though his well-man'd Goshauk, or her bold mate the Tarcel, draw a Covert nere so well; yet, no Eye of Phesants will spring, or pearch in these woods.

The Eagle and the Sacre sure, here ever miss their prey.
Since Bustard and the Barnacle, are never in the way.
No Tarcel drawes a Covert here, no Lanner sits a mark;
No Marline flies a Partridge neer, no Hobbie dares a Lark.

Another pleasure, the better sort of the people of *England* take delight in, which, in my opinion, may be rather call'd a toyle then a pleasure, and that is Race-Horses, forcing poor beasts beyond their power, who were given us for our moderate use. These exercises are too violent for hot Countries, and therefore we will forget them.

Shooting and Bowling may very well be used here; but at Butts onely, and in Bares, or close Allies, for the turfe here will never be fine enough for a Green, nor the ground soft enough, for an Arrow to fall on. Amongst all the sports without dores, that are used in *England*, these two are onely sufferable in the *Barbadoes*. But for the sports within the house, they may all be used there, as, all sorts of Gaming, *viz.* Chess, Tables, Cards, Dice, Shovel-abord, Billiards; and some kinds of Dances, but none of those that are laborious, as high and

lofty

loftie Capers, with Turnes above ground; thefe are too violent for hot Countries.

Some other kinds of pleafures they have in *England*, which are not fo fully enjoyed in the *Barbadoes*, as fmooth Champion to walk or ride on, with variety of Landfcapes at feveral diftances; all there being hem'd in with Wood, and thofe trees fo tall and lofty as to hinder and bar the view fo much, as (upon a level of plain) no Horifon can be feen. But upon the fides of Hills which look toward the Sea, your eye may range as far that way as the globical roundnefs of that watry Element will give way to; but that once feen, the eye is fatisfied, and variety in that object there is none; for no fhipping pafs that way, but fuch as arrive at the Ifland. 'Tis true, that Woods made up of fuch beautifull Trees as grow there, are pleafant things to look on, ahd afford a very plentiful delight to the eyes ; but when you are fo enclos'd, as hardly to look out, you will find too quick and too full a fatiety in that pleafure. But as the Woods are cut down, the Landfcapes will appear at far diftances.

Now for the beauty of the Heavens, they are as far tranfcending all we ever faw in *England*, or elfewhere 4c Degrees without the Line, on either fide, as the land objects of the *Barbadoes* are fhort of ours in *Europe*. So he that can content himfelf with the beauties of the Heavens, may there be fufficiently fatisfied. But we Mortals, that Till and love the earth, becaufe our felves are made up of the fame mold, take pleafure fometimes to look downward, upon the fruits and effects of our own labours; and when we find them thrive by the bleffings of the great Creator, we look up to give thanks, where we find fo great a glory, as to put us into aftonifhment and admiration.

Now for the fmelling fenfe, though we have the bloffomes of the Orange, Limon, Lyme, Cittron, Pomgranate, with the fmell of that admirable fruit the Pine, and others: yet, when we confider the infinite variety of the Flowers of *England*, both for beauty and favour, there is no comparifon between them; and the flowers there are very few in number, and in fmell, not to be allowed in competition with ours of *England* : For, fince the differences between the Houfes of *York* and *Lancafter* have been laid afide, no red nor white Rofe have grown there; but the Lillies have taken up the quarrel, and ftrive in as high a conteft there, as the Rofes have done in *England*; for, they are the faireft and pureft, that I have ever feen, both red and white, but no fweet fmell. He that could tranfplant the flowers of *England* to the *Barbadoes*, would do a rare work, but I fear to little purpofe: For, though the virtual beams of the Sun, give growth and life to all the Plants and Flowers it fhines on; yet, the influence is at feveral diftances, and fo the productions varie; fome flowers muft be warmed, fome toafted, and fome almoft fcalded ; and to tranfpofe thefe, and fet them in contrary places, were to ftrive againft nature. 'Tis true, that the Herbs of *England* grow and thrive there, by reafon they are ftronger, and better able to endure that change; but Flowers, that are of a more tender nature, will not endure fo great heat as they find there. But to repair this fenfe, fome will fay, that Perfumes brought out of *Europe*, will plentifully fupply us: But that will not at all avail

us,

us, for what with the heat and moisture of the aire, it is all drawn out, as by my own experience I found it to be most true, though I lapp'd them close up in papers, and put them in drawers of a Cabinet, where no aire could find passage, they were so close;and for Pastills, they lost both their smell and taste.

As for Musick, and such sounds as please the ear, they wish some supplies may come from *England*, both for Instruments and voyces, to delight that sense, that sometimes when they are tir'd out with their labour, they may have some refreshment by their ears; and to that end, they had a purpose to send for the Musick, that were wont to play at the *Black-Fryars*, and to allow them a competent salary, to make them live as happily there, as they had done in *England* : And had not extream weaknes, by a miserable long sicknes, made me uncapable of any undertaking, they had employed me in the busines, as the likeliest to prevail with those men, whose persons and qualities were well known to me in *England*. And though I found at *Barbadoes* some who had musical minds; yet, I found others, whose souls were so fixt upon, and so riveted to the earth, and the profits that arise out of it, as their souls were lifted no higher; and those men think, and have been heard to say, that three whip-sawes, going all at once in a Frame or Pit, is the best and sweetest musick that can enter their ears ; and to hear a Cow of their own low, or an Assinigo bray, no sound can please them better. But these mens souls were never lifted up so high, as to hear the musick of the Sphears, nor to be judges of that Science, as 'tis practised here on earth; and therefore we will leave them to their own earthly delights.

For the sense of feeling, it can be applyed but two wayes, either in doing or suffering ; the poor Negres and Christian servants find it perfectly upon their heads and shoulders, by the hands of their severe Overseers; so that little pleasure is given the sense, by this coercive kind of feeling, more then a plaister for a broken Pate; but, this is but a passive kind of feeling: But take it in the highest, and most active way it can be applyed, which is upon the skins of women, and they are so sweaty and clammy, as the hand cannot passe over, without being glued and cemented in the passage or motion; and by that means, little pleasure is given to, or received by the agent or the patient: and therefore if this sense be neither pleased in doing nor suffering, we may decline it as useless in a Country, where down of Swans, or wool of Beaver is wanting.

Now for the sense of Tasting, I do confes, it receives a more home satisfaction, then all the rest, by reason of the fruits that grow there; so that the Epicure cannot be deceived, if he take a long journy to please his palate, finding all excellent tastes the world has, comprehended in one single fruit, the Pine. And would not any Prince be content to reduce his base coyne, into Ingots of pure gold? And so much shall serve touching the *Barbadoes*.

Some men I have known in *England*, whose bodies are so strong and able to endure cold, as no weather fits them so well as frost and snow; such Iron bodies would be fit for a Plantation in *Russia* : For, there is no traceing Hares under the Line, nor sliding on the Ice under either Tropick.

Tropick. Others there are that have heard of the pleafures of *Barbadoes*, but are loth to leave the pleafures of *England* behind them. Thefe are of fluggifh humour, and are altogether unfit for fo noble an undertaking; but if any fuch fhall happen to come there, he fhall be tranfmitted to the innumerable Armie of Pifmires, and Ants, to fting him with fuch a reproof, as he fhall wifh himfelfe any where rather then amongft them. So much is a fluggard detefted in a Countrey, where Induftry and Activity is to be exercifed. The Dwarfe may come there, and twice a year vie in competition with the Giant: for fet them both together upon a level fuperficies, and at noon, you fhall not know by their fhadowes who is the tallest man.

The voluptuous man, who thinks the day not long enough for him to take his pleafure. Nor the fleepie man, who thinks the longeft night too fhort for him to dream out his delights, are not fit to repofe and folace themfelves upon this Ifland; for in the whole compafs of the Zodiack, they fhall neither find St. *Barnabies* day, or St. *Lucies* night, the Sun running an eeven courfe, is there an indifferent Arbiter of the differences which are between thofe two Saints, and like a juft and cleer fighted Judge, reconciles thofe extreams to a Medium of 12 and 12 hours, which equality of time is utterly inconfiftent to the humours and difpofitions of thefe men.

But I fpeak this, to fuch as have their fancies fo Aereal, and refin'd as not to be pleafed with ordinary delight, but think to build and fettle a felicity here: above the ordinary level of mankind. Such Spirits, are too volatile to fix on bufinefs; and therefore I will leave them out, as ufelefs in this Common-wealth. But fuch as are made of middle earth, and can be content to wave thofe pleafures, which ftand as Blocks, and Portculliffes, in their way; and are indeed the main Remora's in their paffage to their profits. Such may here find moderate delights, with moderate labour, and thofe taken moderately will conduce much to their healths, and they that have induftry, to imploy that well, may make it the Ladder to climb to a high degree of Wealth and opulencie, in this fweet Negotiation of Sugar, provided they have a competent ftock to begin with; fuch I mean as may fettle them in a Sugar-work, and lefs then 14000l. fterling, will not do that: in a Plantation of 500 acres of land, with a proportionable ftock of Servants, Slaves, Horfes, Camels, Cattle, Affinigoes, vvith an Ingenio, and all other houfeing, thereunto belonging; fuch as I have formerly nam'd.

But one vvill fay, vvhy fhould any man that has 14000l. in his purfe need to run fo long a Rifco, as from hence to the Barbadoes: vvhen he may live vvith eafe and plenty at home; to fuch a one I anfvver, that every drone can fit and eat the Honey of his ovvn Hive: But he that can by his ovvn Induftry, and activity, (having youth and ftrength to friends,) raife his fortune, from a fmall beginning to a very great one, and in his paffage to that, do good to the publique, and be charitable to the poor, and this to be accomplifhed in a fevv years, deferves much more commendation and applaufe. And fhall find his bread, gotten by his painful and honeft labour and induftry, eat

fvveeter

sweeter by much, than his that onely minds his ease, and his belly.

Now having said this much, I hold it my duty, to give what directions I can, to further any one that shall go about to improve his stock, in this way of Adventure; and if he please to hearken to my directions, he shall find they are no Impossibilities, upon which I ground my Computations: the greatest will be, to find a friend for a Correspondent, that can be really honest, faithful and industrious, and having arriv'd at that happiness, (which is the chiefest,) all the rest will be easie; and I shall let you see that without the help of Magick or Inchantment, this great purchase of 14000 l. will be made with 3000 l. stock, and thus to be ordered.

One thousand pound is enough to venture at first, because we that are here in *England*, know not what commodities they want most in the *Barbadoes*, and to send a great Cargo of unnecessary things, were to have them lye upon our hands to loss. This 1000 l. I would have thus laid out: 100 l. in Linnen Cloth, as Canvas and Kentings, which you may buy here in *London*, of French Merchants, at reasonable rates; and you may hire poor Journy-men Taylors, here in the City, that will for very small wages, make that Canvas into Drawvers, and Petticoats, for men and women Negres. And part of the Canvas, and the whole of the Kentings, for shirts and drawvers for the Christian men Servants, and Smocks and petticoats for the women. Some other sorts of Linnen, as Holland or Dowlace, will be there very usefull for Shirts and Smocks for the Planters themselves, with their Wives and Children. One hundred pounds more I would have bestow'd, part on woollen cloath, both fine and course, part on *Devonshire* Carsies, and other fashionable stuffs, such as will well endure wearing. Upon *Monmoth* Caps I would have bestowed 25 l. you may bespeak them there in *Wales*, and have them sent up to *London*, by the waynes at easie rates. Forty pound I think fit to bestow on Irish Ruggs such as are made at *Kilkennic*, and Irish stockings, and these are to be had at St. *James*'s fair at *Bristoll*; the stockings are to be worne in the day by the Christian servants, the Ruggs to cast about them when they come home at night, sweating and wearied, with their labour, to lap about them when they rest themselves on their Hamacks at night, than which nothing is more needful for the reasons I have formerly given. And these may either be shipt at *Bristoll*, if a ship be ready bound for *Barbadoes*, or sent to *London* by waynes, which is a cheap way of conveyance. Fifty pound I wish may be bestowed on shooes, and some boots to be made at *Northampton*, and sent to *London* in dry fatts by Carts; but a special care must be taken, that they may be made large, for they will shrink very much when they come into hot Climates. They are to be made of several sizes, for men, women and children; they must be kept dry and close, or else the moistness of the Ayre will cause them to mould. Gloves will sell well there, and I would have of all kinds, and all sizes, that are thinne; but the most useful, are those of tann'd leather, for they will wash and not shrink in the wetting, and wear very long and supple; you may provide your self of these, at *Evil*, *Ilemister* and *Ilchester* in *Somerset-shire*, at reasonable rates. Fifteen pound I would

would beftow in thefe Commodities. In fafhionable Hats and Bands, both black and coloured, of feveral fifes and qualities, I would have thirty pounds beftowed. Black Ribbon for mourning, is much worn there, by reafon their mortality is greater; and therefore upon that commodity I would beftow twenty pound; and as much in Coloured; of feveral fifes and colours. For Silks and Sattins, with gold and filver-Lace, we will leave that alone, till we have better advice; for they are cafual Commodities.

Having now made provifion for the back, it is fit to confider the belly, which having no ears, is fitter to be done for, then talxt to; and therefore we will do the beft we can, to fill it with fuch provifions, as will beft brook the Sea, and hot Climates: Such are Beef, well pickled, and well conditioned, in which I would beftow 100l. In Pork 50l. in Peafe for the voyage 10l. In Fifh, as Ling, Haberdine, Green-fifh, and Stock-fifh, 40l. In Bisket for the voyage 10l. Cafes of Spirits 40l. Wine 150l. Strong Beer 50l. Oyle Olive 30l. Butter 30l. And Candles muft not be forgotten, becaufe they light us to our fuppers, and our beds.

The next thing to be thought on, is Utenfils, and working Tooles, fuch are whip-Sawes, two-handed Sawes, hand-Sawes, Files of feverall fifes and fhapes; Axes, for felling and for hewing; Hatchets, that will fit Carpenters, Joyners, and Coopers; Chifels, but no Mallets, for the wood is harder there to make them: Adzes, of feveral fizes, Pick-axes, and Mat-hooks; Howes of all fifes, but chiefly fmall ones, to be ufed with one hand, for with them, the fmall Negres weed the ground: Plains, Gouges, and Augurs of all fifes; hand-Bills, for the Negroes to cut the Canes; drawing-Knives, for Joyners. Upon thefe Utenfils I would beftow 60l. Upon Iron, Steel, and fmall Iron pots, for the Negroes to boyl their meat, I would beftow 40l. And thofe are to be had in *Southfex* very cheap, and fent to *London* in Carts, at time of year, when the wayes are drie and hard. Nailes of all forts, with Hooks, Hinges, and Cramps of Iron; and they are to be had at *Bermingham* in *Staffordfhire*, much cheaper then in *London*: And upon that Commodity I would beftow 30l. In Sowes of Lead 20l. in Powder and Shot 20l. If you can get Servants to go with you, they will turn to good accompt, but chiefly if they be Trades-men, as, Carpenters, Joyners, Mafons, Smiths, Paviers, and Coopers. The Ballaft of the Ship, as alfo of all Ships that trade there, I would have of Sea-coals, well chofen, for it is a commodity was much wanting when I was there, and will be every day more and more, as the Wood decayes: The value I would have beftowed on that, is 50l. which will buy 45 Chauldron, or more, according to the burthen of the Ship. And now upon the whole, I have outftript my computation 145l. but there will be loffe in that; for I doubt not, (if it pleafe God to give a bleffing to our endeavours) but in twelve or fourteen months, to fell the goods, and double the Cargo; and, if you can ftay to make the beft of your Market, you may make three for one.

This Cargo, well got together, I could wifh to be fhip't in good order, about the beginning of *November*, and then by the grace of God,

the

the Ship may arrive at the *Barbadoes* (if fhe make no ftay by the way) about the middle of *December*; and it is an ordinary courfe to fail thither in fix weeks: Coming thither in that cool time of the year, your Victuals will be in good condition to be removed into a Store-houfe, which your Correfpondent, (who, I account, goes along with it) muft provide as fpeedily as he can, before the Sun makes his return from the Southern Tropick; for then the weather will grow hot, and fome of your Goods, as, Butter, Oyle, Candles, and all your Liquors, will take harme in the remove.

The Goods being ftowed in a Ware-houfe, or Ware houfes, your Correfpondent muft referve a handfome room for a Shop, where his fervants muft attend; for then his Cuftomers will come about him, and he muft be careful whom he trufts; for, as there are fome good, fo there are many bad pay-mafters; for which reafon, he muft provide himfelf of a Horfe, and ride into the Country to get acquaintance; and half a dofen good acquaintance, will be able to enform him, how the pulfe beats of all the reft: As alfo by enquiries, he will finde, what prices the Goods bear, which he carries with him, and fell them accordingly, and what valews Sugars bear, that he be not deceived in that Commodity; wherein there is very great care to be had, in taking none but what is very good and Merchantable and in keeping it drie in good Casks, that no wet or moift aire come to it; and fo as he makes his exchanges, and receives in his Sugars, or what other commodities he trades for, they lie ready to fend away for *England*, as he finds occafion, the delivering of the one, making room for the other; for Ships will be every month, fome or other, coming for *England*. If he can tranfport all his goods, raifed upon the Cargo, in eighteen months, it will be very well. This Cargo being doubled at the *Barbadoes*, that returned back, will produce at leaft 50 *per cent.* And then your Cargo, which was 1145l. at fetting out, and being doubled there to 2290l. vvill be at your return for *England* 3435l. of vvhich I vvill allovv for freight, and all other charges 335l. fo there remains to account 3100l. clear. By vvhich time, I vvill take for granted, that your Correfpondent has bargained, and gone through for a Plantation, vvhich vve vvill prefuppofe to be of five hundred acres, Stock't as I have formerly laid dovvn; (for vve muft fix upon one, that our computations may be accordingly) if it be more or lefs, the price muft be anfvverable, and the Produce accordingly. And therefore as vve began, vve vvill make this our fcale, that 1400l. is to be paid for a Plantation of 500 acres Stock't. Before this time, I doubt not, but he is alfo grovvn fo vvell verft in the traffick of the Ifland, as to give you advice, vvhat Commodities are fitteft for your next Cargo; and according to that inftruction, you are to provide, and to come your felfe along vvith it.

By this time, I hope, your remaining 1855l. by good employment in *England*, is raifed to 2000l. So then you have 5100l. to put into a nevv Cargo, vvhich I vvould not have you venture in one Bottom. But if it pleafe God, that no ill chance happen, that Cargo of 5100l. having then time enough to make your beft Market, may very vvell double, & 1000l. over; vvhich 1000l. I vvill allovv to go out for fraight,
and

and all other charges. So then, your Cargo of 5100 l. being but doubled, will amount unto 10200 l. But this Cargo being large, will require three years time to ſell; ſo that if you make your bargain for
14000 l. to be paid for this Plantation, you will be allowed three
dayes of payment; the firſt ſhall be of 4000 l. to be paid in a year after you are ſetled in your Plantation; 5000 l. more at the end of the
year following, and 5000 l. at the end of the year then next following.
And no man will doubt ſuch payment, that ſees a viſible Cargo upon
the Iſland of 10200 l. and the produce of the Plantation to boot. Now
you ſee which way this purchaſe is made up, *viz.* 4000 l. the firſt
payment, 5000 l. the ſecond, and ſo there remains upon your Cargo
1200 l. towards payment of the laſt 5000 l. and by that time, the profit of your Plantation will raiſe that with advantage; and then you
have your Plantation clear, and freed of all debts. And we will account at the loweſt rate, that if two hundred acres of your five hundred, be planted with Canes, and every Acre bear but three thouſand weight of Sugar, valuing the Sugar but at three pence per pound,
which is thirty ſeven pound ten ſhillings every acre, then two hundred acres will produce 7500 l. in ſixteen months; that is, fifteen months
for the Canes to grow and be ripe, and a month to Cure the Sugar
that is made.

But if you ſtay four months longer, your Muſcavado Sugar, which
I valued at three pence per pound, will be Whites, and then the price
will be doubled, and that you ſee is 15000 l. Out of which we will
abate ¼ part for waſte, and for the tops and bottomes of the Pots,

$$
\begin{array}{r}
15000 \\
3750 \\
\hline
11250 \\
2400 \\
\hline
13650
\end{array}
$$

$$
\begin{array}{l}
3\!\!\!\!/\,2 \\
1\!\!\!/5\!\!\!/0\!\!\!/0\!\!\!/0\,(3750 \\
4\!\!\!/4\!\!\!/4\!\!\!/4
\end{array}
$$

which may be rank'd with the Muſcavadoes, and that is 3750 l. and
then there remains 11250 l. to which we will adde the value of the
Drink that is made of the ſkimmings, at 120 l. per month, which in
twenty months comes to 2400 l. and then the whole revenue will
amount unto 13650 l. in twenty months. But this profit muſt come
ſucceſſively in, as the Sugars are made, and they work all the year,
exeept in *November* and *December*, when the great downfalls of rain
come: and if they pave the wayes between the Canes, for the Slids
and Aſſinigoes to paſſe, they may work then too; for, little elſe hin-
ders them, but the unpaſſableneſs of the wayes.

So then you ſee, that upon the venturing, and well husbanding of
3000 l. ſtock, you are ſetled in a revenue of 682 l. a month, of which
months we will account 13 in a year, ſo that after your work is ſet in
order, and that you will account the yearly revenue, you will find it
8866 l. *per annum.*

Now let us conſider what the certain charge will be yearly, to
keep

keep the Plantation in the condition we receive it, which we will suppose to be compleatly furnished, with all that is necessary thereunto : And first, of all manner of houseing, as convenient dwelling houses, the Mill-house, or Grinding-house where the Sugar is prest out ; the boyling house, with five sufficient Coppers for boyling , and one or two for cooling, with all Utensills, that belong to the Mill, and boyling-house ; the filling room, with stantions; the Still-house with two sufficient Stills, and receivers to hold the drink, with Cisterns to all these rooms, for holding liquor, and temper; the Cureing house fill'd with stantions, two stories high, and commonly in it seventeen or eighteen hundred pots for cureing ; the Smiths forge, with room to lay coales , Iron , and Steel ; the Carpenter , and Joyners houses , where they lodge and lay their tools, and much of their fine worke; with sufficient store-houses , to lay such provision as we receive from forrain parts, as Beef, Pork, Fish, Turtle; and also to keep our drink which is made of the Sugar, to the repairing of all which , the premises with the Appurtenances, we will allow no less then 500 l. *per Annum.*

To this, there is yet more to be added : for though we breed both Negres, Horses , and Cattle ; yet that increase , will not supply the moderate decayes which we find in all those ; especially in our Horses and Cattell , therefore we will allow for that 500 l. *Per Annum.*

The next thing we are to consider is, the feeding of our servants and slaves , over and above the provisions which the Plantations bear, and that will be no great matter , for they are not often fed with bone-meat ; But we will allow to the Christian servants , (which are not above thirty in number,) four barrels of Beef, and as much of Porke yearly , with two barrels of salt Fish, and 500 poor-Johns, which we have from New *England* , four barrels of Turtle, and as many of pickled Makerels , and two of Herrings , for the Negroes; all which I have computed , and finde they will amount unto 100 l, or there abouts ; besides the fraight, which will be no great matter ; for you must be sure to have a Factor , both at New *England* and *Virginia* , to provide you of all Commodities those places afford, that are useful to your Plantation ; or else your charge will be treble. As from New *England,* Beef, Porke, Fish, of all sorts, dried and pickled; from *Virginia* live-Cattle , Beef and Tobacco ; for theirs at *Barbadoes* is the worst I think that growes in the world ; And for Cattle , no place lyes neerer to provide themselves , and the Virginians cannot have a better market to sell them; for an Oxe of 5 l. pound price at *Virginie,* will yield 25 l. there.

But to go on with our computation : for as we have given order for feeding our people, so we must for their cloathing; and first for the Christians, which we will account to be thirty in number, whereof ⅔ shall be men, and ⅓ women, that we may make our computation the more exact; and for the men, (which are twenty in number,) we will allow one for the supreame Overseer, who is to receive and give directions, to all the subordinate Overseers , which we allow to be be five more; and those he appoints to go out with several Gangs, some ten, some twenty, more or less, according to the ability of the overseer he so imployes ; and these are to go out upon several Imployments, as he gives them directions, some to weed, some to plant, some to fall wood, some to cleave it, some to saw it into boards, some to fetch home, some to cut Canes, others to attend the Ingenio, Boyling-house, Still-house, and Cureing-house; some for Harvest, to cut the Maies, (of which we have three Crops every year,) others to gather Provisions, of Bonavist, Maies, Yeames, Potatoes, Cassavie, and dress it at fit times for their dinners and suppers, for the Christian servants; the Negres alwayes dressing their own meat themselves, in their little Pots, which is only Plantines, boyl'd or roasted, and some eares of Maies toasted, at the fire; and now and then a Makerel a piece, or two Herrings.

The Prime Overseer may very well deserve Fifty pounds *Per Annum*, or the value in such Commodities as he likes, that are growing upon the Plantation ; for he is a man that the master may allow sometimes to sit at his own Table, and therefore must be clad accordingly. The other five of the Overseers, are to be accounted ia the ranke of Servants, whose freedome is not yet purchased, by their five years service, according to the custome of the Island. And for their cloathing, they shall be allowed three shirts together, to every man for shifts, which will very well last half a year, and then as many more. And the like proportion for drawers, and for shooes, every month a paire, that is twelve pair a year; six pair of stockings yearly, and three *Monmouth* Capps, and for Sundayes, a doublet of Canvas, and a plain band of Holland.

An

An account of Expences issuing out yearly for Cloathing, for the Christian Servants, both Men and Women, with the Wages of the principal Overseer, which shall be 50 l. sterling, or the value in such Goods as grow upon the Plantation.

To the five subordinate Overseers, for each mans cloathing.

	l.	s.	d.
Six shirts, at 4 s. a piece	1	04	0
Six pair of Drawers, at 2 s.	0	12	0
Twelve pair of Shoes, at 3 s.	1	16	0
Six pair of Linnen or Irish stokings, at 20 d.	0	10	0
Three *Monmouth* Caps, at 4 s.	0	12	0
Two doublets of Canvas, and six Holland bands	0	15	0
Sum totall for each man	5	9	0
Sum total for the five Overseers	27	5	0

To the fourteen common servants.

	l.	s.	d.
Six Shirts to each man	1	04	0
Six pair of drawers to each man	0	12	0
Twelve pair of shoes, at 3 s.	1	16	0
Three *Monmouth* Caps, at 4 s.	0	12	0
Sum totall to each man	4	04	0
Sum total, of the fourteen servants by the year	58	16	0

Now for the ten women servants, we will dispose of them, thus: Four to attend in the house, and those to be allowed, as followeth in the first Columne, *viz.*

The four that attend in the house to each of them

	l.	s.	d.
Six smocks, at 4 s. a piece	1	04	0
Three petticoats, at 6 s.	0	18	0
Three wastcoats, at 3 s.	0	09	0
Six coifes or caps, at 18 d. a piece	0	09	0
Twelve pair of shoes, at 3 s.	1	16	0
Sum is	4	16	0
Sum total of the four women that attend in the house	19	4	0

The other six that weed, and do the common work abroad yearly.

	l.	s.	d.
Four smocks, at 4 s. a piece	0	16	0
Three petticoats, at 5 s. a piece	0	15	0
Four coifs, at 12 d. a piece	0	04	0
Twelve pair of shoes, at 3 s.	1	16	0
Sum is	3	11	0
Sum totall of the six common women servants	21	06	0

Thirty Rug Govvnes for these thirty servants, to cast about them vvhen they come home hot and vvearied, from their vvork, and to sleep in at nights, in their Hamock, at 25 s. a Govvn or mantle. — 37 10 0

Now for the Negres, vvhich vve vvill account to be a hundred of both Sexes, vve vvill divide them equally; The fifty men shall be allovved yearly but three pair of Canvas dravvers a piece, vvhich at 2 s. a pair, is 6 s.

The women shall be allowed but two petticoats a piece yearly, at 4 s. a piece, which is 8 s. yearly.

So the yearly charge of the fifty men Negres, is	15	00	0
And of the women	20	00	0
Sum is	35	00	0

Now

Now to fum up all, and draw to a conclufion, we will account, that for the repairing dilapidations, and decayes in the houfeing, and all Utenfills belonging thereunto,

	l.	s.	d
We will allow yearly to iffue out of the Profits, that arife upon the Plantation	500	00	00
As alfo for the moderate decayes of our Negres, Horfes, and Cattle, notwithftanding all our Recruits by breeding all thofe kinds	500	00	00
For forraign provifions of victualls for our fervants and fome of our flaves, we will allow yearly	100	00	00
For wages to our principal Overfeer yearly	50	00	00
By the Abftract of the charge of Cloathing the five fubordinate Overfeers yearly.	27	05	00
By the abftract of Clothing the remaining 14 men-fervants yearly	58	16	00
By the Abftract of Cloathing four women fervants that attend in the houfe	19	04	00
By the Abftract of the remaining fix women-fervants, that do the common work abroad in the fields.	21	06	00
The charge of thirty Rug Gowns for thefe thirty fervants	37	10	00
By the abftract of the cloathing of fifty men-Negroes	15	00	00
By the abftract for the cloathing of fifty women-Negroes	20	00	00

Sum total of the expences is	1349	01	00

Sum total of the yearly profits of the Plantation	8866	00	00

So the clear profit of this Plantation of 500 acres of land amounts to yearly	7516	19	00

A large Revenue for fo fmall a fum as 14000 l. to purchafe, where the Seller does not receive two years value by 1000 l. and upwards; and yet gives dayes of payment.

I have been believed in all , or the moft part, of my former defcriptions and computations, concerning this Ifland, and the wayes to attain the profits that are there to be gathered; but when I come to this point, no man gives me credit, the bufinefs feeming impoffible, that any underftanding man , that is owner of a Plantation of this value, fhould fell it for fo inconfiderable a fum : and I do not at all
blame

blame the incredulity of these persons; for, if experience had not taught me the contrary, I should undoubtedly be of their perswasion. But lest I should, by an overweening opinion, hope, that my experience (which is only to my self) should mislead any man besides his reason, which every knowing man ought to be guided and governed by, I will vvithout straining or forcing a reason, deliver a plain and naked truth, in as plain language, as is fitting such a subject, which I doubt not will persuade much in the business.

'Tis a knovvn truth there, that no man hath attained to such a fortune as this, upon a small beginning, that hath not met with many rubs and obstacles in his way, and sometimes fallings back, let his pains and industry be what it will : I call those fallings back, when either by fire, which often happens there; or death of Cattle, which is as frequent as the other; or by losses at Sea, which somtimes vvill happen, of vvhich I can bring lively instances : If either of these misfortunes fall, it stands in an equal ballance, whether ever that man recover, upon whom these misfortunes fall : But, if two of these happen together, or one in the neck of another, there is great odds to be laid, that he never shall be able to redeem himself, from an inevitable ruine; For, if fire happen, his stock is consumed, and somtimes his house; if his Cattle dye, the work stands still, and with either of these his credit falls; so as, if he be not well friended, he never can entertain a hope to rise again.

These toyles of body and mind, and these misfortunes together, will depress and wear out the best spirits in the world, and will cause them to think, what a happy thing it is, to spend the remainder of their lives in rest and quiet in their own Countries. And I do believe, there are few of them, whose minds are not over-ballanc'd with avarice and lucre, that would not be glad to sell good penni-worths, to settle themselves quietly in *England.* Besides the casualties which I have named, there is yet one of nearer concern than all the rest, and that is, their own healths, than which nothing is more to be valued ; for, sicknesses are there more grievous, and mortality greater by far than in *England* , and these diseases many times contagious : And if a rich man, either by his own ill dyet or distemper, or by infection, fall into such a sickness, he will find there a plentiful want of such remedies, as are to be found in *England.* Other reasons, and strong ones, they have, that induce them to hanker after their own Country, and those are, to enjoy the company of their old friends, and to raise up Families to themselves, with a Sum which they have acquired by their toyle and industry, and often hazards of their lives, whose beginnings were slight and inconsiderable; and what can be a greater comfort, both to themselves and their friends, than such an enjoyment ? But I speak not this to discourage any man, that hath a mind to improve his Estate, by adventuring upon such a Purchase ; for, though the Planter, by long and tedious pain and industry, have worn out his life, in the acquist of his fortune; yet the Buyer, by his purchase, is so well and happily seated, as he need endure no such hardships, but may go on in the managing his business, with much ease, and some pleasure ; and in a dosen years, return back with a

very

very plentiful fortune, and may carry with him from *England*, better remedies for his health, then they, who for a long time had neither means to provide, nor money to purchase it; for though some Simples grow there, that are more proper to the bodies of the Natives, than any we can bring from forreign parts, and no doubt would be so for our bodies too, if we knew the true use of them; yet wanting that knowledge, we are fain to make use of our own.

But when able and skilful Physitians shall come, whose knowledge can make the right experiment and use of the vertues of those Simples that grow there, they will no doubt find them more efficacious, and prevalent to their healths, than those they bring from forraign parts. For certainly every Climate produces Simples more proper to cure the diseases that are bred there, than those that are transported from any other part of the world: such cure the great Physitian to mankind takes for our convenience.

Somewhat I have said of the diseases that reign in general in that Island, but have fallen on no particular, though I have felt the power and Tyranny of it upon mine own body, as much as any man that hath past through it to death, though it pleased the merciful God to raise me up again : for I have it to shew under the hand of Colonel *Thomas Modiford*, in whose house I lay sick, thar he saw me dead without any appearance of life, three several times, not as in sounding, but dying fits, and yet recovered at last.

To tell the tedious particulars of my sicknes, and the several drenches our ignorant Quacksalvers there gave me, will prove but a troublesome relation, and therefore I am willing to decline it : Only this much, that it began with a Fever, and as it is the custome of that disease there to cause bindings, costivenes, and consequently gripings and tortions in the bowels, so it far'd with me, that for a fortnight together had not the least evacuation by Seige, which put me to such torment, as in all that time I have not slept; and want of that, wore me out to such a weakneffe, as I was not then in a condition to take any remedy at all. This excessive heat within begat a new torment within me, the Stone; which stopt my passage so as in fourteen dayes together no drop of water came from me; But contrary to my expectation, God Almighty sent me a Remedy for that, and such a one as all the whole world cannot afford the like: for in ten houres after I took it, I found my self not only eas'd, but perfectly cur'd of that torment, at least for the present, for it not only broke, bur brought away all the Stones and Gravel that stopt my passage, so that my water came as freely from me as ever, and carryed before it such quantities of broken stones and gravel, as in my whole life I have not seen the like. About three weekes or a month after this, I became in the same distres, and felt the like torment, whereupon I took the same medicine; which gave me the same help. Now if it did thus to a body so worn out as mine, where Nature was so decayed as it could operate little to the cure ; what will this Medicine do, when it meets with such Organs as can contribute mainly to affist it ? But I give the Reader but a footy Relatiou of my

Maladies

Maladies, and indeed very unfit for his eares, yet when I shall prescribe the Remedy, which may happen to concern him, I may hope to make him amends : for truly my touching upon the disease, was but to usher in the cure, which shall follow close after, and 'tis briefly thus. Take the Pisle of a green Turtle which lives in the Sea, dry it with a moderate heat, pound it in a Morter to powder, and take of this as much as will lye upon a shilling, in Beer or the like, Ale or Whitewine, and in a very short time it will do the cure. If this secret had been known in *Europe* but a dozen years since, no doubt we had been well stor'd with it by this time, for 'tis to be had both at the *Charibby* and *Lucayick* Islands, where these fishes abound.

Yet so slow was my recovery of the main sickness, and my relapses so frequent, as I was ever and anon, looking out to meet my familiar Companion Death ; my Memory and Intellect suffering the same decayes with my body, for I could hardly give an account of $\frac{1}{2}$ of the time I was sick ; but as my health increast, they return'd. In three months more I was able to ride down to the Bridge, where finding a Ship bound for *England*, I agreed for my passage and dyet by the way ; and (as the manner of all Masters of Ships is) he made me large promises of plentiful provisions aboard, as Beefe, Porke, Pease, Fish, Oyle, Bisket, Beere, and some Wine. This Ship had been fifteen months out of *England*, and had traded at *Guinny* and *Binny* for Gold and Elephants teeth, but those commodities taking up but little room, the Captain made the *Barbadoes* in his way home, intending to take in his full lading of Sugar, and such other Commodities as that Island afforded, and so being ready to set Sayle, my self and divers other Gentlemen embarkt, upon the fifteenth of *April* 1650, at Twelve a Clock at night, which time our Master made choyce of that he might the better pass undescry'd by a well known Pirate, that had for many dayes layn hovering about the Island, to take any Ships that traded for *London*, by vertue of a Commission as he pretended, from the Marquess of *Ormond*. This Pirate was an Irish man, his name *Plunquet*, a man bold enough ; but had the Character of being more merciless and cruel, than became a valiant man. To confirm the first part of his Character ; he took a Ship in one of the Harbors of the Island, out of which he furnisht himself with such things as he wanted, but left the carkase of the Vessel to floate at large. He had there a Frigot of about 500 Tunns, and a small Vessel to wait on her, but the night covered us from being discerned by him, and so we came safely off the Island. About a fortnight after we had been at Sea, our Master complained that his men had abus'd him, and (for some Commodities useful to themselves) had truckt away the greatest part of his Bisket ; so that instead of bread, we were serv'd with the sweepings and dust of the Bread-Roome, which caused a general complaint of all the Passengers, but no Remedy : our Pease must now supply that want, which with some Physical perswasion of the Master, that it was hearty and binding as bread, we rested satisfied, with this Motto, *Patience upon force.* The next thing wanting, was Fish, an excellent food at Sea ; and the want of that troubled us much, yet the

same

same Remedy muſt ſerve as for the other, Patience. The next thing wanting was Porke ; and the laſt, Beere, which put us clean out of Patience ; ſo that now our ſtaple food of the Ship , was onely Beefe, a few Peaſe, and for drink, water, that had been fifteen months out of *England :* finding how ill we were accommodated, we deſired the Maſter to put in at *Fiall,* one of the Iſlands of *Azores,* a little to refreſh our ſelves, which Iſland was not much out of our way ; but the Maſter loth to be at the charge of re-victu-alling, and loſs of time, refus'd to hearken to us ; and being a requeſt much to his diſadvantage, ſlighted us, and went on, till he was paſt recovery of thoſe Iſlands, and then a violent ſtorm took us, and in that ſtorm a ſad accident , which happened by meanes of a Por-tugal, who being a Seaman, and truſted at the Helme , who though he have a compaſs before him, yet is mainly guided by the Quarter Maſter that Conns the Ship above , upon the Quarter Deck ; whoſe Directions the Portugal miſtook, being not well verſt in the Engliſh tongue, and ſo ſteer'd the Ship, ſo neer the wind, that ſhe came upon her ſtayes, which cauſed ſuch a fluttering of the Sayles, againſt the Maſts, (the Wind being extream violent) as they tore all in pieces ; Nor was there any other Sayles in the Ship, all being ſpent in the long voyage to *Guinny* ; nor any thread in the ſhip, to mend them , ſo that now the Maſter (though too late) began to repent him of not taking our Counſel to go to *Fiall.*

But how to redeem us out of this certain ruine, neither the Maſter, nor his Mates could tell ; for though the Winds blew never ſo faire, we lay ſtill at Hull ; and to make uſe of the Tyde, in the Maine , was altogether vaine and hopeleſſe. Our Victuals too, being at a very low ebb, could not laſt us many dayes. So that all that were in the ſhip, both Sea-men and Paſ-ſengers , were gazing one upon another, what to doe when our ſmall remainder of proviſion came to an end. But the Sea-men, who were the greater number, reſolv'd, the Paſſen-gers ſhould be dreſt and eaten, before any of them ſhould goe to the Pot ; And ſo the next thing to be thought on was , which of the Paſſengers ſhould dye firſt , for they were all deſign'd to be eaten : So they reſolved upon the fatteſt and healthfulleſt firſt, as likelieſt to be the beſt meat, and ſo the next, and next, as they eate Cherries, the beſt firſt : In this Election I thought my ſelf ſecure, for my body being nothing but a bagg-full of Hydro-pick humours, they knew not which way to dreſs me, but I ſhould diſſolve and come to nothing in the Cooking ; At laſt the Cooper took me into his conſideration, and ſaid, that if they would hearken to him, there might be yet ſome uſe made of me ; and that was in his opinion the beſt ; that ſeeing my body was not of a conſiſtence to ſatisfie their hunger , it might ſerve to quench their thirſt. So I ſaying a ſhort prayer againſt drought and thirſt, remain'd in expectation of my doome with the reſt ; So merry theſe kind of men can make themſelves, in the midſt of dangers, who are ſo accuſtomed to them ; and certainly thoſe men, whoſe lives are ſo

frequently

frequently expofed to fuch hazards, do not fet that value upon them as others, who live in a quiet fecurity ; yet, when they put themfelves upon any noble action, they will fell their lives at fuch a rate, as none fhall out-bid them ; and the cuftome of thefe hazards, makes them more valiant then other men ; and thofe amongft them, that do found their courage upon honeft grounds, are certainly valiant in a high perfection.

At laft, a little Virgin, who was a paffenger in the Ship, ftood up upon the quarter deck, like a fhe-Worthy, and faid, that if they would be rul'd by her, fhe would not only be the contriver, but the acter of our deliverance. At whofe fpeech, we all gave a ftrict attention, as ready to contribute our help to all fhe commanded ; which was, that the Ship-Carpenter fhould make her a Diftaffe and Spindle, and the Saylers combe out fome of the Occome : with which inftruments and materials, fhe doubted not, but to make fuch a quantity of thread, as to repair our then ufelefs Sailes ; which accordingly fhe did, and by her vertue (under God) we held our lives.

Though fuch an accident as this, and fuch a deliverance, deferve a gratefull commemoration ; yet, this is not all the ufe we are to make of it, fomewhat more may be confidered, that may prevent danger for the future ; and that is, the great abufe of Captaines and Mafters of Ships, who promife to their Paffengers, fuch plenty of victuals, as may ferve them the whole voyage : But, before they be half way, either pinch them of a great part, or give them that which is naftie and unwholfome. And therefore I could wifh every man, that is to go a long voyage, to carry a referve of his own, of fuch viands, as will laft, and to put that up fafe ; for, if it be not under lock and key, they are never the neer ; for, the Saylers will as certainly take it, as you truft it to their honefties : Complaine to the Mafter, and you find no remedy. One thing I have obferved, Let a Sayler fteal any part of the Ships provifion, he fhall be fure to have fevere punifhment ; but, if from a Paffenger, though it concern him never fo neerly, his remedy is to be laughed at. Thefe enormities are fit to be complained on at the Trinity-houfe, that fome redrefs may be had ; for, the abufes are grievous.

Out of this danger at Sea, it has pleafed the God of all mercy to deliver me, as alfo from a grievous and tedious ficknefs on land, in a ftrange Country ; For which, may his holy Name be eternally bleffed and praifed, for ever and ever.

I am now caft in Prifon, by the fubtle practices of fome, whom I have formerly called Friends : But the eternal and merciful God has been pleafed to vifit and comfort me, and to raife me up fuch friends, as have kept me from cold and hunger, whofe charities in an Age, where cruelties and tyrannies are exercifed in fo high a meafure, may be accounted a prodigie. But, I doubt not of my releafe out of this reftraint, by the power of him,

who

who is able to do all in all. For, as *David* said to *Saul*, that God, who had delivered him out of the paw of the Lion, and out of the paw of the Bear, would deliver him from that uncircumcised Philiſtine, *Goliah* of *Gath:* So may I now ſay; that God, which has delivered me from a ſickneſs ro death, on land, and from ſhipwrack and hazards at Sea, will alſo deliver me from this uncircumcised Philiſtine, the *Upper Bench,* than which, the burning fire of a Feavor, nor the raging waves of the Sea, are more formidable: But, we have ſeen and ſuffered greater things. And when the great Leveller of the world, Death, ſhall run his progreſs, all Eſtates will be laid eeven.

Mors Sceptra Ligonibus æquat.

THE CASS LIBRARY OF WEST INDIAN STUDIES

As interest grew in the history and experiences of the black population of the world, attention increasingly focused on the islands of the Caribbean. Essential source material was largely inaccessible. In response to this interest Frank Cass Publishers have sought, through this series of reprints, to make available a thoroughly comprehensive selection of the historically most important 18th, 19th and early 20th century accounts and narratives. Supplementing these sources are works of more recent scholarship which have become out of print. These volumes are an invaluable source to scholars and students in this field as well as to those with a more general interest in the subject.

No. 12. Edward Long

The History of Jamaica, or General Survey of the Antient and Modern State of that Island; with Reflections on its Situation, Settlements, Inhabitants, Climate, Products, Commerce, Laws, and Government (1774).
With a new introduction by George Metcalf
New Edition 1970 (ISBN 0-7146-1942-6)

No. 13. E.L. Joseph

History of Trinidad (1838).
New Impression 1970 (ISBN 0-7146-1936-6)

No. 14. Alfred Caldecott

The Church in the West Indies (1898).
New Impression 1970 (ISBN 0-7146-1932-9)

No. 15. C.S. Salmon

The Caribbean Confederation. A plan for the union of the fifteen British West Indian Colonies, preceded by An Account of the Past and Present Condition of the European and the African Races Inhabiting them, with a true explanation of the Haytian Mystery (1888).
New Impression 1971 (ISBN 0-7146-1947-7)

No. 16. Lilliam M. Penson

The Colonial Agents of the British West Indies; a study in Colonial Administration, mainly in the Eighteenth Century (1924).
New Impression 1971 (ISBN 0-7146-1944-2)

No. 17. William James Gardner

A History of Jamaica from its Discovery by Christopher Columbus to the year 1872. Including an account of its trade and agriculture; sketches of the manners, habits and customs of all classes of its inhabitants; and a narrative of the progress of religion and education in the island (1909).
New Impression 1971 (ISBN 0-7146-1938-8)

No. 18. Sir William Young

An Account of the Black Charaibs in the Island of St. Vincent (1795).
New Impression 1971 (ISBN 0-7146-1955-8)

No. 19. Sir Robert Hermann Schomburgk

The History of Barbados, composing a geographical and statistical description of the Island; a sketch of the historical events since the settlement; and an account of its geology and natural productions (1848).
New Impression 1971 (ISBN 0-7146-1948-5)
Reprinting 1998

No. 20. Lionel Mordaunt Fraser

History of Trinidad from 1781 to 1839 (1891 and 1896).
New Impression 2 volumes 1971 (ISBN 0-7146-1937-X)

No. 21. Thomas Coke

A History of the West Indies, containing the Natural, Civil and Ecclesiastical History of each Island: with an account of the Missions which have been established in that Archipelago by the Society late in connexion with the Rev. John Wesley (1808-1811).
New Impression 3 volumes 1971 (ISBN 0-7146-1933-7)

No. 22. John Davy

The West Indies, before and since Slave Emancipation, comprising The Windward and Leeward Islands' Military Command; founded on notes and observations collected during a three years' residence (1854).
New Impression 1971 (ISBN 0-7146-1935-3)

No. 23. Charles Shephard

Historical Account of the Island of Saint Vincent (1831).
New Impression 1971 (ISBN 0-7146-1951-5)
Reprinted 1997

No 24. Richard Pares

War and Trade in the West Indies (1936).
New Impression 1963 (ISBN 0-7146-1943-4)

No. 25.

Not Published

No.26. John Poyer

The History of Barbados, from the First Discovery of the Island, in the year 1605, till the Accession of Lord Seaforth, 1801 (1808).
New Impression 1971 (ISBN 0-7146-1945-0)

No.27. Thomas Atwood

The History of the Island of Dominica. Containing a Description of its Situation, Extent, Climate, Mountains, Rivers, Natural Productions, etc. Together with An Account of the Civil Government, Trade, Laws, Customs, and Manners of the different inhabitants of that Island. Its Conquest by the French, and Restoration to the British Dominions (1791).
New Impression 1971 (ISBN 0-7146-1929-9)

No. 28. Henry Iles Woodcock

A History of Tobago (1867)
New Impression 1971 (ISBN 0-7146-2765-8)